Richard A. Henshaw
1100 South Goodman St.
Rochester, New York 14620
(716) 271-1320

Stony the Road We Trod

Stony the Road We Trod

African American Biblical Interpretation

Edited by Cain Hope Felder

FORTRESS PRESS   **Minneapolis**

STONY THE ROAD WE TROD:
African American Biblical Interpretation

Scripture quotations unless otherwise noted are from the Revised Standard Version of the Bible, copyright © 1946, 1952, and 1971 by the Division of Christian Education of the National Council of Churches.

Biblical citations for chapter 9 are from the Good News Bible, Today's English Version, copyright © 1966, 1971, and 1976 by American Bible Society, used by permission.

Interior design: ediType

Cover design: Patricia Boman

Cover art: E/THEBES. Tomb of Huy, hall, north wall, west of the passage. Dynasty XVIII, ca. 1342–1333 B.C.E. Mural painting. Bearing tribute from the South to Tutankhamun. Detail: five black prisoners followed by two women with children. Reproduction courtesy of the Menil Foundation, Houston/Mario Carrieri, Milan. Used by permission of the Egyptian Organization of Antiquities, Cairo.

Decorative border: E/CAIRO. Egyptian Museum. Inv. JE62045. Dynasty XVIII, ca. 1342–1333 B.C.E. Provenance: Thebes, tomb of Tutankhamun. Footstool: wood overlaid with gilt stucco and blue glass. Reproduction courtesy of the Menil Foundation, Houston/Mario Carrieri, Milan. Used by permission of the Egyptian Museum, Cairo.

Library of Congress Cataloging-in-Publication Data

Stony the road we trod : African American biblical interpretation /
    edited by Cain Hope Felder.
        p.   cm.
    Includes bibliographical references and indexes.
    ISBN 0-8006-2501-3 (alk. paper)
    1. Bible—Criticism, interpretation, etc.   2. Blacks in the Bible.
1. Felder, Cain Hope.
BS511.2.S84   1991
220'.089'96—dc20   91-19567
                                                              CIP

The paper used in this publication meets the minimum requirements of American National Standard for Information Sciences—Permanence of Paper for Printed Library Materials, ANSI Z329.48-1984   (∞)™

Manufactured in the U.S.A.   AF 1-2449

95   94   93   92   91   3   4   5   6   7   8   9   10

We dedicate this volume to our parents.
They have helped greatly
to bring us "thus far along the way."

— The Authors

Contents

Preface

Slowly, but perceptibly, the world is changing—and in some respects the changes are not a cause for alarm or fear. By 2056, for example, Hispanic, black, and Asian people will together outnumber whites in the United States of America, if present population levels and immigration patterns continue. While such a prospect frightens some who have grown accustomed to being part of the dominant political and economic group in North America, the change in demographics offers a range of creative opportunities for the more enlightened within universities, theological centers of higher education, and the churches and synagogues. Modern technologies and political economies have converted the world into a "global village." Such a development yields new opportunities to get to know the erstwhile "estranged others," their stories, their hurts, and—not least—their interpretations of the Bible. The present period affords all a creative challenge to reexamine the ways in which the Bible has been traditionally interpreted *within* and *for* mainstream (i.e., white/Eurocentric) academic curricula and churches.

Although it may surprise some well-meaning Christians and Jews in America today, much of what is regarded as legitimate and objective biblical analysis (exegesis) and interpretation (hermeneutics) has been done for the distinct purpose of maintaining Eurocentrism. The biblical role of non-Europeans in general and blacks in particular has thereby been trivialized and left in the margins, as has their role in salvation history subsequent to the redaction of the Bible. Within this framework, *Stony the Road We Trod* offers a fresh challenge to all Bible interpreters— a challenge that intends to be thoroughly constructive as a preliminary bridge to celebrating not *"his*-story" alone, but *all of "our*-stories" as the people of God. The presupposition for this book is that we must engage the new challenge to recapture the ancient biblical vision of racial and ethnic pluralism as shaped by the Bible's own universalism. We must also gain a new appreciation for the varied uses of Scripture within the Bible itself as a means of developing more sensitivity for the positive elements in such phenomena as modes of African American biblical interpretation, which at times are close to scriptural usage within the Bible and within first-century churches. Thus, we arrive at the burning question that makes this volume distinctive: How can the Bible break down the "dividing walls of hostility" (Eph. 2:14) that recent centuries of Eurocentric biblical translations and interpretations have, however unwittingly in some cases, erected between us? To this question, the present volume attempts to provide some answers; in this regard, such answers take the form of both descriptive and prescriptive narratives and studies.

Stony the Road We Trod is the culmination of a difficult five-year process of collaboration between African American Bible scholars in the United States. Many of us are professors who are isolated in large, predominantly white faculties; a lesser number of us are members of faculties at small, predominantly black theological institutions. We convened, beginning in the summer of 1986, at the Institute for Ecumenical and Cultural Research near St. John's University in Collegeville, Minnesota. Our ranks were augmented by a few black Ph.D./Th.D. students in the biblical field who indicated that they, too, bore the marks of a lonely intellectual faith-journey without much prior opportunity for or benefit of interaction with fellow African American Bible scholars or graduate students in the biblical field. Each summer from 1986–89, the group gathered at Collegeville for a week of deliberations, sharing common experiences about the formative stages of our academic preparation—the joyous breakthroughs and occasional encouragement, but more often the obstacles and low self-esteem that were subtly reinforced by faculty discouragements about considering anything black worthy of more than a passing comment in class, much less a dissertation project. The group, moreover, discussed similarities and differences in professional experiences whether as teachers of the Bible, researchers, or members of one or more of the biblical academic guilds.

Some members of the group dropped out either because they were uncomfortable in the sharing and interrogation of one another as blacks (we were used to receiving scholarly critiques only from nonblacks) or because they simply had scheduling difficulties. The paucity of black women Bible scholars among us reflected in part a continuing problem within the black church, which still does not fully encourage and support its female potential scholars. The group itself agonized over its own male-dominated socialization that, at times, made it quite painful for our female colleagues as they struggled to participate. By no means was the group preoccupied with "white-bashing" or telling endless horror stories of gross insensitivities from white mentors and colleagues. On the contrary, the group diligently sought for what Howard Thurman has called "common ground"—between its members to be sure but also with our colleagues of other races with whom we must continue to work. In the early sessions, some speculated about a book that we would produce out of this continuing consultation. By 1988, however, no other conclusion seemed warranted but to develop a book-length manuscript that would serve as a lasting descriptive and prescriptive testimony of this unique consultation. Our shared experiences and resulting growth required a formal commitment to move from our historic "oral tradition" proclivities to codifying, in book form, a precedent that would begin a tradition of African American collaboration in biblical scholarship generally and biblical interpretation in particular.

Each of the authors who contributed a chapter to this volume wishes to express her or his gratitude to those who helped to make the entire project a memorable success. First, we are extremely grateful to Dr. Thomas Hoyt, Jr. (New Testament), and the Rev. Dr. John W Waters (Old Testament), who conceived the idea for the consultation series. With unusual dedication and vision, they tracked down possible invitees, developed mailing lists, worked with officials in the Society of Biblical Literature, and, not least, helped draw the proposal for funding. Second, a special word of eternal thanks is in order for the Institute for Ecumenical and Cultural Research and especially Dr. Patrick Henry (New Testament), its executive director, who brought uncommon sensitivities to his unenviable task of being a white staff resource to a black group filled with tension, suspicion, and uncertainty about the motives and possible outcomes of the consultation as a whole and about the motives of its staff host and resource in particular. Despite this, Patrick Henry brought a congenial spirit and consistently offered a helping hand when most mortals would have abandoned the entire affair. In a sense, Dr. Henry became a representative of part of the solution for the problem that the consultation was seeking to solve. Third and finally, we wish to thank the officers and staff of the Lilly Endowment in Indianapolis—not only for their grant for the consultation series, but especially for their willingness to allow the group to adjust the grant in such a manner as to make this collaborative book possible.

CAIN HOPE FELDER

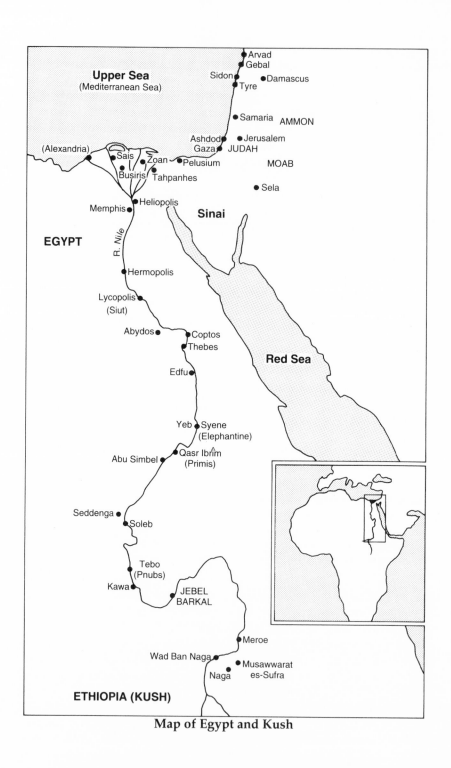

Map of Egypt and Kush

Introduction

Cain Hope Felder

African American biblical scholarship is steadily becoming a fully grown tree near the dense forest of Eurocentric biblical exegesis and interpretation. Only a few decades ago white Bible scholars, who held exclusive prerogatives as the academic elite, would have found it unthinkable that African Americans could be bona fide Bible scholars. The very notion would have brought either laughter or some condescending quip from members of the Euro-American biblical academies, which were then composed entirely of white males. Until recently, the idea of a black Bible scholar—whether Protestant, Catholic, or Jewish—was something of a novelty, an aberration. The tragedy in this aspect of American and Western religious history is that such attitudes totally ignore the simple fact that African Americans have long been students and "scholars" of the Bible. While African Americans for most of their history in the United States have been treated as second-class citizens of both the nation and the church, they have not infrequently been extraordinary interpreters of the Bible, often making profound scholarly insights that are now being more fully documented and proven correct.

With the publication of *Stony the Road We Trod*, we arrive at a new phase in the tradition of black biblical scholars, who have, by dint of historical circumstances unfavorable to them, tended to work virtually in isolation from one another. There are today just a little more than thirty black North Americans with a completed Ph.D./Th.D. in biblical studies (less than one-fifth of 1 percent in North America alone). As of this writing, there are but two African American female Ph.D.'s in New Testament and two in Old Testament. Clearly, there has been a critical need for blacks in the biblical field to become acquainted with and thereby become resources for each other. The pattern of isolation, damaging in many ways, has resulted from three factors. First, African American graduate students in the biblical field have been few due to economic

1

and political conditions that have kept their ranks small, since heavy language requirements and minimal financial support have proven obstacles too great to surmount. Lacking also were role models from the African American community itself and scholarly publications on subjects such as the Bible in relation to blacks in antiquity. In one way or another, the political economy of North America traditionally forced blacks to seek short-term survival and immediate gratification, rather than the long-term, delayed gratification that may or may not ever come if one is black in North America.

Second, African Americans who do gain entrance to graduate programs in biblical studies must do so in overwhelmingly white graduate programs, since there is *no* Bible studies Ph.D./Th.D. degree-granting institution in the world that is predominantly black or where nonwhites constitute the majority of the faculty.

Third, those African Americans with the Ph.D. or Th.D. in biblical studies have often had to work in diverse settings—most in predominantly white seminaries, colleges, and universities, a few in predominantly black institutions of higher education or local congregations—due to their temperament or hermeneutical orientation. Such factors as the foregoing help one to understand how remarkable it is that despite all of these formidable barriers to collaboration among African American Bible scholars, this book, nevertheless, emerges to reestablish the foundations of African American biblical interpretation.

At the beginning of this century, the prolific black historian, political philosopher, and educator W. E. B. Du Bois in his *The Souls of Black Folks* asserted that "the problem of the twentieth century is the problem of the color line." Now that we are near the end of this century, it is woefully apparent that white racism is, at least for African Americans, the most pervasive problem. For many of us, it remains not only unresolved but is often quite subtle, thus all the more pernicious. This is so because, more often than not, white racism is *denied* or *trivialized* by those who perpetuate it through their family socialization, the mass media, corporate life, curricular emphases, and religious separatism. In different ways, each section of this book exposes the continuing problems of racism and "the color line" that seem to be almost second-nature to many white Christians in North America. Some would say that it is not so much that whites are against blacks; rather, whites are just so completely for themselves that, by any means at their disposal, they will protect their privileges in a society designed to work for them. In this reasoning, all blacks have to do is to deny their own history and identity and thus to act like they are part of the American dream so that "the system" can work for them too. Yet for African Americans, this type of reasoning has more often than not led only to a nightmare of self-abasement, a valuation of all other racial and ethnic groups except their own, and a crisis of expediency overwhelming integrity.

Having traveled the "long road" of being trained and credentialed to teach Bible in higher education, the authors in this book have testimonies of record that are at times disturbing and at other times exhilarating. These testimonies inform the ranging presuppositions of their writings. They are collected here with a memory of how all the authors individually survived the variegated assaults upon their history, identity, and sense of integrity as African Americans trying to make sense of the history of biblical interpretation as well as their evolving socio-political context in a nation invariably resistant to their highest social ideals. Before I offer a chapter-by-chapter overview of this book, it might prove helpful to present the tenor of the reflections of the authors as they have traveled this "long and stony road" to become African American Bible scholars.

The Long and Stony Road

For African Americans the road to a doctorate in biblical studies has not been a much-traveled one. Not a few have fallen along the way, often because they did not have the benefits of strong support and encouragement from mentors—but also because the long road was simply too stony. The authors who have collaborated in producing this book thus understand particularly well the second stanza of the Negro National Anthem, "Lift Every Voice and Sing," written by that bard of the black renaissance, James Weldon Johnson. The beginning of that stanza is "Stony the road we trod, bitter the chast'ning rod, felt in the days when hope unborn had died!" Somehow, these words seem to epitomize our struggle as African American scholars who have made biblical interpretation a daily vocational struggle. This explains the title of the present volume. While the struggles that have brought us thus far along the way together have been "stony," we have kept on a road that others of our forebears have trod so nobly. Listen to some of the testimonies from our consultation, and in these find ample evidence of our song along the stony road:

- From fifth to eighth grade I had two subjects, arithmetic and spelling. I spent time trying to learn on my own. There were ancient and medieval history books in our home. On the front pages there were pictures of different races; blacks were depicted as hideous. It was stated that all races, except blacks, had contributed something to civilization; blacks were meant to be hewers of wood and carriers of water for others. From an early age, I thought I would be a minister, but in my teenage years I became an agnostic while still teaching Sunday school. The many questions that haunted me caused me to feel that I would die if I could not go to a place where theology was taught. There was one black person with a Ph.D. in my city's public school system. When the Depression hit, he said if I could get fifty dollars together he would be sure that I would get into a nearby university. I worked two years as a porter in an office building to earn that money.

- When I was about eight years old, I lived in a world of separate water fountains and back doors. I walked five miles and past white schools to get to the black school. One day a bunch of white folks wanted to hang me because I had refused to cross the street when I was supposed to.

- In 1969, when James Forman issued the "Black Manifesto," my denomination put out a warrant for my arrest if I should show up at one of the national church offices. It was peculiar that, having just been ordained to ministry, I was then subject to arrest by officials of the church!

- My father was in an altercation with the person in charge of the farm where he worked; he left in the dead of night so as not to get killed. All of his sisters, brothers, and cousins had to leave too. It was like the biblical migrations.

If the road has been crossed and made arduous by all sorts of barriers, there have also been persons who cleared barriers away:

- My father was a pastor for forty years. When I was growing up, sometimes he and I would be the only ones at the weekly prayer meetings. He would ask me to sing a song and pray, and then he would do the same. "Didn't we have a glorious time!" he would say on the way home. Sometimes I did not want to be there. But we *did* have a glorious time.

- My mother, by the grace of God, was able to keep the household together. She had an eighth-grade education but knew the classics (Greek plays, Shakespeare). She was able to become erudite by working as a personal domestic and reading books from her employers' personal libraries. When I was small, she saved money now and then to take me to hear the symphony orchestra.

- Dead people were segregated, very severely so. Cemeteries were clearly marked, indicating racially who went where. My father, a funeral director, buried a white person. This unheard-of breach of custom provoked a meeting of all the city's funeral directors. My father's response: "If they pay me their money, I don't care what they look like; I'll bury them."

- I grew up in Atlanta in the Depression, in very segregated conditions. Everything was segregated, even banks and insurance companies. But I learned through my family life that there was nothing wrong in being black. I have never had trouble with my identity. I had six brothers who fought in World War II for a country that had made so much trouble for us.

In many stories, the turning point was a mentor, a guide along the road who at a critical juncture showed the way:

- A teacher said, "Everybody in this room comes with a question to this text. If they are different questions, that is because of differences in experience, and all are valid." That affirmation got me through the rest of the program.

- When I was in seminary, I went to a meeting of the Society of Biblical Literature. I heard a black biblical scholar give a talk and realized: "It is possible, it has been done before."

- Graduate school was one of the most frightening experiences of my life. A white professor, whom I trusted then and still trust, passed on to me the oral lore of what it means to survive in this kind of system.

- Benjamin Mays and Howard Thurman showed me that the pursuit of scholarship is itself an act of piety.

- As I took in what the black biblical professor was saying, all doubts that I could be a pastor and a scholar disappeared.

- We black biblical scholars stand in a long tradition of stellar achievement and in a tradition of unrelenting struggle against the forces of racism. All black biblical scholars are charged to proceed boldly forward with "blood-stained torches" in hand. We recognize our continuity in a tradition of black scholars, male and female, who have endured for us things "eyes have not seen and ears have not heard."

- The black religious community is not monolithic. Black Catholics and black Protestants have widely differing views; and among the Protestants there is enormous variety. But there still is something African about the black Episcopalian, the black Catholic, the black Pentecostal. It is more a matter of cultural continuity and social location than of denomination.

- Because the Bible functions so pervasively in the black community we black biblical scholars are relieved of the impossible burden of carrying on the task of interpretation alone. It is exciting to think about real collegiality, wherein individuals don't have to be responsible for everything.

Despite the pluralism within the black community, black scholars recognize at a deep level an affinity, a shared perspective, that has survived despite the way they have been formally trained. Like many feminist scholars, blacks report dissonance between what they know and what they were taught, and they tell of a kind of profound liberation when they finally are able to challenge substantially some of the conventions of the biblical field. Breakthrough comes when scholars no longer bury what they know in submission to the traditional "experts." They begin to question the subtle biases and the very management of the departments and guilds of biblical scholarship.

European Scholarship as the Norm

Eurocentric is not an everyday word, but it aptly describes the world in which biblical scholars, including black biblical scholars, move every day. There is, of course, much biblical study that goes on in North America and other regions besides Europe, but the conventions, the standards, the procedures, and the assumptions of biblical scholarship, like those of nearly every field, have been set and fixed by white, male, European academics over the past several centuries. The extent of uniformity in scholarly norms throughout the world is striking evidence of persisting Euro-American domination. Indeed, the worldwide uniformity itself reinforces the academic prejudice that the European way of doing things is "objective" and somehow not culture bound. When we black biblical scholars discussed these issues, the following remarks arose:

- We must take seriously the politics of interpretation. Even the apparently nonprejudicial search for "the original meaning" of a text is usually driven by a desire to demonstrate that the Eurocentric interpreter's own favored position is closest to that "original meaning."

- We must challenge head-on the blindness in the claim that there is something called "hermeneutics" and then *deviations* (e.g., feminist hermeneutics or black hermeneutics) from it. What passes for normative hermeneutics is in fact white, male, Eurocentric hermeneutics.

- There are significant differences in the European and African mytho-poetic world views. For instance, miraculous deliverance (the transrational) is expected, even normal, in the latter; while in the former whites tend to rely exclusively on empirical procedures, planning, and verification. How can we wrest our understanding of the prophets and miracles from the Euro-American interpretation, and how can we develop and encourage that understanding?

- We must remind our people that there is a glorious and rich history of people of color in antiquity; and there has been a carefully orchestrated effort in Western historiography to hide this fact.

- Intellectuals have difficulty even talking about imagination, much less exercising it. The whole person needs to be addressed in the interpretive process. The Eurocentric mind-set seems more visual, while our viewpoint depends more on what is heard.

- The white, male, Eurocentric model is flawed because it is imperialistic. Also, as a point of view, it is basically irrelevant to our black churches.

- If black folks are going to have to face the white perspective, white folks in my classes are going to have to deal with the black perspective.

- When I put the black perspective at the core of my course in a predominantly white seminary, enrollment dropped from fifty to ten.

The Eurocentric mind-set has tended to prescribe the rhythms, specify the harmonies, and determine the key signatures for everyone's scholarship. Clearly much of lasting value has been composed in this mode. But, as one participant put it, "There is a politics of knowledge in the academy." Just as feminism has challenged patriarchy and shown how patriarchy and androcentrism warp the world for everyone, men as well as women, so black scholars must challenge the Eurocentric mind-set not only for the sake of the black community but also for the health of *all* scholarship.

Academy and Church, Scholarship and Preaching

For several decades biblical scholars have been disturbed by the question of the influence that the seminary model has exerted over the field. Many vocal spokespersons in the professional guild have proclaimed that it will be a bright new day when study of the Bible is finally freed from the doctrinal/dogmatic concerns of churches and seminaries. Only then, these people argue, will biblical study fully take its place alongside other academic disciplines in the university. Some black scholars share this view, but even those who regret church influence on academic study readily admit that any black interpretation of the Bible must take into very serious account the peculiarly intimate link between black biblical understanding and the vital life of the black church. Many black biblical scholars consider that the black church, far from being a liability requiring apology, is in fact one of the greatest contexts for black biblical interpretation. The historic witness of the black church affords black Bible scholars a rich framework for studying the Bible.

There are certainly tensions within the black community over biblical interpretation, theology, and ethics, as over so many other concerns. Sometimes scholars are held suspect (as they also are in white communities); clergy and professors at times can see themselves as competing for the allegiance of laity. But to a remarkable degree, there is a spirit of collective engagement with the biblical text in the black community. Even persons who question the continuing power of the black church in the black community cannot miss the influence of the Bible in providing the language, the imagery, and the cadences in which black people, inside and outside the church, communicate their experience.

When these issues were discussed at the consultations, remarks such as the following were made:

- To seek refuge in the academy from the difficulties of the church is not to assure that you will attain greater clarity in your scholarly work. The academy needs to be put on notice about its own presuppositions; there is often no more clarity there than anywhere else. I have been "schooled" and work now in places that are powerful centers of the professional academic guild, and such settings have convinced me of the guild's inability to offer an honest and convincing critique of what it is we do as African American biblical interpreters.

- It is good that in the academy we are in dialogue with other scholars, but we must beware of making the mistake—a mistake that black theologian James Cone now admits he made—of disregarding the black church in the interest of addressing an agenda set by whites. We must start speaking of black concerns as they relate to the academy. We need to raise some new kinds of questions and propose other options and agendas than those of white scholars.

- If the scholar interprets from an elitist point of view, the black church will know that the scholar's version of the story is not its story. This has happened often enough so that churches may say, "All the academy does is complicate our life. As long as we can pack them in without the academy, what use do we have for it?"

- In some churches, those of us who teach are seen as freaks. People may say of me, "You are a scholar, but are you also a pastor, can we trust you?" Scholarship ought to serve, but it should also perform a healthy critical function that clergy may not always like or have time to perform themselves, but which is necessary. There are still people who ask me as a professor, "When are you coming back to the ministry?"

"What Is at Stake Is the Importance of Our History"

The shared pain and dismay were not the only story. In Collegeville, the discussions were relieved by a ringing affirmation. There is a great tradition of black biblical understanding. It is our calling in our time and place in history to recover, enlarge, and proclaim that tradition. We must use the training that we have received, but we must also argue with and correct such training, so we can apply our tools, language, and theological sensitivity to those realities that we were not taught to take seriously academically. "What is at stake is the importance of our history."

Speaking on this topic of the long heritage of black biblical interpretation, the scholars at Collegeville made the following kinds of comments:

- There is a connection between African Americans' use of the Bible and our self-understanding. When I recognize this, I have to begin my study not with categories that come from afar, from without (e.g., authority, inerrancy), but with the way individuals and groups of persons have used the texts. I must discern the levels of value in historical and existing biblical usage.

- We do not begin as if black people have just started reading the Bible. There is already a tradition. What can we learn from your grandfather and my aunt about what the Bible means?

- We need to avoid a "trickle-down" theory of interpretation, in which the scholar gives and the people eventually receive. There has to be real, on-going interaction. The experience of the black church has given to some kinds of sources—sermons, call narratives, the spirituals—an authority almost on a par with the books of the biblical canon. What does this say about the Bible as a way of communicating? Are there patterns in the kinds of things that are joined together? Over and over again, the message is clear: What happened long ago is also my story—my Lord delivered Daniel, why not me?

- Our common experience of the black struggle for freedom links us to earlier centuries. Does it also give us access to revolutionary biblical insights? Do the ministry and outreach styles of the black church appropriate the biblical Word in ways we do not see in other communities? Black biblical history, neglected so long in the academy and now admitted only reluctantly, has in fact been taught for generations in the "auxiliary curriculum" furnished by the black church.

New Interpretations of Scripture: The Format of This Volume

This book is not a mere anthology of independently composed articles. Rather, we present in these pages a truly collaborative work, since each contribution originated as a paper circulated and criticized by other prospective contributors within the group. Invariably, the initial group critiques led to revisions. (Some original submissions were not sufficiently developed to be considered further and were eliminated.) The arrangement of the chapters and the choice of part titles were also group decisions. An editorial committee composed of select contributors worked with the editor in assuring that certain revisions on original drafts of manuscripts were made. Then, the editor was charged to conduct a final detailed review of the whole manuscript, while editing and proofreading the same for consistency in style and documentation. As African American Bible scholars working in such tedious ways together, we have to "sit back and simply wonder how we got over!"

We have organized our essays into four major parts. The book begins with the broad questions, and then throughout the rest of the book the focus gradually narrows. Part 1 consists of three essays that through different lenses survey the "lay of the land." In attempting to identify the problems and contours of what we are calling African American biblical hermeneutics, each author addresses the question of the pertinence of biblical scholarship. These beginning chapters also focus on the matter of the Bible's authority as sacred canon and Word of God. Although most members of the consultation agreed that the Bible has had and still exerts an enormous "authority" within the black church, we widely believed that greater precision was necessary in determining the nature and source of that authority. We open with a broad survey by Dr. Thomas Hoyt, Jr., professor of New Testament at Hartford Seminary, who provides the nonspecialist with a helpful review of different methods by which Scripture has been interpreted and reinterpreted. He shows how ancient the process of interpreting Scripture really is, for the Bible begins as reinterpretation of an earlier ancient past. Hoyt does not restrict himself to a litany of interpretive methods, however. His principal aim is to demonstrate how African American biblical hermeneutics has learned from and supplemented many of these methods as it sought to emphasize God's liberating activity against oppression, especially white racism. Professor Hoyt then suggests that the authority of Scripture within a group is best measured by the way a given group associates its own compelling central story with the Bible's story. He concludes by identifying three specific methods of biblical interpretation contributed over the years by African Americans—the socio-cultural, the socio-political, and the mytho-poetic.

The subjects of scholarly method and biblical authority are further developed in chapter 2, by Dr. William Myers, founder of the McCreary Center for Theological Study in Cleveland, Ohio, and professor of New Testament at Ashland Theological Seminary. Myers, who holds the D.Min. and Ph.D. degrees, is close enough to the "student experience" to serve as an eloquent spokesman for it as regards biblical studies. After alerting readers to the pervasive Eurocentrism in existing biblical studies, Myers raises a full range of thorny problems that such Eurocentrism poses for African Americans who want to be serious students of the Bible. Professor Myers captures the dual nature of the dilemma, but is not satisfied merely with the descriptive. As his argument moves from methods of interpretation to "canonical stance and perspective," he offers several prescriptions for African Americans to clarify and affirm the Bible's authority by reappraising the great value already given in the black church to both "the call and conversion narratives."

In chapter 3, Dr. Renita Weems, assistant professor of Old Testament at Vanderbilt University (Divinity School), probes the ways by which African American women have developed strategies for *hearing* and *reading* the Bible. She poses a threefold challenge—to scholars, to feminists, and, not least, to the black church. Men have allowed themselves to become too comfortable with texts that have virtually terrorized women. White women simultaneously have not sufficiently acknowledged their tacit benefits from the same system that has oppressed so heavily black and other women of color. Professor Weems illustrates, with Old and New Testament passages, the important ways in which black women acknowledge and yet harbor some ambivalence about the Bible's authority. Then Weems argues that African American women, over the years, have consistently identified with the voices of the oppressed within and behind many of the biblical narratives. Weems decries the fact that the Bible as "authoritative canon" too often comes to black women as preserved by a triumphalist, male-dominated church tradition, and as interpreted by Eurocentric scholars who have tended not to display much regard for the historic roles of African American women. Weems encourages black women, as Myers encourages black students, to bring the "authority" of their own experiences of God and of suffering to illuminate the Bible's own distinct message of liberation for them.

Part 2 of this book shifts the discussion to the kinds of sources, biblical and extrabiblical, that African Americans have used in their own history of biblical interpretation. Dr. Vincent Wimbush, professor of New Testament and Christian Origins at Union Theological Seminary (New York), is the author of the sobering essay that appears as chapter 4. Noting that the role of the Bible in the religious traditions of African Americans has not been adequately studied, Wimbush outlines an interpretive history that roughly conforms to five historical periods. He also calls attention to a range of sources seldom considered in biblical hermeneutics. Wimbush thereby centers on the ways that the Bible, as an adaptable "language-world," has functioned among African Americans for the past four hundred years. In his view, African Americans through spirituals, work songs, sermons, denominational addresses, mottos, and creeds developed their own forms of Christianity that, at times, were accommodationist, oppositional, and even assimilationist. Particularly striking is Wimbush's suggestion that the resent resurgence of fundamentalism among black Americans bespeaks a crisis of insecurity, a lack of confidence, and a crisis in thinking.

Chapter 5 offers a detailed case study of an African American sermon. Readers would want to explore the extent to which this sermon analysis by Dr. David Shannon, president of Andover-Newton Theological School and former professor of Old Testament at the Interdenominational Theological Center, Atlanta, Georgia, confirms insights from the preceding chapter by Wimbush. Following a brief sampling of seminal aspects of early American black preaching, Shannon provides an extended commentary on one of Paul Laurence Dunbar's stylized "sermons." Shannon suggests that in Dunbar's sermon, as in many such

African American sermons, four issues predominate: namely, contextuality, correlation, confrontation, and consultation. These, he argues, are four significant modes of African American biblical interpretation.

Part 3 presents three chapters under the rubric of "Race and Ancient Black Africa in the Bible." We specify "Black Africa" because centuries of European and Euro-American Bible scholars, Egyptologists, archaeologists, and Greco-Roman classical scholars, among others, have tended to confuse modern readers with explicit claims or strong implications that parts of ancient Africa, north of the Sahara, were not "black." My own extended rejoinder to such perplexing suggestions (presupposed to be valid by too many Euro-American Bible scholars) appears in chapter 6. Readers familiar with my *Troubling Biblical Waters: Race, Class, and Family* will recognize the broad arguments regarding the dual processes of "sacralization" and "secularization" that I advance in chapter 3 of that book. With greater attention to the New Testament, I have expanded and otherwise revised portions of the previous version of the essay. Now I stress, as do more recent studies, that, quite unlike today, the biblical world was essentially without color prejudice. Systematic treatments of "race" or exotic theories of racism were alien to the ancient biblical authors who knew of the greatness of ancient African blacks and their glorious cultures, as reflected throughout the Bible.

Chapter 7 is by Dr. Charles Copher, professor of Old Testament (Emeritus) at the Interdenominational Theological Center. Drawing on three decades of experience in teaching and research in the field, Copher takes up the delicate and (to the modern Eurocentric mind) complex matter of the black presence in the Hebrew Bible. Through references to Hamites and Elamites in Genesis 10, Old Testament usage of other Hebrew words, and varied testimonies (Hebrew, Greek, Roman, and Talmudic) by ancient authorities, Copher demonstrates that there is, in fact, an extensive participation by blacks in the salvation drama of ancient Israel—from rulers to slaves, from court officials to authors who wrote part of the Old Testament itself.

In chapter 8, Dr. Randall Bailey offers more evidence on the distortions of the Bible by Eurocentric scholars. Bailey, associate professor of Old Testament at the Interdenominational Theological Center, does more than show the existence of blacks in the Hebrew Bible; he presupposes this as he seeks to demonstrate the ranging *significance* of specific African individuals in the Hebrew canon. The significance that he reveals is a revelation about the function of these Africans in the intentions of the ancient biblical authors. Accordingly, ancient blacks are shown to be the source of political and military hope, known for their wealth, respected for their wisdom, and a norm of valuation to such an extent that ancient Israel associated with blacks, it appears, to raise its own self-esteem. Focusing especially on the poetic passages of prophetic, psalmic, and wisdom literature, Bailey provides refreshing insights through original research.

Part 4 is the final segment of the volume, having three chapters under the heading of "Reinterpreting Biblical Texts." Here the focus narrows to detailed analysis and discussion of specific biblical books and passages that have special interest to African American interpreters of the Bible. The opening salvo by Dr. John Waters, former professor of Old Testament at the Interdenominational Theological Center, is an eminently fitting transition from subjects discussed in part 3. For most of chapter 9 Dr. Waters concerns himself with the Hebrew Bible's presentation of the Hagar cycle of stories found in Genesis 16:1-16 (J) and Genesis 21:8-21 (E). In recent years, there has been a renewed interest in the relationship between Sarah and Hagar within the different versions of this ancient story. Waters attempts, through extended analysis, to ascertain the social (domestic) status and significance of these two women, challenging the commonly held view that Hagar was a slave. Marshaling a variety of evidence, he shows not only that in the earlier of the two accounts (J) was Hagar not a slave, but also that the later retelling of the story (E) that depicts her as such was a reinterpretation with much social and theological significance. The dynamics of these stories, in his view, enhance our understanding of ancient social customs, the status of subjugated people, and the limits and implications of ancient conditions of inheritance. Dr. Waters closes with an excursus that confirms our general contention that modern Western (Eurocentric) interpreters have been much less than kind or accurate in reporting on ancient blacks in the Bible.

Chapters 10 and 11 shift to passages in the New Testament. The author of chapter 10 is Dr. Clarice Martin of Princeton Theological Seminary (New Testament). With great precision, she takes up the frequently misunderstood "household codes" (literally: "the house/ domestic tables" [German, *die Haustafeln*]) that have been often abused by interpreters seeking to justify the submissive role that women should allegedly assume in society and within the church. Dr. Martin properly limits her focus to the codes that appear in Colossians 3:18—4:1; Ephesians 5:21—6:9; and 1 Peter 2:18—3:7. Fully aware that many interpreters have long used these codes to justify the enslavement of African Americans, she challenges, in a creative manner, black men to reassess their own glaring inconsistencies in interpreting these texts. She points out, for example, the ways they very often selectively reject some of these codes, yet are willing to accept others quite literally. By explaining the original function of these codes in the ancient social context of the New Testament world, Professor Martin invites the black church to reassess what often appear to be self-serving and unfair hermeneutical procedures that adversely affect the dignity of African American women.

Students and general readers alike will want to pay close attention to this excellent contribution to our book.

From the deutero-Pauline, we turn back to a New Testament letter written by Paul himself, namely, the Epistle to Philemon; and we are helped in doing so by Dr. Lloyd Lewis (New Testament) of Virginia Theological Seminary in Alexandria. Professor Lewis's title for chapter 11 may suggest that his exegesis is limited to the Epistle to Philemon, but the truth is that he establishes his thesis, in part, also by an analysis of what Paul says in Galatians 3:1—4:7. Lewis contends that a special *new* relationship is depicted in this epistle; this relationship between Paul (apostle and prisoner), Philemon (Christian slave owner), and Onesimus (once slave, now Paul's "child" and "brother") is that of "family." Professor Lewis dissects Paul's "family language" and the image of the church as "family." In Lewis's view, Paul's terminology is strategically chosen to convey his sentiments that by all means Philemon should acquiesce to the freedom of his former slave, Onesimus. Unlike some New Testament scholars, Lewis avoids both the extreme that portrays Paul as sanctioning slavery and the other extreme that depicts the apostle as a first-century abolitionist. It is appropriate to follow Professor Martin's challenge and appeal in chapter 10 with Professor Lewis's closing reminder that Paul the apostle was "unwilling to canonize the social roles found in his environment."

The authors of this book join me, as editor, in expressing our collective thanks to the staff at Augsburg Fortress Publishers, particularly J. Michael West, who encouraged us by finding more of that which was right than wrong in our humble efforts. For my part, let me again thank Dr. Patrick Henry of the Institute for Ecumenical and Cultural Research, for I have been immeasurably helped in my work on this introduction by his extensive notes on our consultations in Collegeville, Minnesota. For all of us as contributors, this five-year project in African American biblical hermeneutics has been a long and stony road indeed; yet, how wonderful to see a bend in the road and know that the sight of "home" is not too far ahead.

PART I

The Relevance of Biblical Scholarship and the Authority of the Bible

— 1 —

Interpreting Biblical Scholarship for the Black Church Tradition

Thomas Hoyt, Jr.

Various methods have been used to interpret the biblical text in its own context and to explore its contemporary relevance. Whether the biblical interpreter has been a lay person reading the Bible "devotionally," a pastor preparing a sermon, or a trained scholar doing technical exegesis, some method or methods of interpretation have always been operative. Black biblical interpreters have developed their own unique interpretative tradition based on ancient, recent, and contemporary scholarship. The task of this chapter is to survey traditional scholarship and to see how it was used to develop a school of interpretation informed by the black experience.

Interpretation within the Text

We know that biblical writers were themselves interpreters, for the historical-critical method has shown us how writers in both testaments exercised a certain freedom in building upon traditions that they received.[1] Let us look briefly at several models from the Old and New

---

1. There are those who think that scriptural meanings are best derived from investigation of community experiences within the texts themselves. These scholars (Childs,

Testaments where interpretation is transpiring within the text itself. These include (1) texts that reenact tradition, (2) texts that have layers of ancient contexts, (3) the contemporary application of a text, and (4) the perennial problem of proof-texts. In both the Old and New Testaments, examples abound of what may be called "reenactment." For example, historical-critical scholars have shown that Deuteronomy is not simply a compilation of laws. Its nature is made clear in the introductory verses, "Beyond the Jordan, in the land of Moab, Moses undertook to explain this law" (1:5). The Law is being restated and applied to the generation about to enter the land. From the point of view of modern scholarship, this is a patent example of the Deuteronomic school updating and explaining an already ancient tradition in relation to a new situation.

The same point was made by Gerhard von Rad as he exercised his traditio-historical approach to Scripture. He stressed the manner in which Israel remembered the bases of salvation: the covenant with the patriarchs, Sinai, the covenant with David, and the establishment of the special status of Zion. All of these bases of salvation were reenacted and reinterpreted in the context of worship in order to confront new events in the acts of God toward God's people.[2] The same process of interpretation and reinterpretation transpired within the New Testament. The writers took traditions and shaped them according to their own contexts. For example, the New Testament writers, who were dedicated to Jesus, exercised a new freedom in their use of the traditions that they had received. Let us look briefly at a Pauline model within the New Testament.

Paul, a mere two decades removed from Jesus, discovered that the tradition of Jesus' teaching about marriage was not sufficient to deal with the specifics of the Corinthian problem. In 1 Corinthians 7, he cannot simply repeat the "command of the Lord" but must also use his own considered judgment. On matters of divorce, Paul said, "not I but the Lord" (7:10). He quoted the prohibition against divorce that is found also in Mark 10:29. Yet Paul makes some concessions. An unbelieving partner had a right to ask for divorce. Married Christians should not divorce, but if they did, there should be no remarriage (7:10-16). His counsel is derived from bringing the tradition of Jesus' command into direct relationship with the complex problems in Corinth.

Sanders) advocate canonical criticism that takes seriously the life of the community in forming the canon and the authority of intracanonical dialogue for understanding specific texts.

2. On purpose, and inadvertently, blacks have made historical-critical, analogical, topological, moral, and allegorical interpretations of both the Old and New Testaments in order to translate past happenings to their own situation. One need only note black slave narratives, gospel songs, spirituals, sermons, and prayers. Building on the historical bases of biblical salvation, the black religious experience resulted in something new yet continuous with the originating events.

This Pauline model commends itself to us in our interpretation of Scripture. Paul tried to ascertain which understanding took seriously both the tradition and the special situation with which he was faced. Unafraid to take personal responsibility, he regarded himself as account-able to his risen and living Sovereign. Paul could, then, use traditions in a creative manner because of the freedom that he had experienced in the risen Lord. Likewise, the contemporary interpreter, though bound by Scripture, tradition, and commitment to the risen Lord, is also free to make judgments in light of the present situation.

Those employing the historical-critical method can discern how Paul refused to give exegetical warrant for what the Corinthians were already doing. By following and adapting Paul's method one might, in a measure, avoid becoming merely an ideological interpreter of the tradition and avoid a tendency toward interpretative stagnation.

Let us now consider another type of interpretation, namely, that found in the layers of contexts within and behind a given text. Find-ing the context of specific passages can get rather complicated. Take, for example, the Sermon on the Mount (Matt. 5–7). It is a collection of di-verse materials compiled and edited by the writer of Matthew's Gospel. The literary context of any given teaching within the sermon *is*, there-fore, chapters 5–7, and the Gospel of Matthew as a whole. Similarly, the situational and cultural background of the sermon is Matthew's own day, the latter decades of the first century. The theological context is also supplied by the Gospel itself, but we cannot stop there. We must place specific sayings of Jesus in the sermon in the situational and cultural con-text of Jesus' own ministry and in the theological context of Jesus' own proclamation of the kingdom of God. If, therefore, the church is going to reclaim the Sermon on the Mount for today, it must also reclaim its multiple contexts or the text itself does not "live."

In Scripture we find our predecessors in the faith struggling to hear, to interpret, and to obey God's Word in the midst of the realities and demands of the times and places in which they lived. They offer us no ready-made answers for the specifics of the issues and situations we face today. They do, however, offer us the witness of their faith, of their experience of God's gift and claim, of their commitment to understand the meaning of the gift and claim, and of their endeavor to be responsive to God's call in the midst of their world.

If interpretation is a part of the internal operation of the canon itself, as the historical-critical method has shown, what is the interpretative task for today? How can texts written thousands of years ago in ancient Israel speak to the life of faith of a twentieth-century person? That is the problem of hermeneutics. The more specifically relevant a biblical teaching was for its own time, place, and circumstances, the less specif-ically relevant it is apt to be for our time, place, and circumstances. The logic of this proposition is clear enough, but we seldom take time to think it through. Some interpreters would prefer merely to ignore the literary, cultural, and theological context of a text and resort to the arbitrary use of allegorical, proof-textual, typological, and analogical modes of biblical interpretation.

In order to allow the text to speak for their generations, the early church fathers like Augustine and Origen utilized the allegorical method. According to this method, each concrete or historical element of a scriptural story possesses also a meaning that lies outside the text. This method seeks a "spiritual" meaning behind the concrete and historical meaning of a text. This manner of scriptural interpretation is illustrated by Saint Augustine's rendition of the parable of the good Samaritan, a rendition composed during the latter part of the fourth century:

> The wounded traveller is fallen man, half alive in his knowledge of God and half dead in his slavery to sin; the binding up of his wounds signifies Christ's restraint of sin; the pouring in of oil and wine, the comfort of good hope and the exhortation to spirited work. The innkeeper, dropping his incognito, is revealed as the Apostle Paul; and the two pence turn out to be the two commandments of love.[3]

The allegorizing here is so dense that one loses sight of the original text. To allegorize is to lose the reader in the game of "this means that" so that the reader completely forgets that God is speaking *directly* through the parable of the good Samaritan. The meaning of the parable for our daily moral, physical, and spiritual concerns is lost. It is on this account that allegorizing abuses the Scriptures; it misleads and distorts the Word.

Origen, in his use of the method, distinguishes between two levels of meaning in the text: the literal and spiritual. The literal meaning is that which the text had in its original context (the meaning one seeks to discover through exegesis). Origen realized that what the words meant was not always clear and, if clear, what they meant was not always meaningful to the contemporary situation. This reality led him to use "spiritual exegesis" to bridge the gap between the distant text and the present. Allegory made it possible to translate the text in a way that would be applicable to Origen's situation. He held the conviction that the Scriptures were inspired and were meant to reveal; therefore, he believed the words must have some meaning for today. He knew that the spiritual and literal meanings were neither identical nor had any direct relationship. What validated the allegorical interpretation was not the literal sense, but God's desire to reveal.

As we shall see, with the rise of historical criticism, the demand for a correspondence between exegesis and interpretation became acute.

---

3. See *Quaestiones Evangeliorum* 2.19 (*Patrologia Latina*, ed. Migne, 35, 1340), as summarized in A. M. Hunter, *Interpreting the Parables* (London: SCM, 1960), 26.

Allegory did not have such a correspondence. Someone may rightly ask, "Who are we to suggest in the twentieth century that the church fathers' method is obsolete and ours is more valid?"

The same question can be asked about those in the black tradition who did not adhere to the historical-critical method and, at many points, allegorized the text. One may have to conclude that for Origen and others in the tradition of allegory, the method is not wrong because they were true to their understanding of reality. With the rise of historical consciousness, the need to show a correlation between our time and that of the text became more important. Luther and Calvin rejected allegorizing both the Old and New Testaments. They argued rightly that it is the duty of the interpreter of the Bible to offer "the plain sense" of the text, presumably the meaning intended by the author.

The method of proof-texting involves taking a text completely out of context in order to validate one's own subjective views (pretexts) or one's understanding of doctrine, tradition, and the like. This method results from a fundamental misunderstanding of the nature of the Christian canon. It assumes, falsely, that the text exists chiefly to buttress, to support, to sanction one's own point of view. Consequently it is used to judge or criticize an opponent. So the text becomes a weapon used to attack the opponent and to justify one's own life and thought.

Even with the establishment of a canon the church has agreed to live by diverse norms since the same problems and conflicts may be dealt with differently in different biblical writings or even in different places within a writing. When the diversity of this canon is not obscured, we are reminded that the New Testament can help us recover a "catholicity" (a universal spirit) in diversity. Ernst Käsemann helps us here in his article on the canon. He contends that within the canon of the New Testament we find, side-by-side, doctrines and interpretations that are not only at variance with one another in essential points but are also irreconcilable with each other.[4] But witnesses from the black church help us also. Black theologians have given consistent witness in their writings to the diversity inherent in scriptural texts, but they have also revealed that within that diversity there are universal themes. Who can deny James Cone's insistence that "Christian theology is a theology of liberation"?[5] He has consistently developed the biblical claim that God came in Christ to set the captive free. Before him, the theme of liberation as a socio-political factor was not often made the organizing principle of a systematic theology. Black scholars who developed similar themes include: Martin Luther King, Jr. (theme: love of God, Christ, and human beings); J. Deotis

---

4. See Ernst Käsemann, "The Canon of the New Testament and the Unity of the Church," in his *Essays on New Testament Themes*, Studies in Biblical Theology, no. 41 (Naperville, Ill.: Allenson, 1964), 95–107.

5. James H. Cone, *A Black Theology of Liberation* (Philadelphia: Lippincott, 1970), 17.

Roberts (theme: reconciliation through liberation); Joseph Washington, Jr. (theme: blacks as God's chosen people); Albert Cleage (theme: Jesus as the black Messiah); Major Jones (theme: freedom and salvation in the context of love); Cecil Cone (theme: an almighty sovereign). White scholars similarly stress various themes as organizing principles for their theological agendas.[6] While it is important to understand that there are overarching themes within the Bible, it is also important not to succumb to proof-texting or manipulating texts so that they will support one's theological agenda.

It is understandable that readers of Scripture would want to select certain writings that appeal to their special need; the diversity of the text invites such selectivity. Robert S. Bilheimer, in describing the various spiritualities in biblical texts, emphasizes the diversity of the text. He suggests that Scripture gives both a clear warrant for struggling against oppression and resources for meeting life's doubts and sufferings. Furthermore, he writes:

> Scripture gives reason to adopt a spirituality of obedience to the law, whether the law of Moses or the new law of Christ. The spirituality of the priest, the lonely calling of the prophet, and the reassuring guidance of the lover of wisdom all stand side by side in Scripture. The inwardness of prayer and praise, the surrender of self, the agonies of struggle, and the power of spiritual transformation are also present. Hope, which implies a spirituality of future expectation, overarches all. One need not look to discover strands in Scripture that define varied spiritual attitudes and styles.[7]

The danger of being overtly selective of sources can lead to a preoccupation with ideology that leads to proof-texting as a biblical norm. Bilheimer's warning is appropriate:

> If my spirituality is drawn chiefly from a few passages of my own choosing, I short change myself. If my own needs and, even more, my own view of my own needs determine which portion of Scripture is most gratifying, I slip into a spirituality of personal preference, molding God to my own desires.[8]

When we begin reclaiming Scripture for today's witness, we must reclaim the whole of the scriptural witness. We must not try to short-cut the process by searching out only those passages that seem to hold promise of being specifically "relevant" for a particular social issue.

In order to allow the Scriptures to serve as the Word of God that sanctions the church as well as judges it, the historical-critical method

---

6. Cf. John Calvin (theme: sovereignty of God); Walther Eichrodt (theme: covenant); and Karl Barth (theme: the Word).

7. Robert S. Bilheimer, *A Spirituality for the Long Haul: Biblical Risk and Moral Stand* (Philadelphia: Fortress Press, 1984), 10.

8. Ibid.

was devised. A child chiefly of nineteenth-century Europe, this method has shown conclusively that Scriptures had their genesis in various ancient faith communities. The various traditions were shaped and conveyed by oral communication prior to being written. When they were written, various documents and traditions accumulated and were subsequently shaped and edited by an author or group of authors. The study of the authorship, date, and content of these is called Higher Criticism. Manuscripts of different editorial traditions are grouped into families. Scholars seeking to ascertain the more authentic manuscripts use techniques of textual criticism (Lower Criticism). Briefly described, these are concerns of the historical-critical method and include textual, source, form, and redaction criticism. This method seeks to clarify the meaning of texts in their own settings and to minimize the need for the allegorical, proof-texting, typological, and analogical modes of interpretation.

While many have vigorously criticized the historical-critical method as inadequate for one reason or another, one cannot ignore it. Many scholars have developed variations on the method and have suggested other perspectives in connection with it. Some would interpret the biblical text based on individual or group experiences. Friedrich Schleiermacher readily comes to mind. Experience expressed in or by the text dominates his methods of biblical interpretation. Other interpretative methods include those of Immanuel Kant and Albrecht Ritschl, who emphasize moral values and disposition articulated in the text. Gustavo Gutiérrez, José Míguez Bonino, Juan Luis Segundo, and Frederick Herzog focus on the struggle against oppression. John Gager, Robert R. Wilson, Norman Gottwald, and Gerd Theissen see the key to interpretation as being the social world of the biblical text. Paul Rubenstein, Robin Scroggs, and Walter Wink emphasize psychological facets of Scripture, especially those that enable a person to find healing for one's own broken self. Finally, James Cone, J. Deotis Roberts, Juan Luis Segundo, and Elisabeth Schüssler Fiorenza use more of a sociological/psychological analysis with a strong emphasis on economic and political factors in their basic interpretative method.

Concern for language (its structure, dynamics, and power) is a key element in biblical interpretation today. We can trace discussions of language in interpretation from Schleiermacher's essay on hermeneutics through Wilhelm Dilthey to Gerhard Ebeling, Ernst Fuchs, Robert Funk, Dan O. Via, Paul Ricoeur, and so on. Closely aligned with the stress on language is the call for new models of literary study of the texts, focusing upon the shape and structure of the text to determine its meaning (Amos Wilder, John Dominic Crossan, Dan O. Via, Sallie McFague, Mary Ann Tolbert, and so on) and upon larger units of total narrative structure and themes (Frank Kermode, Norman Peterson, Robert M. Fowler).[9] Need-less to say, *black biblical hermeneutics can learn from all of these methods, especially the "praxis-liberating activity" in the struggle against racism.* This praxis-liberating methodology uses the interpretative principle of experience in the religious, social, political, and economic arenas. When one surveys the history of blacks in the United States, one can readily understand this strong influence and the dynamics of language that have been stressed in the interpretation of Scripture.

The above discussion of various methodologies has necessitated a rehearsal of the nature of Scripture and the biblical witness, reiteration of the manner in which individual passages must be interpreted in their many contexts, a determination of how we must listen for and be respon-sive to God's Word in our own time and place, and an emphasis upon *the necessity of the historical-critical method as a basis for other related methodologies.* Lurking behind our concern for interpretative principles is the issue of authority of Scripture.

Authority of Scripture and Culture

The authority of Scripture is displayed not so much in the answers that are given but in the questions that are raised. As one understands more deeply the Christian faith, discipleship, and the world in which that discipleship is to take place, these questions summon us to responsible decisions in Christian freedom. In the hands of certain interpreters, the historical-critical method and variations stemming from that method promise a sense of freedom for those who wish to act responsibly as disciples of Jesus Christ.

The historical-critical method also serves as a hedge against the charges of biblicism (literal, dogmatic readings of texts) and fundamen-talism. By discovering and enumerating ways of interpreting Scripture in the contemporary world, one encounters a kind of excitement in biblical hermeneutics today. African American Bible scholars say "Amen" and seek to contribute to the promising directions in which biblical interpre-tation seems to be headed. Even so, the question of biblical authority for African Americans, it appears to me, relates to the issues of culture and imagination.

Some contemporary scholars are putting more emphasis on the influ-ence of cultural perspectives when reading and understanding Scripture. It is becoming clearer that Eurocentric scholars, who typically reflect their

9. David L. Bartlett ("Biblical Scholarship Today: A Diversity of New Approaches," *Christian Century*, October 28, 1981, 1090–93) enumerates five new directions in biblical interpretation. Each of these perspectives motivates biblical interpreters to go beyond the historical-critical method or at least manage the method differently.

cultural preferences, do not provide the only perspective or even the best one for interpreting Scripture. African American, Latin American, and feminist theologians have all stressed rightly that the text is not the only focus for biblical interpretation; both the text and the interpreter must be examined. The sociology of knowledge is quick to focus upon the interpreter as well as the socio-cultural context of both text and interpreter. Many of us think that this emphasis has been neglected for too long in biblical scholarship. Scholars have discussed the factor of environment and its influence on the author and content of various biblical texts. However, Bible scholars have not gone far enough; that is, they need to focus also on the cultural contexts of those who read the Bible. For example, it may enhance meaning to know how a story functioned in the context of ancient customs of the biblical world. In the ancient Near East, where oral communication was valued, it was not unusual to answer a question by telling a story. By telling a story, one could create or destroy a world view. The creation stories of Genesis, for example, were used to destroy the world view of one culture and establish one more attuned to the monotheism of the ancient Israelites. That is all well and good, and important for interpretation, but it is also important to understand how stories function within the cultures of those who read the Bible today.

In black culture "the story" is that which establishes the authority of the Bible, for in its story, blacks find the essence of their story in modern life. Blacks are excellent story-communicators and in many respects are, as Africans, understandably closely related to the world view of the ancient Near East. Biblical interpreters could profit from a more intense exploration of the relationship of oral forms to textual forms. Such an approach to the text would focus on the underside of history in an attempt to explore the meaning of the text for those who are on the margins. In an exploration of the cultural experiences of blacks, who represent the margins of American society, one may see more clearly the crucial importance of cultural questions in biblical interpretation.

Among black people, cultural sharing transcends religious affiliation. One would think, theoretically, that a study of black religion in relation to the Bible would exclude a number of blacks who are religious but who are not Christians. There is, however, a shared, transcendent cultural reality experienced by black Christians and non-Christians alike: black suffering. Black suffering bears and has borne a double burden. On the one hand, black suffering shares the suffering that is common to all human beings, sickness, broken homes, tragedies of death, accidents, wars, etc. On the other hand, that suffering has been compounded by slavery, discrimination, and racism. This sociological grid of blacks provides a solidarity that transcends even membership in the Christian religion.

The Bible has been both primer, culturally speaking, and sacred "authoritative" book for black people. Its character as primer relates to the history of slavery in American culture and its practice of restricting slaves from reading and writing. Having been uprooted from West Africa, black Americans had a rich history of oral communication. The popular African literature included tales, proverbs, and riddles preserved and transmitted from one generation to another by either trained narrators or, more commonly, amateur storytellers. In African culture, the person in the community who serves as the repository of community customs, history, and traditions is the *groit*. He is pivotal for remembrance of past events and the re-creations of the community traditions and so provides occasion for tribal reflection, appreciation, and celebration. When Africans were brought to Jamestown in 1619 as slaves, they brought this oral style of historical-cultural transmission with them.

The African was brought to a land where literacy was highly valued and where the presence and use of Africanisms were frowned upon by whites. This resulted in a more crystallized and sophisticated oral tradition among blacks. The oral stage of communication was complicated because of certain actions by the dominant white group. White owners prohibited blacks from reading because they felt it dangerous to the status quo. Whites felt that blacks who could read would be led to read the Scriptures and would become "infected" by their explicit and implicit teachings on human equality and liberation. Once those held as slaves could read, then who could keep them from writing? The ability to write would open up channels of communication that could result in insurrections. Little wonder, therefore, that state and local laws were passed throughout the South forbidding the teaching of slaves to read and write. Of course, there were notable exceptions to this practice of restrictions on teaching slaves to read and write. The historian Benjamin Quarles points out that the New England colonies had no such restrictions. Cotton Mather, a Puritan, established charity schools where Bible study was given to slaves. The Anglicans established a school for black slaves in 1705 in New York City and forty years later established one in Charleston. During this early period of American history, Quakers were also very instrumental in providing some training for slaves in terms of reading and writing. Anthony Benezet, a Quaker who was one of the most prominent antislavery propagandists in pre–Revolutionary War America, helped establish schools to enable black slaves to read and write. In the South, however, Bible reading was taught primarily by Anglican clergymen to their own slaves; all the clergymen could do was to encourage other slaveholders to teach the Bible to their slaves.[10]

---

10. Benjamin Quarles, *The Negro in the Making of America* (New York: Collier Books; London: Collier-Macmillan, Ltd., 1970), 41–43.

Not only were reading and writing forbidden among slaves as a rule, but there was an attempt to discourage a common language by inter-mixing persons of different African tribes. Thus, blacks had their own Tower of Babel experience forced upon them. A confusion of tongues was supposed to make communication impossible; without a common language, there would be less chance of rebellions. For the same reason, drums were forbidden on the plantations. However, blacks found ways of communicating, and they became ingenious in their use of symbols. The symbolic thus became a part of their history that is valued even to this day. Where there is a lack of reading and writing, other symbols take on great meaning.

This lack of reading and writing skills plus "exile in a foreign land" where a common language was impossible and African communica-tion forms were forbidden created an inexpressible mode of existence. William H. Grier and Price M. Cobb, who have considered this history, are right to argue against the view that black persons ought to pull them-selves up by their own bootstraps and achieve like others who came to America: "Major differences of background are ignored. The black man was brought to this country forcibly and was completely cut off from his past. He was robbed of language and culture. He was forbidden to be an African and never allowed to be an American."[11]

This black experience in America has certainly conditioned black interpretation of the Bible. Even though influenced by oppressive psy-chological, social, economic, and political forces, blacks have displayed a tremendous transcendent spirit that has enabled them to confront the biblical text creatively.

After it was decided that blacks were worthy of conversion, they were taught the Bible in Sunday schools. Capers's Catechism, a Meth-odist church primer approved by the Methodist General Conference, was used. William Capers wrote this catechism and based it on the prin-ciple of the inferiority of the Negro slave. It was intended to provide a theological justification for the slave's state of bondage and servitude. In his book *The Rise of Colored Methodism*, Bishop Othal Hawthorne Lakey of the Christian Methodist Episcopal Church gives a brief quote from Ca-pers's work: "It is obvious that much of the instruction given . . . must, of necessity, deal in the first principles of Christian truth; must, to a large extent, be adapted to an humble grade of intellect, and a limited range of knowledge; and must make its impression by constant and patient reiteration."[12]

---

11. William H. Grier and Price M. Cobb, *Black Rage* (New York: Bantam Books, 1969), 122.

12. Othal Hawthorne Lakey, *The Rise of Colored Methodism* (Dallas: Crescendo Book Publications, 1972), 37.

Capers's Catechism and another by John Wesley were sometimes printed in the same volume. Some of the questions and answers found in Capers's Catechism were:

Q. What did God make man out of?

A. The dust of the ground.

Q. What does this teach you?

A. To be humble.

Q. What is your duty to God?

A. To love him with all my heart, and soul, and strength, to so worship him and serve him.

Q. What is a servant's duty to his master and mistress?

A. To serve them with a good will heartily and not with eye-service.[13]

Through instruments like these, some blacks converted to the Christian faith and learned about the Bible. But blacks had to demythologize American history before they could appropriate biblical history. It can be shown that blacks did not appropriate the intended meanings of the primers that were imposed upon them. They took the teachings as preached by the plantation missionaries and shaped them to meet their own needs, making a creative synthesis out of what whites taught them, of what they discovered for themselves, and of what they remembered from their African past.

Long before theological institutions in the South increasingly appreciated the historical elements in the Bible, blacks had heard and read the Bible through the existential reality of their own oppression in America, and that reality allowed them to identify readily with the historical oppressions recorded in Scripture. Furthermore, when whites preached to blacks, the white preacher and black congregation tended to interpret biblical events differently—the white preacher interpreting biblical events figuratively while the blacks interpreted the events more literally and concretely. When a white preacher referred to a biblical event, blacks tended to view it in terms of an analogous, concrete, historical event within their own experience.[14] Thus the events in the Bible spoke powerfully and directly to their situation, and that led them to shape a distinct and creative interpretation of the Bible.

Realizing that myth is propagated through the retelling of stories, blacks appropriated the Bible mainly through storytelling. Storytelling assumed great meaning as a form of communication among blacks.

---

13. Ibid., 38.
14. See James H. Cone, *God of the Oppressed* (New York: Seabury Press, 1975), 55.

Blacks read the Bible historically and concretely.[15] It was the black preacher who told the stories of Israel liberated from the bondage of Egypt; of the three Hebrew "boys" in the fiery furnace; of the dry bones in the valley; and of the birth, death, suffering, sorrow, burial, and resurrection of Jesus Christ. These stories provided hope for those who identified with the freed Israelites, the rescued Hebrew boys, the life-giving spirit in the dried bones of the valley, and the hope of the resurrection as experienced in the conquering of the grave by Jesus Christ. The Bible, which blacks were initially forbidden to read, was read by free blacks and was taught to blacks by defiant whites who felt the system of slavery unjust. Even though these factors contributed to blacks' familiarity with the Scriptures, it was the black preacher who was chiefly responsible for transmitting the biblical imagery and its message to the masses of black people.[16]

Among blacks there is a commonality of suffering, and throughout their history in America this has led to a corporate caring for the whole of the community and not a mere personal concern for salvation. The kerygmatic aspect of a suffering messiah, like Jesus, especially serves as an analogue to black suffering. In their suffering, blacks have identified with the birth, life, death, and resurrection of Jesus, and hence in Jesus blacks have found a true friend. While it has taken theologians and biblical scholars a long time to discover the humanity of Jesus, the humblest black Christian has always sung with enthusiasm the song "What a Friend We Have in Jesus." It is almost axiomatic that in interpreting Scripture those who are marginalized and those who have more of a stake in the status quo would bring a different set of questions to the text. Research conducted on blacks and their interpretation of Scripture has shown that the oppressors and oppressed usually raise questions in light of their privilege or lack of it. For blacks, Jesus is human and identifies with the poor by suffering on their behalf. He is the same Jesus who is the risen Christ and is the present and coming judge. This Jesus is presently in solidarity with those seeking to eradicate injustices and gives courage and motivation to those who know that Jesus' eschatological promise is to judge all humanity. By contrast, whites tend to stress the resurrection as the beginning of a triumphalist church tradition that protects the status quo.

Blacks tend to share a perspective on the Bible that celebrates God's liberating action in history. Traditionally, this liberation has centered on salvation from the power of sin and evil, but there has always been a parallel emphasis for blacks on salvation from the evil concretized in

---

15. See James H. Cone, *Black Theology and Black Power* (New York: Seabury Press, 1969), 93; and idem, *God of the Oppressed*, 40, 50.

16. See Henry Mitchell, *Black Preaching* (Philadelphia: J. B. Lippincott Co., 1970); also idem, *The Recovery of Preaching* (New York: Harper and Row, 1977).

racial exclusivity and the dehumanization of the poor. Perhaps because of the real effect of the brutality of slavery, segregation, and discrimination, blacks share a common ethos of salvation in which the biblical story speaks naturally to their story. This is what some call "the hermeneutical privilege of the poor and oppressed."

The story of the Exodus speaks especially to blacks. We know the story of the Exodus is chiefly the reflection of the activity of God in the life of a people, with the supreme example of that activity being manifested in the Exodus of God's chosen people from slavery in Egypt. This activity of God in their affairs provided the core of the confessions they made when they gathered together for worship. When they came to the shrines for renewal, they recited these confessions and pledged themselves anew to God, to keeping God's commandments, and to obeying God's laws. The functional mythology of the Exodus that operated in their lives provided the necessary motivation for the earthly journey of the Jews, and it has provided the same motivation for blacks.

The ancient Israelites were instructed to make the following confession when they presented their firstfruits to the Sovereign One:

> My forebear was . . . homeless [and] went down to Egypt with a small company. They lived there until they became a great, powerful, and numerous nation. But the Egyptians ill-treated us, humiliated us, and imposed cruel slavery upon us. Then we cried to the Lord, the God of our fathers, for help, and God listened to us and saw our humiliation, our hardship and distress; and so the Lord brought us out of Egypt with a strong hand and outstretched arm, with terrifying deeds, and with signs and portents. God brought us to this place and gave us this land, a land flowing with milk and honey.

Through hearing and reading the story of the Jews, blacks were enabled to perceive the activity of God in their own community. It is at this point that black history becomes important for study of the Bible. Blacks can neither properly understand nor appreciate the story found in the Bible without knowledge and understanding of black history.

The stories found in the Bible tell us how to look at the black story, what questions to raise, and even when we have found some of the answers. Furthermore, since the stories describe the intended relationship between God and God's creation and between persons, the larger community is judged at every point where human beings are found to be in living conditions and relationships different from those that the story shows God to have intended. The liberating story found in the Bible, of necessity, contradicts the story of slavery. The interpretative value of the story provides one of the keys for understanding the African American story. We can, therefore, restate the confession of the Hebrews as follows:

Our ancestors were great and powerful people on the continent of Africa. Africa once ruled the world. There, great and mighty empires existed like Egypt, Ethiopia, and Mali. Our fathers and mothers, sisters and brothers were kidnapped, stolen like cattle from their home in Africa and brought to America as slaves. They were beaten, molested, and killed. Yet, all the while they were building America.

In their suffering, they cried out to God and God raised up leaders among them—men and women like Nat Turner, Nathaniel Paul, David Walker, Sojourner Truth, Harriet Tubman, William Miles, Richard Allen, James Varick, Daniel Alexander Payne, James W. C. Pennington, Henry Highland Garnet, Samuel Ringgold Ward, Alexander Crummell, Edward Wilmot Blyden, Henry McNeal Turner, Marcus Garvey, Malcolm X, Rosa Parks, Martin Luther King, Jr., and countless other persons less known but yet of great significance.

These men and women stood up to their oppressors and condemned their inhumanity. They told their oppressed brothers and sisters to fight for their freedom and proclaimed God would give them the victory. They hoped that through God's mighty acts and wondrous deeds freedom would be theirs. Already they knew that God had set them free, according to the grace of God as seen in Jesus Christ. Yet, freedom in terms of justice has been denied. Laws on the books establishing civil rights have not been implemented; therefore, misery, poverty, and unemployment are common experiences. We must prepare ourselves with the skills and knowledge that are needed to be of service to our people and thus bring the living conditions intended by God for all God's children. The struggle continues.

Just as Israel, as a community, became liberated from bondage and oppression, God's work in the world is to liberate all people from oppression in order for them to form a community of political and social partnership. Through the retelling of the biblical story, and the story of the black man and woman in America, the former story may evoke faith in God's activity, but the latter story, when heard and heeded, helps black and white respond more creatively to the divine Word for our present situation. The view of Robert A. Bennett, Jr., is right: "The Black experience in America is not the Jewish-Christian experience of ancient Palestine. But, as the tale of sorrows of a people awaiting deliverance, the Black narrative has a message consistent with the biblical witness though not found in that witness."[17]

The creation myth, generally speaking, is most important for blacks. In the Hebraic tradition, God was known as liberator and creator. God the creator and parent and human beings as brothers and sisters are motifs that were derived from the biblical creation stories. This presupposition helped blacks extricate the gospel from its racist entanglements.

---

17. Robert A. Bennett, Jr., "Black Experience and the Bible," *Theology Today* 27 (April 1970–January 1971): 422.

In the primary sources of Christianity, especially the Bible, blacks discovered a perspective on humanity that was entirely different from that which they experienced in the teaching and practices of white Americans. The universal parenthood of God implied a universal kinship within humankind. Some scholars would consider the creation story as the one undergirding the hermeneutic of blacks and their interpretation of Scripture. Those advocating the importance of the biblical creation stories as primary data for the interpretative paradigm for blacks connect this paradigm with the black experiences, reasoning, feeling, and traditions.

Not all African Americans have shared the enormous possibilities of the creation motif. Some African Americans' view of eschatology has foreclosed consideration of the importance of creation and their role as cocreators with God. One example will suffice. William Banks, a black minister whose sincerity no one would question, raises questions with "social gospelers" who emphasize abundant life in this world. Feeling that sin is so pervasive and impossible to eradicate by human effort, he uses the Bible to show how "social gospelers" are wasting their time in the arena of socio-political endeavors. Such passages as Mark 16:15; Acts 6:4; 1 Corinthians 1:17; Ephesians 4:11-12; and 2 Timothy 4:2 are used to play down the mundane and emphasize the spiritual. The following opinion represents the view of one who has spiritualized Scripture to the extent that creation is viewed as evil, and consequently the fight for justice seems irreligious and futile. Banks says:

> The Evangelical recognizes that the world system is in the lap of the devil, and that injustice, war, poverty, and prejudice are all parts of the system. But the social gospeler appears to be deluded. He thinks God has left it up to man to make the world a better place in which to live. Surely there is little evidence today that man is succeeding. Indeed, the idea of man's improving the world is not biblical. It is a poor concept, certainly not based upon the truths of Scriptures, and it has led some men to assume roles God never intended or called them to have. God's plan is to let things get worse and worse (2 Tim. 3:13), and only the return of Jesus Christ will alter world conditions for the better. The social gospeler's failure at this point finds him seeking an imaginary pot of gold at the end of the rainbow of humanism.[18]

William Banks and others sympathetic with his view have unwittingly stressed an exclusive eschatology and have not taken seriously either the incarnation or the Hebraic-Christian concept of creation that declares the work of God to be "very good" (Gen. 1:31). This politically reactionary view has been detrimental to blacks and the poor because the concern has been for the "souls" of human beings to the exclusion

---

18. William Banks, *The Black Church in the U.S.: Its Origin, Growth, Contributions, and Outlook* (Chicago: Moody Press, 1972), 87.

of oppressive and dehumanizing socio-economic, environmental, and political structures.

In spite of the opinions of some black interpreters of Scripture who stress eschatology as opposed to creation or liberation, it is apparent that fundamental to any black biblical hermeneutic are the universal parenthood of God and the concomitant universal kinship of humankind. Consequently, blacks have been able to: (l) allow the Bible to speak both constructively and critically to each new situation; (2) strive for political and social justice, confident of the presence of the God spoken of in the Bible; (3) solidify theological grounds for opposing racism; and (4) establish the *authority* of the Bible on grounds they can understand. This latter point relates to the fact that for blacks the Bible attains its authority as that authority conforms to the black story through experience and culture. The biblical stories make sense to blacks because these have inspired blacks with a retrospective view of their own history, have given them a confession that tells of what God has done in the history of another people, have evoked a telling of what God has done in their own history, and have provided a perspective of faith and hope with regard to what God will do for their freedom. In this respect, the Bible is one of the chief components of the black experience; it enables myth to function coherently in the lives of blacks.

The story of civilization, including its rise, success, and eventual decline, is summed up and encapsulated in the biblical story; this story relates to a basic myth that enables any people to function in society. This is not to deny the influence of forces like economic need, political pressure, class and race conflict, or the desire for power. But these never produce any great, lasting, historic shapes unless they are configured by a story of compelling power, giving them direction. This is why we must agree with Carl Marbury, who writes about Alex Haley's *Roots* and the black theologian:

> Perhaps it is the mythic component that has the deepest implications for the black theological enterprise. Black theology up to this point has been of necessity ideological-reactional and overly apologetic within the American-European theological context. Haley's epic places the black search and struggle within a mythological and typological stream of consciousness that is at once universal, Judeo Christian and/or biblical as well.[19]

Marbury believes that as a basis for biblical hermeneutics, mythology holds the most promise for black theology and, by implication, *black* biblical hermeneutics. This is the case because: "A serious attempt at developing black theologies will of necessity place special use on myths,

---

19. Carl H. Marbury, "Myth, Oral Tradition and Continuity: A Biblical-Theological Response to *Roots*," *The Church and the Black Experience Bulletin* (February 1977): 21.

folklore, folk music, oral traditions, literature, cultural linguistics within the African languages tradition, social anthropology, African religions, the family structures and value systems."[20] If blacks' mythologies and stories have functioned to interpret the Bible, biblical mythologies have also functioned to interpret blacks' story, language, and imagery.

Images and Imagination in Biblical Interpretation

Vivid images are crucial for comprehension and transmission of stories. Scholars should, without apology, advocate using imagination to interpret Scripture. Although in the past some scholars have stressed imagination, many in the rationalist tradition thought this inappropriate and beneath a truly educated person. Emphasis was on the intellect. Because the Scriptures are theological documents it was and is natural that systematic, dogmatic, and pastoral theologians engage in critical reflection. As I said above, scholars were formerly interested solely in the historical facts and putting the text in historical perspective. This is important and necessary, but such a process does not go far enough.

Scripture is more than a body of abstract thought and generalizations. It is usually very concrete, especially in the narrative parts. There are many images and a rich deposit of symbolic language. These are not grasped with only the intellect but also with the imagination. The Scriptures, as historical documents, were composed by authors using the historical methods and purposes current in various cultures at various times. The difference between their view of history and ours is great. They were not interested in historical facts in the way we are, but in the meaning of historical events. In presenting history, they used many images and symbols that confronted the readers with the meaning of that history and enabled them to associate it with their own historical lives. To relate the history in the Scriptures to our own time, we need to use our imagination while reading them, just as their original readers did.

We need an approach to hermeneutics that builds on what historical study has disclosed while also providing a basis to relate present experiences to the text of Scripture. The role of imagination can help us in that endeavor.

To use the imagination means that we must allow the verbal images of the text to evoke mental images in the interpreter and the hearer. The black preacher was and is a master of this use of Scripture.[21] My father, who was a minister in the Christian Methodist Episcopal Church

---

20. Ibid., 23.
21. Ibid., 26.

for over thirty-five years, did not have a seminary education, but had a basic love for Scripture and could tell the biblical stories in such a way that one would walk around in the images and find oneself caught up in the events of the Bible. He would often say, "In my mind of imagination, I can see. . . . " The intent was to evoke a picture that corresponded to what the text said. The preacher is especially called upon to use imagination in interpreting Scripture. For the congregation, Scriptures come to life through the images used by the preacher.

Joseph Johnson, Jr., who was a black biblical scholar and bishop in the Christian Methodist Episcopal Church, recorded some principles of scriptural interpretation that were conveyed to him as a legacy by his father. These principles suggest a way of preparation for the imaginative use of Scripture:

1. Prepare yourself with devotion and prayer prior to your encounter with the Scriptures.

2. Read the entire *chapter* in which the text is located.

3. Become acquainted with all of the stories which lead up to the text and those that follow.

4. What were the problems, the situation of the participants in the story?

5. Read the biblical passages aloud, so as to hear the Scriptures and permit them to speak to you.

6. Discover the human element and the Divine element in the situation.

7. You must see what the writer saw, feel what the participants in the story felt, and hear what they heard.

8. Use your imagination and put yourself in the place of the writer and participants of the story.

9. Assume the different roles of the principal characters in the story and act as if you were present when the story was first told.

10. Ask yourself this question, "What special message does this passage of Scripture bring to your people for their healing and renewal?"

11. Then wait for God to speak.[22]

Someone will quickly object: This use of imagination may work well for the homiletical task, but for scholars, the interpretative value of imagination is minimal. Let us, in answering this objection, take an example from the resurrection passage in John 20:1-2, a very short account of the first visit to the tomb of Jesus. The event took place early in the morning on the first day of the week, while it was still dark. We are told that Mary

---

22. Joseph A. Johnson, Jr., *Proclamation Theology* (Shreveport, La.: Fourth Episcopal District Press, 1977), 46–47.

Magdalene came to the tomb and that when she saw that the stone had been moved away, she ran to Simon Peter and the other disciple, the one Jesus loved, and told them that the Lord had been taken from the tomb and that she and the others did not know where they had placed his body.

The usual interpretations of this passage focus especially on historical problems arising from a comparison with other accounts in the Synoptics. They concentrate on such issues as: Why is Mary Magdalene alone on the visit? (The Synoptic Gospels say she had companions.) How is it that the event does not include a proclamation or manifestation of the resurrection as we are accustomed to read in the Synoptics? In John, the visit to the tomb is highly problematic. Based on the fact that the tomb is open, Mary Magdalene concludes that it is empty and that some have taken away the Lord's body. This reference to Jesus' body as the Lord's body is full of irony. Since she refers to Jesus as "Lord," Mary should have assumed that he was no longer in the tomb. Of course, even as he describes Mary's problem, the author witnesses to his own faith in the resurrection by using the title Lord.

Commentators also show that the event must be understood as relative to what follows. It introduces further accounts that show how the first Christians came to have faith in and to recognize the risen Lord. Given the introductory function of 20:1-2 and the text's historical problems, the tendency is to pass on quite quickly to the rest of the chapter, which is extremely rich theologically.

While insights from the historical-critical method can be rich, they can be made richer by an imaginative study of images in the text. Notice the observation that Mary came to the tomb while it was still dark. In the other gospel accounts, where the empty tomb is good news and a sign of life and hope, she comes to the tomb at dawn or shortly after sunrise. Here in John, it is still dark, a reality grasped by the imagination and readily associated with presentation of the empty tomb as bad news and a sign of hopelessness and death. Also, this darkness is symbolically rich in a Gospel that presents Jesus as the Word that came into the world as the life that gives light to humankind, a light that the darkness (night) could not ultimately overcome (John 1:4-5). At this point in the account, the light has yet to dispel the night. Granted, this imagery of light and darkness may be interpreted differently by blacks and whites, but one can hardly interpret these images in John as racist. The extent to which we share in the experience of darkness enables us to appreciate the light of the risen Lord's manifestation.

Imagination can also deepen our understanding of the fact that Mary went to the tomb, a symbol of death, but never entered the tomb. To experience the risen Lord and share in Christ's life, is it not necessary to enter the tomb, to die and be buried with Christ? In the Synoptic

Gospels, the visit to the tomb is a life-giving experience. But in those Gospels, the women enter the tomb.

We see from this illustration how the imagination opens the text toward the transformation of the person and the society. Interpretation must move from an explanation of the text to genuine understanding and the transformation of the interpreter. This kind of thinking corresponds with fulfillment of the purpose of Scripture, which is not to give information, but to form the church and every person in it. Black theologians have been called pastoral theologians. J. Deotis Roberts does not particularly like that title, but it may be closer to the nature of the Scriptures than the titles "systematic" or "dogmatic" theologian. This is because the Scriptures are pastoral documents intended to shape, orient, strengthen, and inspire the church in the process of addressing the whole person.

If Scripture addresses the whole person, then intellect alone is not enough. The imagination, in conjunction with the intellect, makes it possible for the whole person to be addressed. Images address the person in the concreteness of life, putting one in touch with the senses in a holistic manner. In 1976, Amos Wilder published a book entitled *Theopoetic Theology and the Religious Imagination*.[23] In that book he emphasizes the importance of imagination in biblical interpretation.

Wilder argues that religious communication has been addicted too long to the "discursive, the rationalistic, and the prosaic."[24] He makes a plea for "the role of the symbolic and the pre-rational in the way we deal with experience."[25] Recognizing that "imagination is a necessary component of all profound knowing and celebration"[26] and that "when imagination fails doctrines become ossified, consolations hollow, and ethics legalistic,"[27] he states, "it is at the level of the imagination that any full engagement with life takes place."[28] All theologians and biblical scholars, black and white, need to hear Wilder's admonition and veiled warning: "It is at the level of the imagination that the fateful issues of our new world-experience must first be mastered.... Before any new theologies, however secular and radical, there must be a contemporary theopoetic."[29]

This is important for black theology and biblical hermeneutics if we intend to go beyond rhetoric in communicating that which is a part of the

---

23. Amos Wilder, *Theopoetic Theology and the Religious Imagination* (Philadelphia: Fortress Press, 1976).

24. Ibid., 1.

25. Ibid., 2.

26. Ibid.

27. Ibid.

28. Ibid.

29. From the foreword to *Grace Confounding: Poems by Amos N. Wilder* (Philadelphia: Fortress Press, 1972), ix.

black or the biblical tradition. We must begin to ask how people learn, hear, respond, and inculcate new behavioral patterns. The intellect is one way, but it must be complemented by the imaginative faculties.

There are some legitimate cautions to be followed when using the interpretative imagination. One of the more obvious dangers is that a barrage of strange interpretations could result. The church might revert to a kind of subjectivity that would lead to eisegetical fanaticism. In the African American and other traditions, there have always been persons who solely used their imagination, and that to excess. Probably this always will be a problem. One way to curb such occurrences is to inter-pret images in the manner in which other factors are considered in the historical-critical interpretations of Scripture. Since an image occurs in a context, we have to examine that context before seeking to understand the image. For example, we could not have interpreted light and dark-ness as we did above without having first interpreted the total context in which those images occurred.

The tendency to read whatever we want into the text is a problem. Hence, we must begin to train scholars and interpreters of the text to have an aesthetic formation that prepares them for a controlled application of the creative imagination. Artists and poets have been ahead of us in this matter, and we may need to study more about how these persons have used their imaginations in disciplined ways. That study could help us to express the truths of the biblical texts in ways that would improve and vivify our own formation and that of the black church in general. An illustration of an imaginative mode of biblical interpretation by those whom we consider "poor" is the art and text entitled *The Gospel in Art by the Peasants of Solentiname*.[30]

This book contains excerpts from the four-volume *The Gospel in So-lentiname*, a collection of peasant commentaries on gospel passages read at Mass each Sunday in Nicaragua. The way in which the scriptural in-terpretation of peasants is connected with imagination is very revealing and helpful. In the introduction to the former book, one gets a feel for both interpretation and imagination:

> The peasants' comments on the Gospel—simple, direct, often earthy—
> show forth their deep conviction that Jesus lives and is, indeed, present
> among them. So, too, the paintings reflect the peasants' faith that the
> Gospel is the living Word of the living God heard in their world. Gabriel
> finds Mary at her sewing machine. Bottles of Coca Cola stand, symbol-
> ically, on Herod's table. The troops of Herod/Somoza carry automatic
> weapons and wear uniforms supplied by the United States. And the reader
> will notice in the Resurrection scene that the crude wooden crosses bear

---

30. Philip Scharper and Sally Scharper, eds., *The Gospel in Art by the Peasants of Solentiname* (Maryknoll, N.Y.: Orbis Books, 1984).

the names of Elvis, Felipe, and Donald, young men frequently quoted in the text.[31]

There are three principal virtues in using the imagination in addition to other interpretative strategies already mentioned: (1) We are aided in opening up the Scriptures as they were meant to be read, not because they provide raw material for a theological or ethical system, but for formation of the church, in order that the society might be transformed. (2) The Scriptures are placed at the disposal of all, not just an elite group of specialists. (3) When the Scriptures are allowed to speak through their various images and symbols, the evocative power of these images, coupled with the sociological grid of the reader, leads to new and exciting meanings and ideas. This means that the Scripture can have a myriad of meanings. Images cannot be defined, but ideas can. Sensitivity to images means that we must allow other persons to express their interpretations, which may indeed be of profit to us. Recognizing and adhering to socio-political, socio-cultural, and mytho-poetic bases for biblical interpretation are contributions that African Americans have made and can make to the scholar, preacher, and lay person.

---

31. Ibid., 5. This kind of indigenized use of the Bible portends well for future interpretations.

— 2 —

The Hermeneutical Dilemma of the African American Biblical Student

William H. Myers

Introduction

The amount of literature written on biblical interpretation during the last quarter century alone is staggering. The literature focusing primarily on hermeneutical methodology in one language is legion. Some books are directed at an academic audience,[1] while others are written on a more popular level and are directed at a wider audience.[2] Some of these books are more conservative in their arguments,[3] while others are more

---

1. See, among others, Bernard Ramm, *Protestant Biblical Interpretation* (Grand Rapids, Mich.: Baker Book House, 1970); Anthony C. Thiselton, *The Two Horizons: New Testament Hermeneutics and Philosophical Description* (Grand Rapids, Mich.: Wm. B. Eerdmans Pub. Co., 1980); Hans-Georg Gadamer, *Truth and Method* (New York: Crossroad, 1984); Paul Ricoeur, *The Conflict of Interpretations* (Evanston, Ill.: Northwestern University Press, 1974); idem, *Essays on Biblical Interpretation* (Philadelphia: Fortress Press, 1980).
2. See, among others, Gordon D. Fee and Douglas Stuart, *How to Read the Bible for All It's Worth* (Grand Rapids, Mich.: Zondervan Publishing House, 1982); Terence J. Keegan, *Interpreting the Bible: A Popular Introduction to Biblical Hermeneutics* (New York: Paulist Press, 1985); R. C. Sproul, *Knowing Scripture* (Downers Grove, Ill.: InterVarsity Press, 1977); A. Berkeley Mickelsen and Alvera M. Mickelsen, *Understanding Scripture* (Ventura, Calif.: Regal Books, 1982).
3. D. A. Carson and John D. Woodbridge, eds., *Scripture and Truth* (Grand Rapids, Mich.: Zondervan Publishing House, 1983); idem, eds., *Hermeneutics, Authority and Canon* (Grand Rapids, Mich.: Zondervan Publishing House, 1986).

liberal.[4] Whereas some are structured chronologically,[5] others are more thematically structured.[6] Although most are written by a single author, increasingly more are collaborative works.[7]

There is much to commend in most of these books. The attempt by scholars to simplify rather complex procedures in a manner that makes them accessible for a wider audience is praiseworthy. However, there is a subtle ideology lying beneath the surface of most of these publications. They presuppose a Eurocentric world view and approach to biblical interpretation. The books emphasize selected events in the history of interpretation (the Reformation, the Enlightenment); selected methodological concerns (biblical criticism in general and the historical-critical method in particular); or selected hermeneutical motifs (authorial intent, inspiration, inerrancy, propositional revelation).

Although one grants that most books will be selective, the result of the Eurocentric approach is the exaltation of one cultural world view over all others. In addition, the approach tends to lock the interpretative task in the past (e.g., in debates over authorial intent) while evading key contemporary issues like racism or intercultural dialogue. Although many of these works suggest that they cover the entire history of interpretation or that they address the full range of contemporary hermeneutical developments, in them one rarely finds any discussion of an African American interpretation of the Scriptures.[8] The subtlety of this politics of omission can be observed in the aforementioned publications.

In a rather insidious way, this approach creates a dilemma for the African American biblical student. Since the literature is dominated by a Eurocentric approach, the lectures, assignments, and examinations in the discipline of biblical studies tend to prepare the African American student to answer more Eurocentric-oriented questions and concerns.[9] I do not suggest that this was some kind of conspiracy or that it was

4. See, for example, Jack B. Rogers and Donald K. McKim, *The Authority and Interpretation of the Bible: An Historical Approach* (New York: Harper and Row, 1979). For a rather exhaustive analysis of this book and a "revisionist historiographical" approach from a conservative perspective, see John D. Woodbridge's review in *Trinity Journal* n.s., 1 (1980): 165–236.

5. Robert Grant and David Tracy, *A Short History of the Interpretation of the Bible* (Philadelphia: Fortress Press, 1984); Stephen Neil, *The Interpretation of the New Testament 1861–1961* (London: Oxford University Press, 1964); Rogers and McKim, *Authority and Interpretation of the Bible.*

6. E.g., Carson and Woodbridge, eds., *Scripture and Truth;* idem, eds., *Hermeneutics, Authority and Canon.*

7. See Willard Swartley, ed., *Essays on Biblical Interpretation* (Elkhart, Ind.: Institute of Mennonite Studies, 1984); Donald K. McKim, ed., *The Authoritative Word* (Grand Rapids, Mich.: Wm. B. Eerdmans Pub. Co., 1983).

8. E.g., see the historical surveys cited in note 5.

9. James H. Cone (*My Soul Looks Back* [Maryknoll, N.Y.: Orbis Books, 1986], 76) says, "The academic structure of white seminary and university curriculums requires that black students reject their heritage or at least regard it as intellectually marginal. When black students study the Bible and church history, almost nothing is said about black people's

done with conscious intention. Nonetheless, I do contend that such an approach can have rather pernicious consequences.[10] This approach suggests to all students that the Eurocentric way of interpreting the text is the normative way by which all other approaches are to be tested. While tacitly implying that the Eurocentric approach is without cultural bias, it also implies that an African American reading of the text is culturally biased.[11] The subtlety of the approach is what makes it so dangerous. So painless is the approach that one is bleeding without knowing one has been cut, and hooked without seeing a ripple in the water.

The dilemma may manifest itself in the ministerial context of the African American believing community when students observe that the Eurocentric approach does not help them address the questions raised in an African American context. Students become painfully aware of the fact that they have been given a "metric" set of "tools" to work with in a "nonmetric" context, and they just don't fit. Should the tools be discarded altogether or merely re-tooled? Can they be re-tooled and still remain useful? How and where does one get such expensive, highly revered tools re-tooled?

Tension may arise as students observe that many raise questions about the appropriateness of such tools in the African American context. Yet, they recognize that the Eurocentric approach is not without merit, especially the critical techniques (both Higher and Lower Criticism) that they mastered in formal theological study. Is a synthesis possible or desirable? Where does one find a model or procedure for bringing about a peaceful coexistence or even a synthesis, since there is a paucity of material on both the problem and solution? The easiest—though most dubious—response to this dilemma may be to repudiate and discard all or most of the critical methodologies in academia and to replace these with learnings garnered on the firing line in the ministerial context.

A similar dilemma may manifest itself in academia when the African American student is appointed to a teaching post in a Eurocentric school. Again, it is an amazingly insidious set of circumstances. Most of the sources, syllabi, models, pedagogical techniques, and teachers that the student was exposed to while in school were Eurocentric. This

---

heritage that would suggest that they have anything to contribute intellectually in those areas."

10. "How is it possible for a black student to get a Ph.D. in theology, biblical studies, or church history and not think that the black church and community have nothing to contribute to those disciplines? Is not an identity crisis inevitable by the very act of becoming a black professor?" (ibid.).

11. The almost innocuously subtle packaging of this approach can be observed in J. I. Packer, "Infallible Scripture and the Role of Hermeneutics," in Carson and Woodbridge, eds., *Scripture and Truth*. In answering his own question about hermeneutically invalid conceptions of biblical hermeneutics, Packer says, "Latin American liberation theology, which sees the bringing in of social and economic justice as the essence of what the Bible teaches that God's work today must be, is an example of this mistake" (p. 354).

changes little with the African American's faculty appointment because she or he is probably the first African American appointee, or if there is another that person probably is not in the biblical studies department. So again, the pedagogical content, style, and tone are set by Eurocentric colleagues. The expressed or implied desire of the academic administration, denominational body, student body, and alumni may dictate to a large degree the dominant subject matter, pedagogical style, and approach of the school. The level of desire for change among this group will determine how quickly change can occur.

As a result of the combination of many of the above-mentioned factors, the African American biblical professor may feel that it is appropriate to start with the Eurocentric approach of biblical interpretation. Furthermore, it may be that during his or her student years the professor embraced the Eurocentric approach far more than is realized or admitted. Where is there an African American biblical professor today who does not teach form, source, textual, or redaction criticism?

As African American biblical professors observe that the pedagogical structure needs altering, they also observe that this is much easier said than done.[12] First, there is a paucity of models and sources. Second, there may be strong resistance to such changes inside the academy (from colleagues and students).[13] Third, it is often difficult to separate method from a tradition of beliefs; hence, it can be very difficult to affirm all students in their own tradition while attempting to do major surgery on their method of interpretation.[14] Finally, there is a difference of opinion among African American scholars as to the appropriate strategies. Some

---

12. Cone (*My Soul Looks Back*, 47) says, "A moral or theological appeal based on a white definition of morality or theology will always serve as a detriment to our attainment of black freedom. . . . Freedom is not a gift, but a responsibility, and thus must be taken against the will of those who hold us in bondage."

13. "Racism runs deep even among seminary professors" (ibid., 28).

14. This is not as easily done as it sounds. Often methodological convictions become so intertwined with the doctrinal and/or ideological convictions of one's tradition that, for that person, they are one and the same. Often it is possible to reduce it to one construct. The "inerrancy" debate today is an example of this interrelationship and reductionistic tendency. See, for example, the debate between James D. G. Dunn and Roger Nicole in *Churchman* 96–98 (1982–83): 104-22, 198–215, 201–25; between Clark H. Pinnock and Rex A. Koivisto in *Journal of the Evangelical Theological Society* 24/2 (June 1981): 139-55; and between Norman L. Geisler and Robert Gundry in *Journal of the Evangelical Theological Society* 26/1 (March 1983); see also Arthur F. Holmes, "Ordinary Language Analysis and Theological Method," *Bulletin of the Evangelical Theological Society* 11 (1968–69): 131–38, and Norman L. Geisler, "Theological Method and Inerrancy: A Reply to Professor Holmes," *Bulletin of the Evangelical Theological Society* 11 (1968–69): 139–48.

Another example would be the debate over whether or not one's presuppositions are separate and distinct from one's methodology. See, e.g., Norman L. Geisler, "Methodological Unorthodoxy," *Journal of the Evangelical Theological Society* 26/1 (March 1983): 87–94. Gadamer (*Truth and Method*, 465) says, "Even a master of the historical method is not able to keep himself entirely free from the prejudices of his time, his social environment and his natural situation, etc." See esp. his "Hermeneutics and Historicism," in *Truth and Method*, 460–91.

see themselves primarily as guardians of the community and believe that a contextual strategy, especially one that begins with African American sources and historical description, is most appropriate.[15] Others may believe that an ecumenical strategy will be more effective.[16] While the latter group may be most concerned with avoiding the error of replacing one imperialistic methodology with another, the former may be most concerned with avoiding enslavement to a Eurocentric approach to biblical interpretation.[17]

In this essay I want to pursue further the methodological dilemma that African American biblical students face in biblical interpretation in the academy as well as in their own believing community of faith.

Method and Methods

I assume that a primary responsibility of the African American biblical scholar is to aid the African American believing community in understanding, surviving, and altering its present socio-political situation through accurate and appropriate interpretation and application of Holy Scripture.[18] It is neither easy nor simple.[19] As soon as one acknowledges this responsibility the obvious question that follows is: How?

As one attempts to answer the "how," one encounters a methodological dilemma. This dilemma raises further questions, all of which this essay cannot address. For example: Is the complexity of African

---

15. See especially James H. Cone, *The Spirituals and the Blues* (New York: Seabury Press, 1972); idem, *God of the Oppressed* (New York: Seabury Press, 1975); Vincent L. Wimbush, "Biblical Historical Study as Liberation: Toward an Afro-Christian Hermeneutic," *Journal of Religious Thought* 42/2 (Fall–Winter 1985–86): 9–21.

16. E.g., J. Deotis Roberts, *Liberation and Reconciliation: A Black Theology* (Philadelphia: Westminster Press, 1971).

17. E.g., Roberts (ibid., 23) feels that "a Black Theology that takes reconciliation seriously must work at the task of inter-communication between blacks and whites.... White Christians may be led to understand and work with blacks for liberation and reconciliation on an interracial basis." However, Cone (*God of the Oppressed*, 238–40) says, "I contend that only black people can define the terms on which our reconciliation with white people will become real.... Whenever black people have entered into a mutual relation with white people, with rare exceptions, the relationship has always worked to the detriment of our struggle."

18. Perhaps what Cone (*My Soul Looks Back*, 76) says about black theology and black theologians is also true for black biblical scholarship: "Black theology must arise out of the struggle of black life. Attending professional societies (white or black), reading and writing books, and teaching in seminaries are not enough. Indeed they must be secondary to our active participation in the praxis of the liberation struggle."

19. Cone gives an excellent insight into the difficulty when he says, "As I reflect over my fourteen years of writing and teaching black theology, I am embarrassed by the extent of my captivation by white concepts. And I realize that I am still partly enslaved by them. The struggle to overcome this enslavement has been a constant struggle in my intellectual development" (ibid., 77).

Americans' situation better served by a method or methods? Should one look for a new method or attempt to reshape an old method? In what ways does one's training as a biblical scholar in Eurocentric institutions help as well as hamper one in shaping a method or methods?[20] In light of African Americans' training and convictions, what is the most efficient way for them to make a contribution? What are the advantages and disadvantages of collaborating with other African American biblical scholars, with Third World biblical scholars, and with European or European-American biblical scholars?[21]

It is within the context of an oppressive society—a society that in many ways diminishes the value of African Americans—that the Scriptures have played an important role in helping African Americans to survive and maintain a healthy identity and hope.[22] The African American biblical scholar has not been exempted from such oppressive treatment.[23] As students, authors, and teachers, most, if not all, of these scholars have shared a common history of overt and subtle forms of racism and rejection of the value of the African American believing community's contribution to the interpretative process.

As the oppressive society seeks to disaffirm the value of African Americans, they by contrast seek to affirm their value. As the oppressive society seeks to deny rights to full participation in the society, African Americans seek to affirm those rights. As the oppressive society seeks to enslave, African Americans seek to liberate. Enslavement and rejection of the rights of others are actuated not only by maintaining control over the political, economic, and social systems, but also by maintaining control over key "charter documents" (such as Holy Scripture or the U.S. Constitution) and especially over the interpretative methodology deemed normative. One is forced to ask if there is not a madness in the very method itself.[24]

The Eurocentric approach to theological hermeneutics has been dominant in Western cultures since the Enlightenment.[25] This dominance

---

20. Cf. especially the works cited in notes 9, 10, and 19 with those cited in note 11.

21. See, e.g., James H. Cone, *Speaking the Truth: Ecumenism, Liberation and Black Theology* (Grand Rapids, Mich.: Wm. B. Eerdmans Pub. Co., 1986), and idem, *My Soul Looks Back*, chap. 4.

22. See Wimbush, "Biblical Historical Study as Liberation."

23. See especially Cone, *My Soul Looks Back*.

24. See the literature in note 14 concerning the debate over the possibility of separating presuppositions from methodology.

25. See, e.g., Gadamer, *Truth and Method*; Peter Stuhlmacher, *Historical Criticism and Theological Interpretation of Scripture* (Philadelphia: Fortress Press, 1977); Bernard Ramm, *After Fundamentalism: The Future of Evangelical Theology* (New York: Harper and Row, 1984). However, see John D. Woodbridge ("Some Misconceptions of the Impact of the 'Enlightenment' on the Doctrine of Scripture," in Carson and Woodbridge, eds., *Hermeneutics, Authority and Canon*) for a discussion on the difficulty of merely defining the term *Enlightenment*.

persists in spite of the many concerns, challenges, and calls for modification leveled against it. Perhaps a few of the challenges are worth noting.

1. It is too exclusive. It lacks appreciation for the development of hermeneutical approaches in non-Western cultures and minority cultures within the Western culture.[26]

2. It is preoccupied with the notion that a text has only one legitimate meaning, which usually means *the* only orthodox meaning.[27]

3. It reads the text solely as a product of history. Thus, in its search for original meaning it effectively locks the text in the past.[28]

4. It overemphasizes text production and text mediation to the exclusion of text reception in the interpretative process. With this kind of emphasis questions of origin, sources, transmission, and preservation dominate.[29]

5. It is too letter-conscious and not narrative-conscious enough. Therefore, it overemphasizes the propositional statement to the exclusion of the historical-experiential event.[30]

6. It is too heavily dependent on the historical-critical method and the historical interpretation theory as a means for appropriating meaning.[31]

---

26. Daniel J. Harrington, "Biblical Hermeneutics in Recent Discussion: New Testament," *Religious Studies Review* 10/1 (January 1984): 7–10; idem, "Some New Voices in New Testament Interpretation," *Anglican Theological Review* 64 (January 1982): 362–70; Wimbush, "Biblical Historical Study as Liberation." In addition, see the works of Cone, esp. *God of the Oppressed* and *The Spirituals and the Blues.*

27. Examples of works that present this position are numerous. See, among others, Geisler, "Methodological Unorthodoxy," 87–94; idem, "The Relation of Purpose and Meaning in Interpreting Scripture," *Grace Theological Journal* 5/2 (1984): 229–45; J. P. Louw, "Primary and Secondary Reading of a Text," *Neotestamentica* 18 (1984): 26–37.

28. James A. Sanders (*Canon and Community* [Philadelphia: Fortress Press, 1984], 3, 25) says: "Biblical criticism has locked the Bible into the past. A critical reading of the Bible for the most part means recovering the points originally scored. That is the thrust of biblical criticism as it has developed since the Enlightenment. The attitude or posture of biblical criticism has been to devalue the pursuit of the meanings the biblical text may have for the believing communities today.... In Enlightenment terms this has meant the recovery of the original intent of the author or the understanding of the original audience."

29. See the excellent introduction to this issue by B. C. Lategan, "Current Issues in the Hermeneutical Debate," *Neotestamentica* 18 (1984): 1–17.

30. Sanders, *Canon and Community;* Paul J. Achtemeier, *The Inspiration of Scripture: Problems and Proposals* (Philadelphia: Westminster Press, 1980); and Wimbush, "Biblical Historical Study as Liberation." See, however, the valuable discussion by Kevin J. Vanhoozer, "The Semantics of Biblical Literature: Truth and Scripture's Diverse Literary Forms," in Carson and Woodbridge, eds., *Hermeneutics, Authority and Canon,* 53–104. Vanhoozer tries to put life back into the propositional statement by combining Carl F. H. Henry's emphasis (i.e., verbal, cognitive communication with authority resting in the text) with speech-act theory as seen in the work of J. L. Austin, John Serle, and Paul Ricoeur.

31. See the importance of the historical-critical method to this type of study as well as an assessment of its possibilities and limitations in Edgar Krentz, *The Historical-Critical Method* (Philadelphia: Fortress Press, 1975); W. S. Vorster, "The Historical Paradigm—Its Possibilities and Limitations," *Neotestamentica* 18 (1984): 104–23; Alan F. Johnson, "The

7. It places the reader in a passive state as opposed to an active state.[32]

8. It tends to cater to a literate bourgeois class while condescending to, de-basing, and/or excluding the oral traditions and methods of interpretation traditionally resident in minority cultures.[33]

It should be evident that the Eurocentric approach to biblical interpretation is under siege in diverse parts of the church.[34] The data suggest that the Eurocentric way of doing theological hermeneutics is inadequate in Third World cultures and minority cultures within oppressive Western cultures. In fact, African American theologians, historians, and biblical scholars alike have argued that the African American's usage and understanding of the text as well as appropriation of Christian constructs developed in an altogether unique manner.[35] Furthermore, the manner in which the African American approach developed and is presently utilized is not incorporated in the Eurocentric method. It is omitted in all major works on hermeneutical methodology.

A key element in the Eurocentrism in biblical interpretation is the manner in which the historical-critical method has yielded conclusions. The Eurocentric approach to the historical-critical method has grown in popularity and use in Western cultures since the Enlightenment. Its growth and popularity continue today in spite of some pronouncements that it is dead, bankrupt, ineffective, irrelevant, and ideologically loaded.[36] The challenge to Eurocentrism as evident in the use of the historical-critical method occurs because opponents and some proponents recognize that few of its results have moved us any closer to an appreciation of other people's (e.g., Latin Americans' or African Americans') ways of interpreting the text. The importance of the historical-critical method for its proponents is captured in James Barr's insistence that "criticism retains an unchallenged freedom."[37] Other pro-

Historical Critical Method: Egyptian Gold on Pagan Precipice?" *Journal of the Evangelical Theological Society* 26/1 (March 1983): 3–15.

32. Lategan, "Current Issues in the Hermeneutical Debate," 10ff.

33. Wimbush, "Biblical Historical Study as Liberation"; see also the other works cited in note 15, above.

34. See Harrington, "Biblical Hermeneutics in Recent Discussion"; see also the other works cited in note 26, above.

35. Wimbush, "Biblical Historical Study as Liberation."

36. Walter Wink (*The Bible in Human Transformation* [Philadelphia: Fortress Press, 1973], 1) says, "Historical biblical criticism is bankrupt." George Soares Prabhu ("Toward an Indian Interpretation of the Bible," *Biblebhashyam* 6 [1980]: 151–70) says the historical-critical method is "ineffective, irrelevant, and ideologically loaded," and Gerhard Maier (*The End of the Historical-Critical Method* [St. Louis: Concordia Publishing House, 1977]) argues for its total rejection, i.e., its death. See the valuable essay by Willard M. Swartley, "Beyond the Historical-Critical Method," in Willard M. Swartley, ed., *Essays on Biblical Interpretation*, 237–64.

37. James Barr (*Holy Scripture: Canon, Authority, Criticism* [Philadelphia: Westminster Press, 1983], 33–34) says, "The concept of freedom is of central importance here, for I wish to suggest that freedom is the central content of the idea of criticism when it is applied to

ponents, though rejecting Barr's call for absolute freedom, nevertheless affirm the importance of the method. The primary reason for this affirmation is the valuable insight that has come from using the method appropriately.[38]

Now we can speak more concretely about the methodological dilemma of the African American biblical student. Although African American believing communities have been interpreting the Scriptures for centuries, the method has not been as systematically articulated or described in literature as has the Eurocentric method. African American biblical students are products of an African American culture that, perhaps imperceptibly, yields a methodological orientation during and after academic training.

African American students are trained in the Eurocentric method in academia and perhaps, like their Eurocentric counterparts, become convinced of its positive contributions and embrace the method. How many African American biblical scholars are there who would advocate jettisoning critical techniques today? Yet, somewhere along their pilgrimage they became aware of the method's limitations for the African American believing community.

Whereas some African American biblical scholars call for the repudiation of the Eurocentric method, others call only for a new set of controllers of the method. Should the African American biblical student's strategy be to offer a complementary critique or a replacement critique of the Eurocentric method? Or should one side with those who argue that the Eurocentric method is so irrelevant, bankrupt, and dead that it should not have a resurrection or, better said, a resuscitation?[39] Or should one side with those who argue that it has its own internal self-corrective possibilities that should be utilized because it is so crucial to sound interpretation that it cannot and should not be dislodged?[40]

The choice may be far more complex and formidable than first meets the eye. Even when African American scholars agree on a given problem (e.g., oppression) and goal (e.g., liberation), often friendship and/or fellowship may be strained when it comes to agreeing on the strategies for obtaining the goal.[41] Sometimes repudiation of a given method as

the Bible. . . . Criticism means the freedom, not simply to *use* methods, but to follow them wherever they may lead." See Raymond E. Brown (*The Critical Meaning of the Bible* [New York: Paulist Press, 1981], 23–44), who argues similarly.

38. E. J. Krentz, *The Historical-Critical Method;* Swartley, "Beyond the Historical-Critical Method"; Ramm, *After Fundamentalism;* Sanders, *Canon and Community;* Stuhlmacher, *Historical Criticism and Theological Interpretation of Scripture.*

39. See note 36, above.

40. See note 38, above.

41. Witness, for example, the clash between James Cone (see especially *God of the Oppressed*) and J. Deotis Roberts (*Liberation and Reconciliation*). Cone (*My Soul Looks Back,* 62) says, "My response to Roberts has been more severe because he seemed to have ignored the obvious by saying what whites wanted to hear." In his most recent book,

well as repudiation of a strategy viewed as ineffective in dealing with the method are made a matter of community allegiance. This is complicated all the more by the fact that some of us are at different stages of awareness of the overall dilemma and its complexity. Hence there is a greater need for patience in the development of solutions.

The situation is even more complex because some African American biblical students who thought they were doing battle with European-oriented interpreters have discovered that they in fact are battling themselves and other African American biblical students. This can be most unsettling, and therefore is rarely publicly acknowledged. No one is more candid about this than James Cone as he narrates his reaction to criticisms of his black theology by other black theologians:

> Much more important than the responses of white theologians were the responses of black theologians. . . . The first radical disagreement came from Charles Long and Carleton Lee. . . . I was shocked that the criticism was so severe and also voiced the concerns of other black scholars. Gayraud S. Wilmore and my brother Cecil joined the dialogue and sided with Long and Lee against me. I was stunned for some time and did not know what response to make. . . . I was embarrassed by this critique, because no one had been more critical of white theology than I. To find out from my black colleagues that I was still held captive by the same system that I was criticizing was a bitter pill to swallow.[42]

Of course I certainly do not know yet how this methodological dilemma will be resolved. However, I would offer the following observations:

1. The way out of this methodological dilemma must come primarily from African American biblical scholars.

2. The solution will probably evolve as a result of a combination of both contextual research and interdisciplinary accord as individuals and groups address the issue.

3. Perhaps the solution will be *methodologies* held in balanced tension with one another as opposed to *a* methodology. If this is the case, then all concerned may be forced to wrestle with the amount of contradiction that each of us can accept.

4. We will have to decide to what degree contributions by (and dialogue with) European, Euro-American, and Third World scholars are helpful or harmful to the resolution of the dilemma. On this point, we must decide

---

Black Theology in Dialogue (Philadelphia: Westminster Press, 1987), Roberts says, "But the oppression-liberation formula does not adequately unlock the biblical message."

It is interesting to note that when it comes to the strategies of liberation, African Americans have always had their Booker T. Washingtons and Martin Luther Kings as well as their H. Rap Browns, Stokeley Carmichaels, Eldridge Cleavers, and Malcolm Xs.

42. Cone, *My Soul Looks Back*, 59–61.

whether we want to be heard only in our community or in the larger community as well. Are we speaking merely to and for ourselves? I hope not!

5. African American biblical scholars must take the lead in restructuring the pedagogical content and structure of academia.[43]

Canon and Canons

It is difficult to separate the discussion of method from that of canonical stance. This interrelationship is captured to a degree by Brevard Childs in his discussion on canon:

> *The issue at stake in canon turns on establishing a stance from which the Bible is to be read as Sacred Scripture.* . . . Attention to canon establishes certain boundaries within which the tradition was placed. The canonical shaping serves not so much to fix a given meaning to a particular passage as to chart the arena in which the exegetical task is to be carried out. Attention to canon is not the end but only the beginning of exegesis. *In one sense the canonical approach sets limits to the exegetical task by taking seriously the traditional boundaries.*[44]

In addition, the arguments of James A. Sanders are helpful. Sanders states:

> Canonical criticism may permit the current believing communities to see themselves more clearly as heirs of a very long line of shapers and re-shapers of tradition and instruct the faithful as to how they may faithfully perceive the Bible even yet as adaptable for life. . . . Canonical criticism focuses on the function of authoritative traditions in the believing communities, early or late. . . . It would appear that once the text became frozen into a final form—there were numerous "final" forms—the communities soon found the hermeneutical means necessary to break it down to reapply to their purposes and needs.[45]

Although there are some similarities in these two scholars' approaches to canon, there is a significant dissimilarity. Whereas Sanders emphasizes the process and functions of the "final form" (i.e., canon) in a believing community, Childs focuses much more on *the* final (literary)

---

43. Regarding structure, African American faculty members must be intentional in their efforts to increase the one-per-faculty appointment of African Americans. Regarding pedagogical content, African American faculty must be intentional in adding *required* works written by African American biblical scholars that reflect their different approach to the text. This must be done early in the degree program and in core courses (e.g., Introduction to New Testament), not merely specialized courses offered later in the program as electives.

44. Brevard Childs, "The Canonical Shape of the Prophetic Literature," *Interpretation* 32 (1978): 54–55; emphasis mine.

45. Sanders, *Canon and Community,* 20, 24, 25.

form. Perhaps there are ways of discussing canonical perspective other than these two, but I am not aware of any that do not in some way fit under the rubric of a "final form" or a "function" type perspective. The dominant perspective without a doubt has been to focus on the final form.[46] As soon as one becomes aware of the fact that there are a variety of final forms ranging from the five books of the Samaritan Pentateuch to the eighty-one books of the African Ethiopian Orthodox Church—the Protestant churches have sixty-six and the Roman Catholic and Eastern Orthodox churches have a different set of seventy-three—one is forced to ask: Whose final form?

When we consider the arguments of both Sanders and Childs on canon, it should be apparent how a particular canonical perspective influences one's method of interpretation. As Childs suggests, one's canonical approach sets the arena—limits, perimeters—in which the exegetical battle can be fought. If one can limit the "boundaries of the dialogue" to *the* final form as well as restrict the hermeneutical means allowable for cracking open *the* final form to *the* method, then the dialogue of pluriform voices is reduced to *the* monologue of power and control.

The arguments of Sanders are particularly helpful because he focuses on the function of canon in believing communities irrespective of final form. This canonical perspective shifts the focus away from an endless debate locked in the past over the final form (usually implying *the* orthodox form) to an emphasis on the way in which canon—irrespective of final form—explains the world to a believing community at any time in history. Canon from this perspective appears to have more of an unbroken life in the believing community, a life cut loose from arguments over a past final form and continuously rejuvenated by each succeeding generation of "shapers and reshapers."

Certainly Childs is correct when he asserts that this matter of canon has to do with "establishing a stance from which the Bible is to be read as Sacred Scripture." However, we must ask: Whose stance? Is it to be the stance of Childs or Sanders, or some other stance? From my experience it seems that the canonical perspective that focuses on final form has aided Eurocentric interpreters in maintaining control over method. This perspective is much more likely to be used to limit the boundaries to past issues (e.g., final form, authorship, past meanings, authorial intent, literary style) while evading present issues (e.g., racism, sexism, classism). Hence it seems that canonical perspective—one's stance "from which

---

46. We didn't hear about the phrase "canonical criticism," with its focus on the "function" and "process" of canonical formation, until *Torah and Canon* (Philadelphia: Fortress Press, 1972) by James A. Sanders. Even today the literature is dominated by the final form perspective. See Sanders's excellent book, *From Sacred Story to Sacred Text* (Philadelphia: Fortress Press, 1987), which collects the various articles that he has published on canonical perspective over the years.

the Bible is read as Sacred Scripture"—is bound up with methodology, and therefore the ability to maintain power and control over the canon being interpreted is reinforced when one method and one canonical perspective are exalted above all others.

How does one break through this control of power? Herein lies another aspect of the hermeneutical dilemma for African American biblical students. It is likely that the canonical perspective that they have had the most exposure to in seminary emphasized final form, perhaps even a final form as *the* orthodox form.[47] Furthermore, they may have become convinced by the arguments and thereby may accept one particular final form theory as *the* final form. The difficulty arises when students are confronted with other final forms that may be radically different from the one they have accepted. The obvious dilemma is that the student has become wedded to a canonical perspective that is very difficult to discard without it affecting other convictions.

The canonical perspective that looks at how canon functions in believing communities is useful to the African American believing community. Sanders's perspective allows far more room for the African American believing community to make contributions to the improvement of method in the interpretative process than does the usual emphasis on final form. It is far more useful as a point of departure in seeking to resolve the canonical perspective dilemma and break through the control of power that is dominant in a Eurocentric methodology.

There is force in Sanders's argument that it is Scripture as canon that explains the world in the ambiguity of reality; that it is the function of canon to address identity and lifestyle; that while the historical-critical method focuses on explaining Scripture, it is the canonical tradition that helps to make sense out of what is going on in the world, giving an illumination on life, not merely Scripture itself; that the books retained in the canonical tradition are those that had value for explaining the world of the present believing community.[48] This is a perspective that focuses on the belief that there is life in the canon that is adaptable enough for any believing community at any time even in different forms. Such an approach allows one to affirm one's own believing community's form without having to disaffirm other believing communities' forms.[49]

---

47. David M. Scholar ("Issues in Biblical Interpretation," *Evangelical Quarterly* 88/1 [1988]: 19n.27) says, "The acceptance of the biblical canon as a particular collection of 66 documents—all these and no others—is itself not a given of any biblical text. Biblical canon is known to us through the histories of Israel and the early church and is accepted as a normative collection by faith as a work of God within historical particularity. Canon history is certainly filled with its own ambiguities and uncertainties."

48. Sanders, *Canon and Community*, chap. 2, esp. 24–28.

49. I am well aware of the potential epistemological issue of mutually exclusive canonical perspectives, but it is beyond the scope of this essay.

African American biblical scholars must attempt to give shape and form to their own unique canonical perspective. A substantial amount of research needs to be done to uncover evidence that describes how canon has functioned in African American communities *throughout their history in this country.* The plethora of questions that need attention are: What is our final form? Has the present form always been our final form? How has our stance regarding the sacred text shaped our exegesis? What boundaries have been fixed as a result of our canonical stance? Should these boundaries be altered? How has our situation as African Americans in an oppressive society affected the shape and form of our canon, the selective use of that canon, and the interpretation of that canon? Can this unique dimension be identified in our sermons, songs, rituals, symbols, conversion and call narratives, scholarly literature, homiletical and liturgical styles? What have we consistently passed on in our canonical tradition and what has dropped out along the way? Have we ever and do we presently operate with a virtual canon within the canon? If so, why? And if so, can that canon be clearly identified? What is the extent of continuity between this canon and the Bible throughout African American history? If there is an African American de facto canon, to what degree is it similar to the recognized canon of other believing communities? Are this possible canon and the African American canonical perspective broad enough to be inclusive, yet narrow enough to have a distinctive meaning?

If we approach the discussion in this manner, we will have something significant to add that is not a mere rehash. This approach will allow us perhaps to do a new and mighty work in our community and in our discipline. As a result, we should be able to demonstrate that an African American canonical stance has as much epistemological validity and value as any other stance.

When we acknowledge that there is more than one final form (shifting emphasis to the function of final forms within believing communities), the question of *other sources* and their relationship to the final form emerges. More basically, we must determine whether there are other sources that have helped to shape the believing community's identity in such a way that they have taken on a near-canonical status in the community. Sanders suggests as much when he says,

> The Mishnah and Talmud have *functioned* for Judaism in precisely the same ways the Bible has functioned in the believing communities but at an authoritative level somewhat below that of the Bible. So in Christianity creeds were developed which functioned as authoritative. Hymns outside the Psalter have functioned in a similar manner, perhaps at what one might call a tertiary level of canonicity. Certainly the *Hodayot* (1Q and 4QH) would have so functioned at Qumran, but similar liturgical collec-

tions grow up in all denominations which reach a certain level not only of authority but of canonicity in the sense that they become difficult to change because they attain a certain status in the communities which revere and use them. All this bespeaks the essentially conservative nature of communities of faith and belief. Even certain translations, such as the Septuagint (LXX) of the OT for early Christians, the Vulgate of Jerome for very conservative Roman Catholics, or the King James Version still for many Christians, attain a certain canonical status.[50]

What are those other near-canonical sources in African American believing communities and what is the relationship between them and the sacred text? Undoubtedly, those sources would include sermons, Negro spirituals, testimonials, conversion narratives, and call narratives. Are there others?

These sources are the media by which we have transmitted—primarily in oral fashion—our traditions that contain vital information about our self-understanding as African Americans in an oppressive Western culture. Paul Achtemeier hints at the importance of "self-understandings" captured by traditions when he says,

> Traditions are the means by which the community understands itself in relation to its past. . . . Traditions guard those past events which give to the community its uniqueness and they aid the community in shaping its life in accordance with those originating events. . . . The origin of a tradition is therefore an event that engenders a hope strong enough to affect the life of a community.[51]

Not only do our sources contain information on African American self-understandings in an oppressive culture, they contain equally vital information on how we have viewed the sacred text as canon, wider sources as canon, and the canon within the canon.

Therefore, our research must not stop at definition and description of the role and value of these sources in helping African Americans to survive and to maintain their identity and self-esteem under oppressive conditions. We must also seek to elucidate how these sources functioned in the interpretative task. We must elucidate the relationship between these other sources and the sacred text. We must inquire about the potential mutual shaping that occurs in the interpretative process as well as the authoritative status of those other sources in our believing community.

For example, the object of my present research is the role and function of the call narrative[52] in the African American believing community.

---

50. Sanders, *Canon and Community*, 14–15.
51. Achtemeier, *Inspiration of Scripture*, 124.
52. I include the call experience itself in the analysis of the call narrative by inquiring into the relationship between the two.

My thesis is that the call narrative has always held and still holds a significantly authoritative canonical status when compared to the sacred text in the sanctioning process of those reputedly "called into the preaching ministry." Moreover, I contend that while this was true for an even larger segment of our believing community in our past, where this tradition is maintained in contemporary settings, the force and authoritative status of the call narrative remain undiminished.[53] One might well argue that the juxtaposition of a different normative canonical stance vis-à-vis the dominant stance is one of the ways to break the latter's control of the interpretative system. This strategy breaks the control of a final form as well as the power of the dominant methodology by merely bypassing that methodology in favor of a direct existential encounter with an even higher power (i.e., God).[54] As an African American female colleague said to me in response to whether or not the women-in-ministry issue could be settled exegetically, "It may be a moot point since women have heard and responded to the call from God."

Another example is the conversion narrative. Anyone who has listened closely to the testimonies of some older African Americans is aware of how important the "mourner's bench" experience was for them as part of the conversion narrative.[55] In some African American believing communities the centrality of that experience and the ability to narrate it for legitimization almost rival the place and role of the sacred text.

We must inquire into the history of this wider canonical perspective in our community, clearly articulating how and why it developed, how it functioned, and how the intricate dynamics and relationships between these various sources helped to give shape to each other, to our hermeneutical methodology, as well as to our self-understanding as African Americans. I am convinced that the results of this kind of inquiry will reflect both our uniqueness as well as a broadening and deepening of the canonical perspective and interpretative methodology.

---

53. As exalted a position as the sacred text holds in African American believing communities, there are many quarters in which a convincing call narrative is so equally hallowed that an aspiring ordinand with M.Div. in hand would not receive ordination if he or she could not articulate an acceptable call narrative deemed to be from the heart. However, an ordinand with a convincing call narrative who does not possess the necessary academic credentials could receive ordination.

54. I am well aware of the subjectivistic extremes to which such a strategy can be taken. The church's history is full of examples of the danger. But I am suggesting that this strategy take place from a canonical stance within a believing community; I am not suggesting private interpretations. Furthermore, it should be noted that no believing community with a given canonical stance has been without its extremes.

55. It is interesting to note that the contemporary call narrative in the African American community has resisted transformation much better than the contemporary conversion narrative when compared to their respective counterparts of the past.

Summary

I have argued that African American biblical students often face a hermeneutical dilemma because their Eurocentric training in seminary does not aid them in the articulation of an African American hermeneutic in their ministerial context or academic position.

I further suggest that there is such an important, perhaps even unique, relationship between a believing community's canonical perspective and its hermeneutical methodology that both must be thoroughly investigated and described if one hopes to do justice to the debate over method.

I also assert that it is up to the African American biblical scholar to pave the way out of this dilemma. And I believe that the way out is more likely to evolve, especially as the African American biblical scholar enumerates and describes the relationships between the canonical and near-canonical sources that influence the interpretative process in the African American believing community. In addition, the African American biblical scholar needs to push for a transformation of the pedagogical content (e.g., through inclusion of the above material) and the structure of academia so that future students are not faced with the same dilemma.

Finally, I hope that we do not embrace only the kinds of offensive strategies and tactics that permit us to talk only to ourselves, and that the larger community does not embrace the kinds of defensive tactics that force us to talk only to ourselves. May we all be both "hearers and doers" of the Word who came and dwelt among us in the flesh that all of us might be set free.

— 3 —

Reading *Her Way* through the Struggle: African American Women and the Bible

Renita J. Weems

An on-going challenge for scholars committed to a liberation perspective on the Bible is explaining how and why modern readers from marginalized communities continue to regard the Bible as a meaningful resource for shaping modern existence. This is a challenge because in some crucial ways not only do biblical authors at times perceive reality very differently from these groups, but the Bible itself is often used to marginalize them. For example, feminist biblical scholars have made the helpful insights that the androcentric milieu of the ancient world pervades biblical texts, and they have convincingly demonstrated that specific texts are unalterably hostile to the dignity and welfare of women; because of these and other similar findings, these scholars are hard pressed to explain why large numbers of religious women (including feminists) still identify with many of the ideals and characters found in the Bible. Likewise, African American scholars have brought eloquent and impassioned charges against the Bible as an instrument of the dominant culture that was used to subjugate African American people. However, the Bible is still extremely influential in the African American religious life, and these scholars are hard pressed fully to explain why. Scholars must realize that something is at work here that involves more than the reader's lack of sophistication, or a slavish dogmatic devotion to the Bible.

Exploring the true reasons, in this post-Enlightenment, postintegrationist, and supratechnological age, becomes important because the Bible is still able to influence, persuade, and arrest so many modern readers.

In this chapter, I wish to explore the rationale by which African American women (marginalized by gender and ethnicity, and often class) continue to regard the Bible as meaningful. This rationale has much to do with how African American women assess the Bible's portrait of how human beings relate to one another. African American women have, in the past, regarded this portrait as credible; they have judged that it coincides with the way they—as African, American, and women—have experienced relationships with other people. I suggest that black women find this portrait especially meaningful because it reflects a distinctive way of living that African American women have valued and continue to advocate with great energy.

Over the last decade or so, a number of illuminating studies have been produced by feminist literary critics who, building upon the discussions taking place in such areas as linguistics, psychology, sociology, and philosophy, have focused attention on the reading strategies of women. Their aim has been to determine whether women interpret literature differently from men, and if so, to what extent gender itself accounts for that difference.[1] Beyond this, other insightful works have focused more specifically on comparing how women read texts written by men and how they read those written by women.[2] Moreover, scholars writing particularly in the area of African American religious history have frequently commented on the different ways in which Anglo- and African Americans have historically interpreted the Bible. These scholars have speculated that the differences may be due in large part to the contrasts in the social and political status of these groups.[3] It is my hope in this

---

1. Working in this important area of reader criticism, Jonathan Culler has raised the provocative question, "Suppose the informed reader of a work of literature is a woman. Might this not make a difference . . . ?" (*On Deconstruction: Theory and Criticism after Structuralism* [Ithaca, N.Y.: Cornell University Press, 1982], 43). For fine anthologies of research devoted to pursuing the implications of this kind of question, see Elizabeth A. Flynn and Patrocinio P. Schweickart, eds., *Gender and Reading: Essays on Readers, Texts, and Contexts* (Baltimore: Johns Hopkins University Press, 1986); Judith Spector, ed., *Gender Studies: New Directions in Feminist Criticism* (Bowling Green, Ohio: Bowling Green State University Popular Press, 1986).

2. See, e.g., David Bleich, "Gender Interests in Reading and Language," in Flynn and Schweickart, eds., *Gender and Reading*.

3. There are many excellent works on the role that so-called slave religion played in shaping and/or sustaining African American history. Two notable examples in this area are Albert Raboteau, *Slave Religion: The "Invisible Institution" in the Antebellum South* (New York: Oxford University Press, 1978); and Mechal Sobel, *Trabelin' On: The Slave Journey to an Afro-Baptist Faith* (Westport, Conn.: Greenwood Press, 1979).

chapter to move such a thesis from the realm of speculation to an insight that is methodologically demonstrated. I will identify a few ways that factors in American society (associated with gender, race, and, in some cases, class) have shaped African American women's relationship with the Bible—a relationship that has some ambivalence. Of course, there are manifold factors inherent to American history that played a role in shaping African American women's consciousness, factors which, in turn, influenced how African American women read literature in general. My scope is necessarily restricted here to a few salient factors that have particular importance for how and why African American women read the Bible.

Reading can be a sublime and complex process. Such sublimity and complexity are magnified all the more when the book is imbued with the kind of power that the Bible has had over Western women's lives. The Bible is in many ways alien and antagonistic to modern women's identity; yet, in other ways, it inspires and compels that identity. An example of the complexity of this situation is this: How African American women read the Bible is a topic that has to do with not only uncovering whose voice they identify with in the Bible—female as opposed to male, the African as opposed to the non-African, the marginalized as opposed to the dominant. It has equally and more precisely to do with examining the *values* of those readers and the corroboration of those values by the text; it has to do with how the text arouses, manipulates, and harnesses African American women's deepest yearnings.

Moreover, African American women have not attempted to negotiate fully the socio-literary universe of the Bible as paradigmatic of a truly liberationist and liberated hermeneutic. Negotiating and interpreting texts are processes that are both empirical and intuitive, rational and transrational, recoverable and unrecoverable. Obviously, many factors, tangible and intangible, cultural and psychological, have shaped African American women's attitudes and reading habits. I will use a select few of these in this study. My discussion is organized in two parts. The first part consists of an examination of the socio-cultural location of African American women against the backdrop of American history. Here, I will show that history has impacted African American women's reading in general, and their reading of the Bible in particular, given the way that the written text has been presented to them as "authoritative." The second part consists of looking at some of the varying types of texts found in the Bible in terms of the voices and values of African American women.[4]

---

4. Throughout this essay, when I speak of African women or African American women, I admit that I am employing language that tends to obscure the enormous differences among African American women in terms of their perspectives, backgrounds, religious traditions, and self-understandings. One might be justified in claiming that, in fact, I am referring to myself (and a small sample of women with whom I am personally familiar)

The African American Female Reader
Confronting the Bible

Only within the last one hundred years or so have African Americans in large numbers been able to read. In America, prior to that time, their enslaved ancestors were not simply unable to read, they were *forbidden* to read.[5] This clarification makes all the difference in the world. In fact, so determined was the American slavocracy to censure reading among slaves that in addition to the laws prohibiting citizens from teaching slaves to read, aggressive, hostile measures were taken to discourage slaves and free Africans from seeking to learn to read. *Forbidding slaves from reading was, undoubtedly, intended to restrict the slave's contact with the outside world and to insure that the slaves were totally dependent upon their slavemasters to interpret and manage their environment for them.* As a result of this aspect of American history, African Americans to this day continue to view reading as an act clouded with mystery, power, and danger. The truth of this is evident in the ambivalence toward reading one can still detect within segments of the African American community—many still view reading as an activity that is at once commendable and ominous.[6]

Because slaves were not permitted to read for themselves, their exposure to ideas, notions, concepts, knowledge, and information was chiefly through word of mouth. Indeed, the one piece of literature that was intentionally and consistently made "available" to them, namely the Bible, was communicated through public readings or sermons. As to be expected, the transmitters of the Bible in a slave culture rehearsed

---

as the surrogate for all African American women. Although this no doubt reflects one of the numerous shortcomings of scholarly discourse, the more modest intention here is simply to call attention to the special circumstances of a segment of readers who previously have been overlooked in biblical and theological studies and to reclaim their presence in American religious history.

5. According to the historian Leon Litwack, at the time of their emancipation, around 5 percent of the emancipated population could read (*Been in the Storm So Long: The Aftermath of Slavery* [New York: Random House, 1979], 111).

6. It is important to point out that those African Americans like myself who were born during or shortly after World War II are a mere two or three generations removed from slavery. For example, my grandfather and his sisters, all in their eighties and with varying literacy skills, can still recall the stories that their emancipated parents and grandparents told them about the hardships of slavery and the measures that were taken to keep them from being able to read. Although African Americans as free citizens have had the right to learn to read for the last one hundred and twenty-five years or so, it has been only since the landmark Supreme Court decision of *Brown v. Topeka Board of Education* in 1954, which declared that segregated schools were unconstitutional (which was translated more specifically to mean that African American children had the right to a quality education), that many of the accoutrements of culture that cultivate and support reading and learning have been made available, even nominally, to African Americans.

and interpreted the contents of the Bible as they saw fit.[7] Thus, what the slaves learned of the Bible's content, however distorted, depended upon an aural tradition for its sustenance, transmission, and assimilation. What the slavemasters did not foresee, however, was that the very material they forbade the slaves from touching and studying with their hands and eyes, the slaves learned to claim and study through the powers of listening and memory. That is, since slave communities were illiterate, they were, therefore, without allegiance to any official text, translation, or interpretation; hence once they heard biblical passages read and interpreted to them, they in turn were free to remember and repeat in accordance with their own interests and tastes. Sermons preached by slave preachers attest amply to the ways in which slaves retold the biblical message in accordance with their own tastes and hermeneutic.[8] Hence, for those raised within an aural culture retelling the Bible became one hermeneutical strategy, and resistance to the Bible, or portions of it, would become another. Howard Thurman's story of his grandmother's listening habits illustrates this last point.

> Two or three times a week I read the Bible aloud to her. I was deeply impressed by the fact that she was most particular about the choice of Scripture. For instance, I might read many of the more devotional Psalms, some of Isaiah, the Gospels again and again; but the Pauline epistles, never—except, at long intervals, the thirteenth chapter of First Corinthians. . . . With a feeling of great temerity I asked her one day why it was that she would not let me read any of the Pauline letters. What she told me I shall never forget. "During the days of slavery," she said, "the master's minister would occasionally hold services for the slaves. Old man McGhee was so mean that he would not let a Negro minister preach to his slaves. Always the white minister used as his text something from Paul. At least three or four times a year he used as a text: 'Slaves, be obedient to them that are your master . . . , as unto Christ.' Then he would go on to show how it was God's will that we were slaves and how, if we were good and happy slaves, God would bless us. I promised my Maker that if I ever

---

7. Scholars frequently comment upon the importance of the Bible and biblical religion in the African American religious experience. A recent article by an African American female scholar involved in theological scholarship deserves special comment. Katie G. Cannon, a womanist ethicist, has written about the hermeneutical strategies that were employed by the hegemonic culture to legitimate and sacralize slavery (see "Slave Ideology and Biblical Interpretation," *Semeia* 49 [1989]: 9–24). Cannon argues that three ideological notions undergirded the exegetical strategies of the slaveholding apologists: (a) the charge that African Americans were not human; (b) the claim that God had foreordained black people to a life of subjugation and servitude to white people; and (c) the assumption that because the Bible does not expressly prohibit the bartering of human flesh, slavery, therefore, was not a violation of divine law.

8. As an example, see John G. Williams, *De Ole Plantation* (Charleston, S.C.: published by the author, 1895).

learned to read and if freedom ever came, I would not read that part of the Bible."[9]

Thurman's grandmother presumably never learned to read the Bible for herself, and it is clear that she never became attached to every word printed in the Bible. In fact, her aural contact with the Bible left her free to criticize and reject those portions and interpretations of the Bible that she felt insulted her innate sense of dignity as an African, a woman, and a human being, and free to cling to those that she viewed as offering her inspiration as an enslaved woman and that portrayed, in her estimation, a God worth believing in.[10] Her experience of reality became the norm for evaluating the contents of the Bible.

It is a fact that the slaves' earliest exposure to the Bible was aural and was set within the context of a slaveholding society that forbade teaching slaves to read. It is also a fact that the Bible was transmitted to slaves in accordance with the interests of slave owners. Both of these facts *must not be underestimated* when considering how modern African American women read the Bible.[11] The strategies one employs in reading a text will depend in large part upon what one's overall disposition is toward the act of reading itself. That is, reading begins with what the reader has been taught about literature and the very act of reading. Texts are read not only within contexts; a text's meaning is also dependent upon the pretext(s) of its readers. Hence, African American women's earliest exposure to the Bible was characterized by their history as a community of enslaved women of color trying to find meaning and hope for their (communal) existence from a text that was held out as congenial to them as long as they remained slaves, but censorious of them should they seek to become free human beings. Indeed, whether one considers their history from the context of North American women's history or African American history, one discovers that the Bible has been the most consistent and effective book that those in power

---

9. Howard Thurman, *Jesus and the Disinherited* (Nashville: Abingdon Press, 1949), 30–31.

10. Deborah Gray White argues that the female slave network was an important institution for the survival and resistance of slaves and one which provided the opportunity for African women to maintain autonomous religious rituals and positions within the community (see *Ar'n't I a Woman? Female Slaves in the Plantation South* [New York: W. W. Norton, 1985], 119–41).

11. Their detachment from the Bible as a textual phenomenon explains in part why African Americans have been absent from doctrinal battles that have characterized American Protestantism, and why, until recently, there has been a paucity of written sermons and exegetical works by African Americans. In an aural culture, textual motifs and fragments predominate. Cheryl T. Gilkes has discussed how one such biblical fragment has imprinted itself upon the African American cultural imagination and has been preserved in a locution, widely repeated in African American religious lore ("Mother to the Motherless, Father to the Fatherless: Power, Gender, and Community in an Afrocentric Biblical Tradition," *Semeia* 47 [1989]: 57–85).

have used to restrict and censure the behavior of African American women.

Thurman's grandmother's refusal to have the Pauline portions of the Bible read to her highlights two important ways in which the experience of oppression has influenced African American women's disposition toward reading the Bible. First, the experience of oppression brought African American women to understand that outlook plays an important role in how one reads the Bible—it became clear that it is not just a matter of whose reading is "accurate," but whose reading is legitimated and enforced by the dominant culture. Second, the experience of oppression has forced the marginalized reader to retain the right, as much as possible, to resist those things within the culture and the Bible that one finds obnoxious or antagonistic to one's innate sense of identity and to one's basic instincts for survival. The latter, however, has not always been easy.

After all, the Bible (rather, its contents) has not been presented to African American women as one of a number of books available to her to read or not read as she pleases. For African American (Protestant) women, the Bible has been the *only* book passed down from her ancestors, and it has been presented to her as *the* medium for experiencing and knowing the will of the Christian God. The Bible's status within the Christian community as an authoritative text whose content is seen as binding upon one's existence always has been a complicated matter. Its role for marginalized readers—especially those who read the Bible in order to get some idea of who they are in the presence of God or who they are in relation to other people—is even more complicated and problematic.[12] Depending upon the social location of the reader, the history of African Americans exemplifies the ways in which the Bible can and has been used, in the name of its supposed authority, to sanction the subjugation and enslavement of people or to instigate insurrection and buttress liberation efforts of oppressed people. Indeed, the seemingly mercurial dexterity of Bible interpreters has had dire implications for both African Americans and women. Nevertheless, the Bible has some power on its own, and it is certainly true that it has been able to arrest African American female readers and persuade them to make their behavior conform according to certain of its teachings. This is due in part to at least two factors. First, the Bible, or portions of it, is believed to provide existential insight into the dilemmas that grip African American women's existence. Second, it reflects values and advocates a way of life to which African American female readers genuinely aspire. But

---

12. For a helpful discussion of the ways in which Protestant biblical tenets have influenced Protestant feminist biblical scholarship, see Mary Ann Tolbert, "Protestant Feminists and the Bible: On the Horns of a Dilemma," *Union Seminary Quarterly Review* 43 (1989): 1–17.

the fact that it has been used most often in American society to censure rather than empower women and African Americans has forced them to approach the task of reading the Bible with extreme caution.

Within recent years, there has been growing attention to the influence that readers themselves exert in interpreting texts. Meaning is no longer seen, as it has been in formalist circles, as the sole property of the text, and the reader is no longer viewed simply as one who is to perform certain technical operations (literary analysis, lexical studies, etc.) upon the text in order to extricate its carefully guarded, unadulterated message. Rather, meaning in contemporary discussions is viewed as emerging in the interaction between reader and text; that is, the stimulus of the text (language, metaphors, literary form, historical background, etc.) interacts or enters into exchange with the stimulus of the reader (background, education, cultural values, cosmology, biases, etc.).[13] From this perspective, moreover, reading is acknowledged to be a social convention, one that is taught, reinforced, and, when "done properly," rewarded. That is, what is considered the appropriate way to read or interpret literature is dependent upon what the dominant reading conventions are at any given time within a culture. Indeed, it should be added, the dominant reading conventions of any society in many instances coincide with the dominant class's interests in that society. In fact, one's socio-cultural and economic context exerts enormous influence upon not only how one reads, but what one reads, why one reads, and what one reads for. Thus, what one gets out of a text depends in large measure upon what one reads into it.

When we consider more specifically the matter of the Bible's status as an authoritative text, again the histories of both African Americans and women in this country show rather clearly that it is not texts per se that function authoritatively. Rather, it is reading strategies, and more precisely, *particular* readings that turn out, in fact, to be authoritative.[14]

---

13. While it shares many of the assumptions of New Criticism, which focused on the autonomy of the text, the contemporary perspective emphasizes the role that the reader plays in construing meaning within texts. Reader-response criticism, as this perspective is called, is considered to have started with the writings of I. A. Richard in the 1920s and in recent times has come to be associated with names like Wolfgang Iser, Stanley Fish, and Michael Riffatere, who, despite the differences in their emphases, share a common interest in such elements as the reader, reading process, and response. One of the more widely commented upon works in the area is Wolfgang Iser's *The Implied Reader* (Baltimore: The Johns Hopkins University Press, 1974). For helpful collections of essays on the development of this perspective, which will simultaneously point out the broad spectrum of viewpoints associated with it, see Susan R. Suleiman and Inge Crosman, eds., *The Reader in the Text: Essays on Audience and Interpretation* (Princeton: Princeton University Press, 1980); Jane P. Tompkins, ed., *Reader-Response Criticism: From Formalism to Post-Structuralism* (Baltimore: The Johns Hopkins University Press, 1980).

14. In other words, even if one concedes that the Bible is authoritative, one still has not said anything about how the Bible should be interpreted. For example, the Bible can be read figuratively or literally, from a christocentric or theocentric perspective, from a

After all, the history of Protestantism aptly points out that different readings (and hence interpretations) of the one fixed text, the Bible, have existed simultaneously. However, in any given period in history, by and large, only one reading convention is deemed to be *the* appropriate way to read (e.g., the allegorical method during the Middle Ages and the historical-critical method during the nineteenth century). What is construed as the appropriate way to read and write is a convention that is passed along during a person's educational and cultural development and is reinforced in the way the dominant culture rewards (e.g., through promotion, public readings, publication) certain readings and penalizes others. And, as we will have occasion to consider shortly, the dominant reading conventions and the dominant class interests in many instances reinforce one another. In other words, readers and reading strategies have far more power than isolated ancient text in themselves.

One distinctive American way of teaching blacks to read has had profound implications upon the way many African Americans view the printed word. This method suggests that in order to read and understand a literary work "properly," one must be prepared to abandon oneself completely to the world of that literary work. Here, the African American woman, when confronted with a work, must agree to renounce her experience of reality, suspend her understanding of life, and waive her right to her own values, so that she may without encumbrances surrender herself to the experiences, world view, values, and assumptions embedded in the work. This, we have been told, is to allow the text to speak for itself; and only under these circumstances, when we permit the text to speak to us on its own terms, without our mediation, do we have the chance, so we have been taught, of apprehending accurately the true meaning of a text. To do otherwise is to impose one's prejudices upon the text. It is a technique for reading that is taught in the schools and reinforced by the dominant culture.

Strongly influenced by eighteenth- and nineteenth-century European historiographic debates, the notion that a text can be properly understood only after one has thoroughly assessed its historical context originally emerged as a challenge to what was, at the time, the doctrinal way of reading. In the case of the Bible, texts were read literally or figuratively to conform to church doctrine without any regard for the way historical settings influenced language and ideas, without regard for the differences that existed among biblical authors, and without regard for the differences between ancient and modern audiences.[15] On the one

---

historical-critical or fundamentalist point of view, and still be viewed as an authoritative book.

15. Arguing that the kind of confessional, precritical reading of the Bible advocated by fundamentalism (a movement to which African Americans have become attracted in recent years due to very particular socio-political reasons) is potentially self-destructive,

hand, the value of the historical-critical technique was to reclaim the autonomy of a historical work by attempting to protect the text for as long as possible from the biases of the reader, so that the work might be appreciated within its own context. On the other hand, the negative result, especially as it has become evident in the way this position has been used by those in power, has been to undermine marginalized reading communities by insisting that their questions and experiences are superfluous to Scripture and their interpretations illegitimate, because of their failure to remain objective. But, as the story of Thurman's grandmother demonstrates, the emotional, psychological, and religious health of African American women has been directly related to their refusal to hear the Bible uncritically and their insistence upon applying what one might call an "aural hermeneutic." This hermeneutic enables them to measure what they have been told about God, reality, and themselves against what they have experienced of God and reality and what they think of themselves as it has been mediated to them by the primary community with which they identify. The community of readers with whom they identify as they read tends to influence how they negotiate the contents and contexts of the Bible.

Describing what reading male texts does to women, Judith Fetterley writes, "The cultural reality is not the emasculation of men by women, but the *emasculation* of women by men. As readers and teachers and scholars, women are taught to think as men, to identify with a male point of view, and to accept as normal and legitimate a male system of values, one of whose principles is misogyny."[16] In other words, according to Fetterley, in order to read texts by men, women have to read like men. That is, the African American female reader of the Bible has, like other women, been taught to suspend her female identity long enough to see the world through the eyes and ears of the male narrator. Failing that, she is expected to agree to become the male reader/audience for whom the text was originally written. As a result of their training in school, church, and the home, African American women, like women everywhere who read and find meaning within the Bible despite the clutter of silenced biblical women, have been taught to and indeed have felt it necessary to identify with the male voice in texts.

Vincent Wimbush maintains that a historical-cultural reading allows African Americans "an increased measure of *hermeneutical control* over the Bible," in a way that allows Afro Christian churches "to articulate self-understanding, maintain integrity as separate communities, and determine their mission in the world" ("Historical/Cultural Criticism as Liberation," *Semeia* 49 [1989]: 47-48). See Wimbush's article for a discussion of the dangers of the fundamentalist interpretative strategies for the survival of the African American community.

16. Judith Fetterley, *The Resisting Reader: A Feminist Approach to American Fiction* (Bloomington, Ind.: Indiana University Press, 1978), xx.

But the male voice in texts is not the problem per se. For man qua man is not for African American women the presumed nemesis. It is rather a certain kind of man. Obviously, when they encounter biblical texts, Anglo-American women, like African American and other culturally marginalized female readers, are confronted with works in which they share neither the author's gender nor, in some cases, cultural viewpoints. However, as I have already pointed out, texts are not the sole determinants of meaning. Reading strategies and social interests are endorsed and enforced by ruling interpreting communities that can be not only androcentric, but also, as in the case of Anglo-feminist readings, class-centered and ethnically chauvinistic. That is, within the Anglo-Saxon religious hegemony, the female voice has been suppressed because it comes from a woman. The Anglo woman has, nevertheless, benefited from (and hence contributed to) the hegemonic legacy of the dominant culture in her complicity in reading the Bible like a man who insists upon securing and retaining his domination over others and his control over his surroundings. Thus, one characteristic of the African American woman's reading of the Bible is that she has refused to read (and respond) like a certain kind of man.[17] Therefore, the insistence on the part of Anglo (Eurocentric) feminists for recognition within the Western religious and literary tradition might be viewed as an unwitting admission that, as Anglos, they too have played a part in shaping the Eurocentric texture of that religious and social hegemony.

Further, how one reads or interprets the Bible depends in large part on which interpretative community one identifies with at any given time. That is, the average reader belongs, in actuality, to a number of different reading communities, communities that sometimes have different and competing conventions for reading and that can make different and competing demands upon the reader. In fact, the interpretative community with which one identifies will have a lot to say about what "reading strategy" one will adopt. For, in the end, it is one's interpretative community that tends to regulate which reading strategies are authoritative for the reader and what ought to be the reader's predominant interests.[18] For example, Christian African American women belong to at least four communities of readers: American/Western, African American, female, and Christian. Each community has its own ideas about what the reader

---

17. Writes one reader-response critic, "A bad book [then] is a book in whose mock reader we discover a person we refuse to become, a mask we refuse to put on, a role we will not play" (Walker Gibson, "Authors, Speakers, Readers, and Mock Readers," in Tompkins, ed., *Reader-Response Criticism*, 5).

18. And within those communities, a reader's identity may be compounded by any number of other factors—class, geography, sexual preference, physical health—all of which may impinge upon what perspective she or he brings to the reading act (see Stanley E. Fish, *Is There a Text in This Class? The Authority of Interpretive Communities* [Cambridge: Harvard University Press, 1980]).

should be reading for in a text, and each one is governed by its own vested interests. Hence, an African American woman, confronted, say, with the Old Testament story of Ruth, may be forced, depending upon the context in which she is reading, to focus predominantly on Ruth the woman, Ruth the foreigner, Ruth the unelected woman, Ruth the displaced widow, or, perhaps, Ruth the ancestress of the king of Israel, King David, to name a few.

Indeed, a full analysis of the ways in which these interpretative communities individually and collectively influence African American women's reading habits is beyond our present scope. Yet, when one looks at how this experience as *women* has shaped their attitude toward reading, one finds that there have been very few incentives for African American women *as women* to read. Until recently, the production of literature of consequence in this culture has been a male enterprise that has left the African American woman, like other female readers, to read about and reflect upon the meaning of her existence through the viewpoint of a largely androcentric canon. It is a canon that has by and large proved itself to be incapable of transcending gender restraints against women in antiquity and, by implication, modern female readers. That canon has consistently assigned women to the category of "the other." Because of that, the African American female reader, in essence, finds herself permanently reading as an outsider as long as she is unwilling and incapable to deal creatively in partitioning out her double identity as woman and African American. She experiences what it means to be a woman as she experiences it as an African American, and her African Americanness as she experiences it as a woman. Admittedly, there is no evidence to suggest that, in addition to the fact that she was a slave, the African woman was prohibited from reading *because* she was a woman. Still, one must consider that (1) the Bible's world view is pervasively androcentric; (2) the official interpreters of the Bible over the centuries have been almost exclusively male; and (3) the Western canon is predominantly male in origin. These facts help one to see that although the African American woman was not forbidden to read *because* she was a woman, the Bible projects her femaleness as a problem. The Bible purports to address the existential dilemmas of its intended audience, but its less than favorable treatment of women, at times, has created some ambivalence in the ways African American women read the Bible. The fact is that the literary canon of Scripture was not written with African American women as the intended audience.

In short, the Bible has often conveyed to the African American woman its mixed messages within a context that has denied that such a woman has any substantive heritage in the printed word. The message of her environment has been that as a woman, she has had no one to write for her, and as an African, she has had no one to write to her.[19] We have seen already in the example of Howard Thurman's grandmother at least one way in which, as African American, a woman responded to the Bible's teaching on slavery. In those contexts, however, where the African American female reader identifies predominantly with the interests of a female interpretative community, she has by and large had the same options for responding to the Bible as Anglo and other female readers. She could elect either to reject totally the Bible on account of its androcentric bias,[20] to elevate portions of the Bible that in her estimation are central for understanding God's liberating activity and allow those passages to become the norm by which all other passages are judged,[21] or to supplant the biblical account of salvation history altogether with extrabiblical accounts that help provide a fuller, more egalitarian reconstruction of biblical history.[22]

To the extent, however, that the African American woman has insisted upon holding in creative tension her African American and female identities simultaneously, her history overwhelmingly shows that—with neither the permission nor paradigms for doing so—*African American women have sought to be sensitive to oppression wherever it exists, whether in society or in narrative plots.*[23] They, like other women

---

19. In the introduction to the volume he edited on the significance of race as a meaningful category in the study of literature and criticism, Henry Louis Gates, Jr., writes: "Race has become a trope of ultimate, irreducible differences between cultures, linguistic groups, or adherents to specific belief systems which—more often than not—also have fundamentally opposed economic interests. Race is the ultimate trope of difference because it is so very arbitrary in its application. The biological criteria used to determine 'difference' in sex simply do not hold when applied to 'race.' Yet we carelessly use language in such a way as to *will* this sense of *natural* difference into our formulations. . . . We must, I believe, analyze the ways in which writing relates to race, how attitudes toward racial differences generate and structure literary texts by us *and* about us. We must determine how critical methods can effectively disclose the traces of ethnic differences in literature. But we must also understand how certain forms of difference and the *languages* we employ to define those supposed differences not only reinforce each other but tend to create and maintain each other" ("Race," in Henry Louis Gates, Jr., ed., *"Race," Writing, and Difference* [Chicago: University of Chicago Press, 1985], 5, 15).

20. If one can use the work of African American female theological scholars as an example, one finds that they have not *as yet* endorsed some of the more radical options taken by Anglo-feminist theological critics, like Mary Daly and proponents of goddess worship, who reject the Bible and biblical religion altogether as hopelessly misogynistic and patriarchal. I believe, at this juncture in their history, African American female theological scholars want to stand, for as long as they can, with their constituency within the Christian and biblical traditions.

21. See Jacquelyn Grant's discussion of the role and significance of the person and ministry of Jesus for the African American female self-understanding in *White Women's Christ and Black Women's Jesus: Feminist Christology and Womanist Response* (Atlanta: Scholars Press, 1989).

22. There are indeed specific occasions when African American women may elect to respond in either of these manners, e.g., in women's Bible study, in the feminist academy.

23. Most recently, the distinctiveness of our message has been underscored by the poet and novelist Alice Walker. She coined the term *womanist* as indigenous to African

marginalized by virtue of sex and culture, have consistently called attention to texts where individuals (both male and female) are slaughtered, subjugated, silenced, or isolated as a result of their identity—and not their deeds.[24] In fact, of all the interpretative communities to which she belongs, the African American female interpretative community (whether in the church, the academy, or the civic club) is the only one that has consistently allowed her to hold in tandem all the components of her identity.[25] It is the only one where, so that she may be included in the universe of readers, she is not required to suppress some one aspect of her identity in order to assert another. Both the feminist and the African American male interpretative communities have seemed unable to tolerate (when not ignoring them altogether) the multiple and simultaneous identities of the African American female reader.

Where the Bible has been able to capture the imagination of African American women, it has been and continues to be able to do so because significant portions speak to the deepest aspirations of oppressed people for freedom, dignity, justice, and vindication.[26] Substantial portions of the Bible describe a world where the oppressed are liberated, the last become first, the humbled are exalted, the despised are preferred, those rejected are welcomed, the long-suffering are rewarded, the dispossessed are repossessed, and the arrogant are prostrated. And these are the passages, for oppressed readers, that stand at the center of the

---

American folklore, and she has captured the commitment of African American women to the survival of all peoples. She writes, "A womanist [is] committed to the survival and wholeness of entire people, male *and* female. Not a separatist, except periodically, for health..." (*In Search of Our Mothers' Gardens: Womanist Prose* [New York: Harcourt, Brace, and Jovanovich, 1983], xi). Almost one hundred years earlier, in 1892, in a speech to the Congress of Representative Women on the status of black women, the educator, suffragette, and "race woman" Anna Julia Cooper sought to broaden the vision of her predominantly white audience by appealing to the example of her constituency: "Now, I think if I could crystallize the sentiment of my constituency, and deliver it as a message to this congress of women, it would be something like this: Let woman's claim be as broad in the concrete as in the abstract. We take our stand on the solidarity of humanity, the oneness of life, and the unnaturalness and injustice of all special favoritisms, whether of sex, race, country, or condition" (*A Voice from the South, by a Black Woman of the South* [1892; reprint, Westport, Conn.: Greenwood Press, 1976], 94).

24. For a fine discussion of the synergistic relationship that has existed between black women's experience and their literary traditions, see Katie G. Cannon, *Black Womanist Ethics* (Atlanta: Scholars Press, 1988).

25. Commenting on the distinguishing feature of black women's literature, Mary Helen Washington writes, "If there is a single distinguishing feature of the literature of Black women—and this accounts for their lack of recognition—it is this: their writing is about Black women; it takes the trouble to record the thoughts, words, feelings, and deeds of Black women, experiences that make the realities of being Black in America look very different from what men have written" (*Invented Lives: Narratives of Black Women, 1860–1960* [New York: Anchor Press, 1987], xxi).

26. For an insightful discussion of the way texts capitalize on the reader's desires, see Frederic Jameson's *The Political Unconscious: Narrative as a Socially Symbolic Act* (Ithaca, N.Y.: Cornell University Press, 1981). Jameson writes: "The effectively ideological is also at the same time necessarily utopian" (286).

biblical message and, thereby, serve as a vital norm for biblical faith. Therein is a portrait of a God that oppressed readers can believe in. In the process of the Bible's description of an ethic of divine reversal, some of those who will be abased may be African or women, and the overthrow of the proud may seem to come about only through more violence, but these factors pale in the face of the overall promise of liberation. The fact that these factors are suppressed in the reading process says more about the depth of human yearning for freedom than it does about any lack of sophistication on the part of the readers. If, therefore, African American women have acquiesced to the dominant reading convention of identifying with the male voice within a text, and, thereby, have read in most cases with the "eyes of a man," and I believe they have, then their indelible status as marginalized readers has seen to it that they have read the Bible by and large with the eyes of an *oppressed* man! This statement should not be construed as an attempt to justify the way African American women read the Bible; rather it is an effort to suggest rather broadly the very complex ways in which those who are multiply marginalized negotiate their multiple identities when reading. That said, let me summarize the discussion so far.

The concentration up to this point has been on the reader in the reading process. I have attempted to outline some of the social factors that have impinged upon the consciousness and reading habits of the African American woman. By situating the African American female reader within the context of the American religio-literary tradition, with its history of systematically denying African Americans access to the world of reading and with its strictly defined androcentric canon, I have contended that the African American woman reads the Bible having on the one hand to resist what she has been taught about her lack of any right to read, and having on the other hand to comply in some critical ways with what she has been taught about how to read. For African American women, therefore, to read the Bible and to presume that they recognize themselves and their world in the socio-literary world they find there are in many respects subversive claims. They are subversive because they run counter to much that African American women have been taught about themselves as potential consumers of literature.

The nature and extent of that subversion can be seen best in the active role African American women who have identified themselves with the Christian faith have played in the major social and civil rights movements of this country.[27] They and others have attributed their activism,

---

27. Some of the more popular collections of testimonies from and biographical information on slave women and their nineteenth-century free colored sisters amply attest to the extent to which these women attributed their heroic and persistent acts of resistance to their faith in God. For example, see Bert Lowenberg and Ruth Bogin, eds., *Black Women in Nineteenth-Century American Life* (University Park, Pa.: Pennsylvania State University,

in many cases, to their reading of the Bible. Indeed, one can find many fine studies devoted to examining from any number of perspectives (e.g., literary, historical, sociological, theological, archaeological) the unique contents of the Bible. The results of that work will be presupposed in the following remarks where I will consider the second half of the reading process, namely, the biblical text. In that discussion I will explore whether and to what extent the social values and perspectives encoded in the text reflect the sentiments of the oppressed.

The Biblical Perspectives Confronting the Reader

Aspects of biblical interpretation in America have definitely impacted the lives of African Americans and women. This would seem to suggest that the Bible has been an important device for shaping social reality. That is, the Bible is not merely an entity of intellectual or religious achievement. It is rather, as canon, a document that was produced to advocate and shape social behavior according to certain ideals. The ideals that the Bible *in the name of God* advocates represent just a few of what no doubt were a number of positions that were at the time advocated by rival thinkers, religious groups, and authors. The production and utilization of the Bible, therefore, were activities whose aim (intentionally or unintentionally) was to take sides in the struggle of one ideological faction against another. While the conspicuous ethos of the Bible is the viewpoints of those in history whose claims won out, close scrutiny of the Bible will yield in some cases sketchy hints of the counterclaims of rival groups.

In the first half of this chapter, I cited one of the ways that we in the West have been taught to read that has been used against the marginalized to the benefit of the hegemony, namely the notion that readers are to subjugate their experiences to those of the dominant voice in a literary work. I have also noted before that the dominant reading conventions within a society often reinforce the dominant class's interests in that society. In the case of biblical literature, the dominant voices are often those whose interest was to undermine counterclaims, to delegitimize counter-revelations, and to control those people who posed a threat to the class interests of the dominant group. The consequence of the above-mentioned reading strategy is that one is not only forced to subjugate oneself to the voice embedded in the text, but by identifying with the dominant voice, the modern marginalized reader is forced to side against the marginalized in the Bible and is made to identify with the ideological

1976); Dorothy Sterling, ed., *We Are Your Sisters: Black Women in the Nineteenth Century* (New York: W. W. Norton & Company, 1984).

efforts of the dominant group. For women, this means identifying with texts written by men, for men; in many instances it means female readers are required to be insensitive to women in texts. For African Americans, this means identifying with texts interpreted by those within the dominant cultural group; for those who belong to the dominant cultural group, it means defending one's claims against rival cultural groups. For African American women, this means identifying with texts written by those in power for those in power against the powerless. *A challenge for marginalized readers in general, and African American women in particular, has been to use whatever means necessary to recover the voice of the oppressed within biblical texts.* Here again, they have had to rely upon their own experience of oppression as their guide.

In an article on the social effects and hermeneutical implications of the Philippians Hymn in Philippians 2:6-11, a hymn that makes its christological statement through the metaphor of slavery, Sheilah Briggs begins her discussion by noting that there are three categories of texts that confront readers committed to a liberationist perspective when they read the Bible. Each one poses a different set of hermeneutical problems, and each one, presumably, requires a different set of hermeneutical operations. In the first category of texts the voice of the oppressed, despite the processes of canonization and redaction, can still be heard. In the second category, the voices and values of the dominant group are clearly reflected. The third category of texts, in which the Philippians Hymn belongs, consists of those texts whose social effects upon their audience were unclear, the language, imagery, and perspective being oblique and incorporating "a range of different performances, hearings, readings."[28]

Briggs, unfortunately, does not cite specific examples of biblical texts that fall under the first and second of her categories. One New Testament text that might qualify for the first category is the Letter to Philemon, which concerns a runaway slave. Admittedly, the text tells us hardly anything about the perceptions and actions of Onesimus, the slave. The brief epistle discloses more about the writer's regard for his friendship with the slavemaster Philemon, and the lengths to which the writer went to protect the reputation of the budding church movement from being seen as a threat to the social and economic fiber of the Roman Empire. Nonetheless, the occasion that gave rise to the letter—from a religious leader to a slaveholding Christian friend—is that a slave who had escaped is now being returned to the latter. From the point of view of the liberationist reader, it is important that however ineradicable slavery might have been in Rome, and however pastoral and tactful the tone of the letter, the runaway slave, Onesimus, ran away in all likelihood

---

28. Sheilah Briggs, "Can an Enslaved God Liberate? Hermeneutical Reflections on Philippians 2:6-11," *Semeia* 47 (1989): 139.

because he did not want to remain a slave, even the slave of a Christian. Moreover, that Paul speaks of returning or "sending" Onesimus to Philemon suggests that Onesimus, despite his conversion or perhaps because of his conversion, is not returning to his slavemaster freely. This is an instance where the voice of the oppressed, despite the considerations of the dominant voices, deserves fuller examination.[29]

African Americans have been ambivalent in their treatment of this story. They have recognized themselves in Onesimus's act of self-determination, and they have been sympathetic to Paul's subtle attempt to hint rather broadly that the good-hearted slavemaster free the slave (1:16, 17). However, the manner in which Paul handles the matter of slavery in the Letter to Philemon has served to remind both African American male and female readers of two things. First, the social location of biblical authors, like those of modern interpreters, can influence their theology. Paul makes much of his persecution and imprisonment for the sake of the gospel, and this fueled his commitment to evangelize the empire and inspired his vision of the imminent return of Jesus as the Lord of all the earth. Nevertheless, he claimed his birthright as a "Hebrew among Hebrews" (e.g., male, educated, Benjaminite [see Phil. 3:4f.]) and as a citizen of Rome (Acts 23:22-29), with social and political privileges. These credentials, in view of his teachings on women and slaves, appear to have restricted his vision of the kingdom of God to that of a vindicated community of religiously oppressed men; it appears, then, that he did not envision the kingdom as a totally reconstructed and reconciled humanity. Second, the Bible attests, however obliquely, that there were some—a segment of society and a subclass within the Christian movement, not unlike modern marginalized readers—who understood their humanity and their religiosity differently from that of the dominant voices of the text, however irretrievable in the end the declarations of the former may be.

As for possible examples in the Old Testament, an obvious and widely commented upon case is the story of the Hebrews' escape from Egyptian slavery. For the Hebrew community, the events told in the Book of Exodus stand at the center of Israel's identity and testimony about the character of Israel's God. In fact, the claim has been made that what one finds in the entire saga of Israel's Exodus from Egypt and its earlier attempts in the wilderness recounts the details of a social revolution. It tells of Israel's efforts to constitute itself as a theocratic community that would be the voice of an oppressed people who sought intentionally to stand in radical contradistinction to the elitist, despotic, totalitarian, oppressive values and policies of neighboring societies. In this way, the Pentateuch in general and particular books, such as Exodus and

---

29. See chapter 11 of the present volume.

Deuteronomy, reflect the hopes, dreams, ambitions, and manifesto of a band of runaway slaves imagining for themselves a new way of being in the world.[30] This explains, in large part, the significance attached to the Exodus event and story by liberation movements and theologians, African, Asian, Latin American, feminist, and African American alike. A reading of slave narratives will show that for African American slave women and men Christian hope was anchored in the story of a God who heard the outcries of the enslaved and in turn delivered them from the bondage inflicted by their taskmasters.[31] For American slaves who were themselves descended from Africans, that the taskmasters in the Exodus story were Africans was subordinate to the fact that the victorious underdog in the story was a people whose plight as slaves was only too well understood.[32]

Within that same larger complex of material in the Book of Genesis is the story of the Egyptian woman Hagar and her slaveholding mistress, the Hebrew Sarah (see Gen. 16:1-16; 21:1-21). Here the status, ethnicity, gender, and circumstances of a biblical character have been seen as unmistakably analogous to those of the African American reader.[33] It is a story of the social and economic disparity between women, a disparity that is exacerbated by ethnic backgrounds. It is the story of a slaveholding woman's complicity with her husband in the sexual molestation of a female slave woman. It is a story of the hostility and suspicion that erupt between women over the plight and status of their male sons. It is the story of an enslaved Egyptian single mother who is subjected to the rule of a vindictive and brutal mistress and an acquiescent master. It is a story familiar, even haunting to African American female readers. Indeed, in actuality the story of Sarah and Hagar is a story about neither woman,

---

30. For the most classic formulation of this viewpoint, see Norman Gottwald, *The Tribes of Yahweh: A Sociology of the Religion of Liberated Israel* (Maryknoll, N.Y.: Orbis Books, 1979). However, this viewpoint has been seriously challenged (see Jan Dus, "Moses or Joshua: On the Problem of the Founder of the Israelite Religion," in *The Bible and Liberation* [Berkeley: Community for Religious Research and Education, 1976]). Of course, this viewpoint is an ideologically motivated, highly idealistic assessment of Israel's history. This becomes clear when one considers that this block of material was probably composed in an early form significantly later in Israel's history, say, during the period of King Josiah's reforms in 621 B.C.E., when Israel had become a political bureaucracy seeking its own self-preservation.

31. One such collection of slave experiences is found, for example, in Charles H. Johnson, ed., *God Struck Me Dead: Religious Conversion Experiences and Autobiographies of Ex-slaves* (Philadelphia: Pilgrim Press, 1969).

32. For illuminating discussion of the significance of race in the Bible for African Americans and Africans, see Charles B. Copher, "3000 Years of Biblical Interpretation," *Journal of the Interdenominational Theological Center* 13, no. 2 (Spring 1986): 225–46; and Cain H. Felder, *Troubling Biblical Waters: Race, Class, and Family* (Maryknoll, N.Y.: Orbis Books, 1989), 37–48.

33. See my comments on this story from the interpretative context of African American Christian women in the chapter entitled, "A Mistress, a Maid, and No Mercy," in my book, *Just a Sister Away: A Womanist Vision of Women's Relationships in the Bible* (San Diego: LuraMedia Publishers, 1988).

but is Abraham's story, and the drama between these two women shows the rival and petty efforts of the two to manipulate the deity's promise of an heir for the patriarch Abraham.[34] Nevertheless, African American female readers have taken the sketchy incidental details of the story of Hagar—a sexually and economically exploited slave woman who first runs away and is eventually banished—and have perceived uncanny parallels between the plight and status of Hagar and themselves. While the details of Hagar's story offer for the African American female reader minimal positive strategies for survival, the story, by way of a negative example, reminds such a reader what her history has repeatedly taught her: *That women, although they share in the experience of gender oppression, are not natural allies in the struggles against patriarchy and exploitation.* The Genesis story of Hagar and Sarah is an important story, therefore, because it reinforces and coincides in some crucial ways with African American women's experience of reality.

Finally, one might object, and correctly so, to this selection of episodic biblical instances of resistance against the hierarchical social structures of the times. The voice of the oppressed in the end is not the predominant voice. In fact, theirs is a voice that could be viewed as random aberrant outbursts in a world otherwise rigidly held together by its patriarchal attitudes and androcentric perspective. "One can talk of more or less androcentric texts," argues Briggs, "but only with the recognition that androcentricism pervades the whole of the New Testament."[35] The same holds true within the Old Testament. Whatever hints of the values and struggles of the oppressed in the Bible that one happens upon, they are, in the end, conveyed to the reader through the perspective of the dominant group. While there is admittedly remarkable variety in their perspectives, the voices that came to dominate and be embedded in the Bible are for the most part male, elitist, patriarchal, and legitimated. About that segment of society and subclass within biblical religion who opposed the voices of the dominant groups, we can say only that they were both female and male and evidently powerless.

It has proved the task and responsibility of marginalized readers today, both female and male, to restore the voices of the oppressed in the kingdom of God.[36] In order to do this, they have had to be able as

---

34. See chapter 9 in the present volume.
35. Briggs, "Can an Enslaved God Liberate?" 137.
36. This is Briggs's position when she argues far more carefully than I have been able to do here that the past that biblical interpretation seeks to recover cannot be made transparent solely through exegetical operations, but requires an intuitive component that in fact only those in analogous circumstances can bring to bear upon texts. Writing about Philippians 2:6-11, Briggs states, "The subjectivity which might have been the slaves' as they subverted the text . . . is not historiographically recoverable. It is a past that can only be invented, a theological task proper to the narrative creativity of biblical proclamation within the communities of the oppressed today" (ibid., 149).

much as possible to read and hear the text for themselves, with their own eyes and with their own ears. And in the final analysis, they have had to be prepared, as I have tried to highlight in this exploration of African American women's reading strategies, to resist those elements of the tradition that have sought, even in the name of revelation, to diminish their humanity. In so doing, African American women have continued to read the Bible in most instances because of its vision and promise of a world where the humanity of everyone will be fully valued. They have accomplished this reading in spite of the voices from within and without that have tried to equivocate on that vision and promise.

PART II

African American Sources for Enhancing Biblical Interpretation

— *4* —

The Bible and African Americans: An Outline of an Interpretative History

Vincent L. Wimbush

Introduction: The Bible as Language-world

There has been no lack of efforts in the last decade or so to make sense of the religious traditions of African Americans. Such traditions have been interpreted, for example, as institutional or denominational history,[1] as a liberation movement,[2] as part of a history-of-religions paradigm for aboriginal America,[3] as sociological phenomena,[4] and as historical manifestations of the African world view and piety in a particular context

---

1. James M. Washington, *Frustrated Fellowship: The Black Baptist Quest for Social Power* (Macon, Ga.: Mercer University Press, 1986).

2. In the modern period beginning with the watershed book of James H. Cone, *Black Theology and Black Power* (New York: Seabury Press, 1969). For a bibliography on the development of black theology see especially James H. Cone and Gayraud S. Wilmore, eds., *Black Theology: A Documentary History, 1966–1979* (Maryknoll, N.Y.: Orbis Books, 1979).

3. Charles H. Long, *Significations: Signs, Symbols, and Images in the Interpretation of Religion* (Philadelphia: Fortress Press, 1986).

4. C. Eric Lincoln, *Race, Religion, and the Continuing American Dilemma* (New York: Hill and Wang, 1984); and Harold D. Trulear, "Sociology of Afro-American Religion: An Appraisal of C. Eric Lincoln's Contributions," *Journal of Religious Thought* 42, no. 2 (Fall–Winter 1986): 44–55.

among the "dispersed."[5] I have learned much about African Americans from these and other studies. But I have been left dissatisfied with what appears in far too many of these studies to be either a total neglect or a superficial treatment of the role of the Bible in the religious traditions of African Americans. The argument here for attention to the Bible among African Americans has less to do with any assumed valorization—"authority," "inspiration," among other concepts now current in religious circles—of the Bible in some timeless, abstract manner, than with concern about an understanding of the range of its functions in the history of African Americans. My suspicions and theses are that greater clarity about the role that the Bible has played in the history of African Americans can shed light on the different responses African Americans have made to the socio-political and economic situations in which they have found themselves. Since every reading of important texts, especially mythic or religious texts, reflects a "reading" or assessment of one's world, and since the Bible has from the founding of the nation served as an icon,[6] a history of African Americans' historical readings of the Bible is likely to reflect their historical self-understandings—as Africans in America.

One useful way of beginning to clarify the issues involved in thinking about the function of the Bible among African Americans is to think of the Bible as a language, even language-world. The experience of being uprooted from their African homeland and forced to labor in a strange place produced in the first African slaves what has been termed a type of disorientation.[7] This disorientation, obviously contrived by the white slavers because of its advantages for them, was most evident in language or powers of communication. Part of the Europeans' and Americans' justification for the enslavement of Africans was the "strangeness" of the latter—their physical attributes and their culture, especially their languages.[8] Of course, many of the Europeans and their counterparts in the "New World" deemed the Africans' physical features and cultures inferior—Africans were considered to be hideous in their looks and barbaric in their ways. Certainly, part of what it meant to be fully enslaved was to be cut off from one's cultural roots.

Although groups of the Africans who were captured and enslaved could have communicated with one another without problem, the slavers took steps to frustrate communication. So being deprived ini-

5. See Albert J. Raboteau, *Slave Religion: The "Invisible Institution" in the Antebellum South* (New York: Oxford University Press, 1978); and George E. Simpson, *Black Religions in the New World* (New York: Columbia University Press, 1978).

6. Martin E. Marty, *Religion and Republic: The American Circumstance* (Boston: Beacon, 1987), 140–67.

7. Long, *Significations*, 97–113, 158–84.

8. Donald G. Matthews, *Religion in the Old South* (Chicago: University of Chicago Press, 1977), 136f.

tially of a language with which meaningful communication could be realized, the first African slaves experienced a type of "social death,"[9] cut off from their roots, including their languages and religious heritage. This is what slavery was supposed to mean in the eyes of many.

But this state of affairs did not always obtain even for the African slaves. A great many of the slaves did adopt—as part of the complex phenomenon of acquiring a number of new skills, symbols, and languages for survival—the Bible as a "language" through which they negotiated both the strange new world that was called America and the slave existence. With this "language" they began to wax eloquent not only with the white slavers and not only among themselves, but also about themselves, about the ways in which they understood their situation in America—as slaves, as freed persons, as disenfranchised persons, as a people. For the great majority of African Americans the Bible has historically functioned not merely to reflect and legitimize piety (narrowly understood), but as a language-world full of stories—of heroes and heroines, of heroic peoples and their pathos and victory, sorrow and joy, sojourn and fulfillment. In short, the Bible became a "world" into which African Americans could retreat, a "world" they could identify with, draw strength from, and in fact manipulate for self-affirmation.

Nearly all interpreters have acknowledged that the Bible has played an important role in the history of African Americans. What remains is a comprehensive effort to relate and then interpret that history through attention to the various ways in which the Bible has been engaged by African Americans. This essay is an attempt to provide only a working outline of such a history. Its importance lies in its suggestiveness, or heuristic value, not its comprehensiveness. It is no more than an outline of what I have isolated as the major types of readings of the Bible among African Americans from the beginning of their introduction to it in the period of slavery up to the modern period. The types of readings actually correspond to different historical periods and are meant to reflect different responses to historical (socio-political-economic) situations and (collective) self-understandings.

Other initial clarifying statements are in order. First, each "reading" is assumed to be public, or communal, not private, or individualistic. Second, each "reading" is assumed to have emerged out of particular life-settings, and to have been more or less manifested and preserved in different types of sources—e.g., songs, sermons, testimonies, addresses. The "more or less" is significant: The sources are not absolutely mutually exclusive of different types of readings. Third, each type of reading is assumed not to be in evidence solely in terms of the direct quotation

---

9. Orlando Patterson, *Slavery and Social Death: A Comparative Study* (Cambridge: Harvard University Press, 1982).

of certain biblical passages—although the occurrence of certain clusters of biblical materials over and over again would obviously be significant, especially in terms of the development of a "canon" (see the discussion below). Again, emphasis will be placed upon the discernment of the range of *functions* of the Bible in African American communities. Fourth, although the discussion to follow is divided according to types of readings, the predominant orientation and method are historical, and are best understood in this way. The ultimate goal is an *interpretative history* of African Americans based on their readings of the Bible.

Having said this, it is important for me to note that even as each type of reading represents a period in the history of African Americans, the types of readings are not strictly chronologically successive—no one reading completely disappears when another begins. There is much overlap of readings in different historical periods. One period differs from another for the most part in terms of emphases. So given the nature of the historical inquiry that this essay represents, strict chronological perimeters or dates to correspond to the different types of readings would not be helpful; they could in fact serve only to frustrate the thesis that will govern the essay—that there is much overlap of readings between periods. Nevertheless, some general dating perimeters will be referenced throughout the essay.

First "Reading":
Rejection, Suspicion, and Awe of "Book Religion"
(Beginning of African Experience in the New World)

What the Africans faced in the New World was what the European settlers had also to face—strangeness. The latter, however, set out from the beginning to conquer the strangeness and bend it to their will and ethos. They conquered native peoples and declared that European customs, languages, and traditions were the law. The Europeans' embrace of the Bible helped to lend this process legitimacy. Since many of them through their reading of and reference to the Bible had already defined themselves as dissenters from the dominant social, political, and religious traditions in their native countries, they found it a rather natural resource in the context of the New World. The Bible functioned as a cultural image-reflector, as a road map to nation-building. It provided the Europeans justification to think of themselves as a "biblical nation," as God's people called to conquer and convert the New World to God's way as they interpreted it.[10]

---

10. Sydney Ahlstrom, *A Religious History of the American People* (New Haven: Yale University Press, 1972), pt. 2.

The Africans could not and did not fail to notice the powerful influence of the Bible upon the Europeans' self-image, culture, and orientation. Their first reaction, as far as evidence allows, to the Europeans and to the Europeans' understanding of themselves can be seen—and, I think, more clearly explicated—in their response to the Bible, referred to by Europeans as "Holy Scripture" or the "Holy Book." For the great majority of the first African slaves the first reaction was an admixture of rejection, suspicion, and awe. On the one hand, they seemed to reject or be suspicious of any notion of "Book Religion." As is the case with most nonliterate peoples with well-established and elaborate oral traditions, the Africans found the notion of piety and world view circumscribed by a book to be absurd.[11] On the other hand, the fact that those who had enslaved them and were conquering the New World were "Bible Christians" was not at all lost on the Africans: It did not take them long to associate the Book of "Book Religion" with power.[12]

Even before the Africans were able to manipulate the Bible in a self-interested, affirming manner, their early capacity and willingness to engage "the Book" were significant, for they demonstrated the Africans' ability to adapt themselves to different understandings of reality. That capacity and willingness also reflected their will to survive, to accommodate themselves to the New World, even as they understood it to be dominated by the European slavers. What form and meaning this "accommodation" would assume would be debated in times—and reflected in "readings" of the Bible—to come.

Second "Reading": Transformation of "Book Religion" into Religion of Slave Experience (Beginning of Mass Conversions in the Eighteenth Century)

It was not until the revival movements—in the North and South—of the eighteenth century that Africans began to convert to Christianity in significant numbers, significant enough to justify labeling this period as the beginning of a type of African American religious ethos. They responded to the Europeans' evangelical preaching and piety, especially the emphasis on conversion experience as the sign of God's acceptance of the worth of the individual, and the often spontaneous formation of communities of the converted for fellowship and mutual affirmation. Because testimony regarding personal experience with God was the single most important criterion—relativizing, though not obliterat-

---

11. Raboteau, *Slave Religion*, 242; and Samuel D. Gill, *Beyond "The Primitive": The Religions of Nonliterate Peoples* (Englewood Cliffs, N.J.: Prentice-Hall, 1982).

12. Harold W. Turner, *Religious Innovation in Africa: Collected Essays on New Religious Movements* (Boston: G. K. Hall, 1979), 271–88; and Gill, *Beyond "The Primitive,"* 226–28.

ing, social status and racial identification—for entry into the evangelical communities, and because that criterion held the promise of a degree of egalitarianism and affirmation, it was no wonder that the Africans began to respond in great numbers to the white Methodists and Baptists.[13]

The sacralization of the Bible among white evangelical Protestants, North and South, could hardly have been ignored by the Africans. The young nation officially defined itself as a "biblical nation"; indeed, popular culture was also thoroughly biblical.[14] It would have been difficult not to take note of the diversity of views that reading the Bible could inspire, not only between North and South as cultural, political readings, but also among evangelical communities—Baptist, Methodist, Presbyterian. The lesson that the Africans learned from these evangelicals was not only that faith was to be interpreted in light of the reading of the Bible, but also that each person had freedom of interpretation of the Bible. Given differences between individuals and different religious groups, the Africans learned that they, too, could read "the Book" freely. They could read certain parts and ignore others. They could and did articulate their interpretations in their own way—in song, prayers, sermons, testimonies, and addresses. By the end of the century "the Book" had come to represent a virtual language-world that they, too, could enter and manipulate in light of their social experiences. After all, everyone could approach the Bible under the guidance of the Spirit, that is, in his or her own way.[15]

And interpret they did. They were attracted primarily to the narratives of the Hebrew Bible dealing with the adventures of the Hebrews in bondage and escaping from bondage, to the oracles of the eighth-century prophets and their denunciations of social injustice and visions of social justice, and to the New Testament texts concerning the compassion, passion, and resurrection of Jesus. With these and other texts, the African American Christians laid the foundations for what can be seen as an emerging "canon." In their spirituals and in their sermons and testimonies African Americans interpreted the Bible in light of their experiences. Faith became identification with the heroes and heroines of the Hebrew Bible and with the long-suffering but ultimately victorious Jesus. As the people of God in the Hebrew Bible were once delivered from enslavement, so, the Africans sang and shouted, would they be delivered. As Jesus suffered unjustly but was raised from the dead to

---

13. Matthews, *Religion in the Old South*, 198f.; and Lawrence W. Levine, *Black Culture and Black Consciousness* (New York: Oxford University Press, 1977), 136ff.

14. Mark A. Noll, "The Image of the United States as a Biblical Nation, 1776–1865," in N. O. Hatch and Mark A. Noll, eds., *The Bible in America* (New York: Oxford University Press, 1982), 39–40; and N. O. Hatch, "Sola Scriptura and Novus Ordo Seclorum," in ibid., 74–75.

15. Raboteau, *Slave Religion*, 239f.; and Matthews, *Religion in the Old South*, 212–36.

new life, so, they sang, would they be "raised" from their "social death" to new life. So went the songs, sermons, and testimonies.

In his classic collection and interpretation of the spirituals James Weldon Johnson captures well the importance of the Bible in the imaginations of the earliest African Americans:

> At the psychic moment there was at hand the precise religion for the condition in which [the African] found himself thrust. Far from ... his native land and customs, despised by those among whom he lived, experiencing the pang of separation of loved ones on the auction block ... [the African] seized Christianity, ... the religion which implied the hope that in the next world there would be a reversal of conditions. ... The result was a body of songs voicing all the cardinal virtues of Christianity ... through a modified form of primitive African music. ... [The African] took complete refuge in Christianity, and the Spirituals were literally forged in the heat of religious fervor. ... It is not possible to estimate the sustaining influence that the story of the Jews as related in the Old Testament exerted upon the Negro. This story at once caught and fired the imaginations of the Negro bards, and they sang, sang their hungry listeners into a firm faith.[16]

Of course, Johnson's interpretation of the function of "otherworldly" religion among oppressed peoples has been significantly modified and corrected by current research in the sociology of religion in general,[17] as well as by studies on African American religion in particular.[18] But very few interpreters of African Americans, from whatever methodological perspective, have captured and articulated so well the importance of the Bible in the imagination of African Americans.

The spirituals reflect the process of the transformation of the Book Religion of the dominant peoples into the religion reflective of the sociopolitical and economic status of African slaves.

> Go down, Moses
> 'Way down in Egypt land,
> Tell ole Pharaoh, Let my people go.
>
> •
>
> Dey crucified my Lord,
> An' He never said a mumblin' word.
> Dey crucified my Lord,
> An' He never said a mumblin' word,
> Not a word—not a word—not a word.

---

16. See James Weldon Johnson, ed., *The Book of American Negro Spirituals* (New York: Viking Press, 1925), 20, 21; Howard Thurman, *Deep River and the Negro Spiritual Speaks of Life and Death* (Richmond, Ind.: Friends Press, 1975); and Benjamin E. Mays, *The Negro's God as Reflected in His Literature* (New York: Atheneum, 1969), 19–96.

17. Bryan R. Wilson, *Magic and the Millennium: A Sociological Study of Religious Movements of Protest among Tribal and Third World Peoples* (New York: Harper and Row, 1973).

18. See Trulear, "Sociology of Afro-American Religion."

Dey nailed Him to de tree,
An' He never said a mumblin' word.
Dey nailed Him to de tree,
An' He never said a mumblin' word,
Not a word—not a word—not a word.

Dey pierced Him in de side,
An' He never said a mumblin' word.
Dey pierced Him in de side,
An' He never said a mumblin' word,
Not a word—not a word—not a word.

•

Sometimes I feel like a motherless child,
Sometimes I feel like a motherless child,
Sometimes I feel like a motherless child,
A long ways from home.

These and other songs, as well as numerous sermons, addresses, and exhortations,[19] reflect a hermeneutic characterized by a looseness, even playfulness, vis-à-vis the biblical texts themselves. The interpretation was not controlled by the literal words of the texts, but by social experience. The texts were heard more than read; they were engaged as stories that seized and freed the imagination. Interpretation was therefore controlled by the freeing of the collective consciousness and imagination of the African slaves as they heard the biblical stories and retold them to reflect their actual social situation, as well as their visions for something different. Many of the biblical stories, themselves the product of cultures with well-established oral traditions, functioned sometimes as allegory, as parable, or as veiled social criticism. Such stories well served the African slaves, not only on account of their well-established oral traditions, but also because their situation dictated veiled or indirect social criticism—"hitting a straight lick with a crooked stick."[20]

That the songs and sermons reflect a type of indirect or veiled commentary on the social situation that the African slaves faced has been noted by most interpreters.[21] But more careful attention to the manner in which the images and language of the Bible were used can shed more light on the question of the oppositional character of African American religion.[22] I would argue that study of both the selection of biblical texts/stories and their redaction by these early African Americans can

---

19. See Mays, *The Negro's God;* and Milton C. Sernett, ed., *Afro-American Religious History: A Documentary Witness* (Durham, N.C.: Duke University Press, 1985).
20. Raboteau, *Slave Religion,* 250.
21. See Johnson, ed., *The Book of American Negro Spirituals;* Thurman, *Deep River;* Mays, *The Negro's God;* Cone, *Black Theology and Black Power;* Raboteau, *Slave Religion;* and Cone and Wilmore, eds., *Black Theology.*
22. Cone and Wilmore, eds., *Black Theology,* 227f.

force entirely different and more illuminating categories upon the discussion. Attention to both biblical story and African American redaction will more likely bring to focus the major emphases and concerns of the African Americans who sang, prayed, and testified in the language of the Bible. Detailed exegetical treatments of the raw materials of the African experience of this period are in order. More specifically, comparative, or redaction-critical studies of biblical text/stories in relation to African American stories drawn from the Bible are in order.

I would also argue that this reading of the Bible on the part of African Americans was foundational: All other readings to come would in some sense be built upon and judged against it. This reading is in fact the classical reading of the biblical text for African Americans; it reflects the classical period in the history of African Americans (the eighteenth century). It reflects what arguably has been so basic to the orientation of the majority of African Americans that all subsequent debates about orientation, world view, and strategies for survival and/or liberation have begun with this period and what it represents. In sum, it represents Africans' pragmatic, relative accommodation to existence in America. "Pragmatic" because it attempts to come to grips with what opportunities were at hand for survival and amelioration of social status; "relative" because it never assumed that persons of African descent could ever be fully integrated into American society. This response, therefore, is at base hermeneutically and socially critical. It reflects the fact that the Bible, understood as the "white folk's" book, was accepted but not interpreted in the way that white Christians and the dominant culture in general interpreted it. So America's biblical culture was accepted by the Africans, but not in the way white Americans accepted it or in the way the whites preferred that others accept it.

My thesis about the general function of the Bible among African Americans makes all the more important the need for the detailed study of African American songs and sermons alongside of the appropriate biblical texts. Such studies should confirm or disconfirm the general thesis.

Third "Reading": Establishment of Canon and Hermeneutical Principle (Beginning of Independent Church Movements in the Nineteenth Century)

In the pre–Civil War northern states, Africans were only slightly less enslaved than their southern counterparts. A few were "allowed" some opportunities to educate themselves both formally and informally. A few were "allowed" access to important public forums—especially those forums dedicated to debating the issue of the morality, social utility, and politics of slavery. And some received good formal education in spite of many frustrations and stumbling blocks. In this climate Africans of the northern states led the way toward the third collective reading of the Bible among African Americans. This reading corresponded to and illuminates the self-understanding of a significant number of African Americans of the period.

In this period, the independent congregations and local and regional denominational bodies developed among African Americans.[23] This development symbolized the oppositional (that is, primarily antiracist) civil rights agenda and character of African American religion.[24] Attention to the nature of the reading of the Bible among the African American churches during this period will shed more light on the nature of the oppositional character of the independent church movements.

Sermon after sermon and oration after oration crafted by slaves and freedpersons reflected concern about the social lot of Africans in America. What for our purposes is striking is that both the explanation for the social situation of the Africans and the solution to their problems were cast in biblical language. Black freedom-fighters waxed biblical about the kinship of humanity under the sovereignty of the one God, about slavery as a base evil in opposition to the will of God, about the imperatives of the teachings of Jesus to make all nations a part of God's reign, and about the judgment that is to be leveled against all those who frustrate God's will on earth.[25]

During this period African Americans seemed anxious to institutionalize as an ethical and moral principle one of the rare New Testament passages they found attractive and even identified as a *locus classicus* for Christian social teaching—"There is neither Jew nor Greek, there is neither slave nor free, there is neither male nor female; for you are all one in Christ Jesus" (Gal. 3:28). Ironically, this biblical verse stressing the principle of Christian unity was embraced and referred to over and over again as the separate church movements got under way. This and other passages were used to level prophetic judgment against a society that thought of itself as biblical in its foundation and ethic.

In a social situation in which the Bible figured prominently in debates about a number of public policy issues, including slavery, African Americans joined the debate with their own reading of the Bible. Since colonial days white Americans had been familiar with reading the Bible from a nationalist perspective. The story of the Hebrews' long struggle to

---

23. Sernett, ed., *Afro-American Religious History*, chaps. 2, 3; see Washington, *Frustrated Fellowship;* and Cone and Wilmore, eds., *Black Theology.*

24. Thomas R. Frazier, "Historians and Afro-American Religion," *Journal of the Interdenominational Theological Center* (Fall 1985): 3–4.

25. Peter J. Paris, *The Social Teaching of the Black Churches* (Philadelphia: Fortress Press, 1985); and Sernett, ed., *Afro-American Religious History*, 188–226.

come into possession of the Promised Land was a paradigm for the Europeans' struggles to come into possession of the American "Promised Land." In the nineteenth century African Americans began to hold forth against such typological claims of white Americans (Protestants, for the most part). African Americans pointed out that their own experience in the New World was an antitype of the ancient Hebrews' experience with respect to Palestine.[26] This they did by applying their favorite biblical passages to an array of social issues—in sermons, prayers, official denominational addresses, creeds, and mottos.

This reading of the Bible among African Americans extends at least from the nineteenth century up to the present. It has historically reflected and shaped the ethos and thinking of the majority of African Americans. If the period of enslavement (certainly eighteenth century through emancipation) represents the classical period, the nineteenth century represents the period of self-conscious articulation, consolidation, and institutionalization. Frederick Douglass and David Walker stand as eloquent examples of nineteenth-century biblical interpreters who took the hermeneutical principle of the kinship of humanity under the sovereignty of God and applied it to the emancipation agenda. These two, among many others, were eloquent in their excoriations of "Christian" and "biblical" America. So Douglass in 1845:

> The Christianity of America is a Christianity, of whose votaries it may be truly said, as it was of the ancient scribes and Pharisees, "They bind heavy burdens, and grievous to be borne, and lay them on men's shoulders, but they themselves will not move them with one of their fingers. All their works they do for to be seen of men." ... Dark and terrible as is this picture, I hold it to be strictly true of the overwhelming mass of professed Christians of America. ... They would be shocked at the proposition of fellowshipping a sheep-stealer; and at the same time they hug to their communion a man-stealer, and brand me an infidel, if I find fault with them for it. They attend with Pharisaical strictness to the outward forms of religion, and at the same time neglect the weightier matters of law, judgment, mercy, and faith.[27]

So also David Walker in 1829:

> Have not the Americans the Bible in their hands? Do they believe it? Surely they do not. See how they treat us in open violation of the Bible! ... Our divine Lord and Master said "all things whatsoever ye would that men should do unto you, do ye even so unto them." But an American minister, with the Bible in his hand, holds us and our children in the most abject slavery and wretchedness. ... I tell you Americans! that unless you speedily alter your course, you and your country are gone!!!! Will not that very

---

26. Marty, *Religion and Republic*, 140–65; and see Noll, "The Image of the United States as a Biblical Nation."

27. Sernett, ed., *Afro-American Religious History*, 105–6.

remarkable passage of Scripture be fulfilled on Christian Americans? Hear it Americans!! "He that is unjust, let him be unjust still:—and he that is filthy, let him be filthy still; and he that is righteous, let him be righteous still; and he that is holy, let him be holy still."[28]

From the nineteenth century into the present, the ideal of the kinship and unity of all humanity under the sovereignty of God has been important to a great number of African Americans, and the official mottos and pronouncements of the independent denominations have reflected that. Two examples will help to demonstrate this.

At the twentieth quadrennial session of the General Conference of the African Methodist Church, in May 1896, the saying of Bishop Daniel Payne, "God our Father; Christ our Redeemer; Man our Brother," became the official motto of the denomination:

> This is the official motto of the A.M.E. Church, and her mission in the common-wealth of Christianity is to bring all denominations and races to acknowledge and practice the sentiments contained therein. When these sentiments are universal in theory and practice, then the mission of the distinctive colored organizations will cease.[29]

In his presidential address before the forty-second annual session of the National Baptist Convention, in December 1922, Dr. E. C. Morris specified how Afro-Baptists understood and justified their separate existence:

> We early imbibed the religion of the white man; we believed in it; we believe in it now.... But if that religion does not mean what it says, if God did not make of one blood all nations of men to dwell on the face of the earth, and if we are not to be counted as part of that generation, by those who handed the oracle down to us, the sooner we abandon them or it, the sooner we will find our place in a religious sect in the world.[30]

The reading of the Bible in evidence here can be characterized as prophetic apology. By this term I mean to refer to African Americans' use of the Bible in order to make self-assertive claims against a racist America that claimed to be a biblical nation. The clamor from African Americans was for the realization of the principles of inclusion, equality, and kinship that they understood the Bible to mandate. In the nineteenth century we see among African Americans the beginnings of more consistent and systematic attempts to make use of the Bible in order to force "biblical" America to honor the biblical principles. The very fact that the Bible was so read revealed African Americans' orientation and collective self-understanding—they desired to be integrated into American society.

---

28. Ibid., 191–92.
29. Cited in Paris, *The Social Teaching*, 13.
30. Cited in ibid., 51.

Their critical, polemical, and race- and culture-conscious reading of the Bible reflected the desire to enter the mainstream of American society. The Bible itself had apparently come to represent American society. So a critical reading of it was a critical reading of American society. That the Bible—and the whole of the tradition of which it was a signal part—was engaged at all signified relative acceptance of American society.

Irony must be seen in the fact that it was from the situation of institutional separatism that the prophetic call went out for the realization of the biblical principles of universalism, equality, and the kinship of all humanity. Perhaps African Americans had begun to see the inevitability of the irony in America: the call for oneness could be made only apart from others, lest particularity be lost; but since particularity in America often meant being left out or discriminated against, an apology for the inclusion was made.

Fourth "Reading": Esoteric and Elitist Hermeneutical Principles and Texts (Early Twentieth Century to the Present)

This reading has its origins in the early twentieth century; it continues to have great influence in the present, especially in large urban areas of the North and South. Included here are a number of different groups with little or no formal ties to one another. What they have in common, however, is a tendency to develop esoteric knowledge or principles of interpretation of the (Protestant and/or Catholic) Bible; to lay claim to the absolute legitimacy of that knowledge and those principles; to claim exclusive possession and knowledge of other holy books, or previously apocryphal parts of the Bible; and to practice bibliomancy (the reading of holy books for the purpose of solving personal problems or in order to effect some wonder from which one can benefit). These are to be seen only as tendencies; not all tendencies would be in evidence among all groups included in this category.

The groups included in this period have often been labeled sects. All African American religious communities have been so labeled by many social-scientific researchers of American religions, since the former were understood to have been founded in response to, and continue to exist on account of, tensions with the dominant society. However, it should be clear at this point that this essay is in part a response to the inadequacy of such labeling of African American religious communities, past and present. What is required is a typology that can more accurately register the religious diversity among African Americans.

In terms of groups that predominate and characterize readings and periods in the religious history of African Americans, the Baptists and Methodists should certainly be placed in the earlier periods and identified with the corresponding readings. They dominated both the classical and institution-building periods and can be classified as a type of mainstream among African American religious communities. But in this fourth reading and in the corresponding historical period, the groups that emerge and predominate are different. Among these groups are the Black Muslims, the Black Jews, the African Orthodox, the Garvey movement, the Holiness/Pentecostal churches, and the Reverend Ike's United Church and Science of Living Institute.[31]

With a more critical perspective of the world and of American society and its biblical self-understanding, these groups are different from the worldly and mainstream Baptists and Methodists, among others. They share a more fundamental disdain for and mistrust of American society. They are less concerned about "cashing the check" on America's promise of democracy, equality, and freedom of opportunity. They tend to be less concerned about holding America to its responsibilities as a biblical nation because they generally do not believe any of America's claims about itself to be true. In sum, such groups can be characterized by their consistent rejection of both American society in general and the older established African American religious communities. The former is rejected on account of its racism; the latter are rejected on account of their accommodationism.

It is their reading of the Bible, or religious texts in general, that more poignantly reflects these groups' difference from the others. Their claims to esoteric knowledge and principles of interpretation of holy books correspond to their rejection of the boundaries that the dominant society and the accommodationist minority communities agree upon for dialogue and debate about key issues. Outright rejection of the canon itself, or additions to the canon, or esoteric principles of interpretation of whatever canon—these tendencies evidence the radical psychic stance of these groups vis-à-vis the dominant society. It should be noted, however, that the irony in this period lies in the fact that the separatism of the groups in this period notwithstanding, many of the groups often called for, and saw partially realized in their boundaries, the integration that yet eludes mainstream religious communities—black and white. And it is the engagement of biblical and other religious texts that clearly reflects this phenomenon. The syncretistic teaching of many of these groups implies a universalism that intends to transcend the limiting historical reality. In other words, through the esoteric books and esoteric knowledge about such books, a new, egalitarian, cosmopolitan community-world

---

31. Hans Baer, *The Black Spiritual Movement: Religious Response to Racism* (Knoxville: University of Tennessee Press, 1984), 8–9.

is envisioned.[32] Rabbi Matthew, an early twentieth-century leader of the Black Jews of Harlem who taught a variant of Ethiopianism, serves as an important example of this type of reading of the Bible and other religious texts:

> I must treat briefly the history of the sons of men, from Adam, of whom it is only necessary to say that when God decided on the necessity of man's existence, He did not choose to make a black man, or a white man: He simply decided to make man—not white nor black—from the dust of the earth, in whom He encased the reproductive power of all colors, all species, all shades of all races and eventual nationalities. From Adam to Noah, there were only two classes of men, known as the sons of God, and sons of men: a Godly and an ungodly group....
>
> The two classes eventually met in Noah and his wife: Noah was a son of the Godly (a son of God), he chose a wife from the daughters of men (the carnal-minded), and to the time of the flood he had three sons: Shem, Ham, and Japheth. After the flood Ham took the lead....
>
> As Cush rose in power, Africa, the entire continent, including Egypt, became the center of the world's cultural and religious education, and thus Ham secured for himself and his posterity for all time, a name—Pioneers of the World's Civilization.[33]

Fifth "Reading": Fundamentalism (Late Twentieth Century)

The fifth and most recent type of African American readings of the Bible has to do with fundamentalism and an attraction to white fundamentalist communities. Not unlike the catalysts for the rise of fundamentalist piety among whites in the early decades of this century, the rise of such piety among African Americans in *significant numbers* in the last few decades signifies a crisis—of thinking, of security.

White America at the end of the nineteenth century and in the first few decades of the twentieth century was faced with the onslaught of change in every facet of life—the scientific revolution, inventions, a world war and the new awesome weapons it introduced, new questions about reality, and new methods of inquiry designed to address these questions in the universities that were becoming more comprehensive and research-oriented. The cumulative change was so great, so radical, that it has been termed a virtual revolution, a "paradigm shift of consciousness."[34]

---

32. Turner, *Religious Innovation in Africa*, 280–81; Baer, *The Black Spiritual Movement*, 133; and Cone and Wilmore, eds., *Black Theology*, 145–66.

33. Sernett, ed., *Afro-American Religious History*, 399–400.

34. Timothy P. Weber, "The Two-Edged Sword: The Fundamentalist Use of the Bible," in Hatch and Noll, eds., *The Bible in America*, 101–20.

The shift took different shapes in different contexts at different times. In religious circles, in theological seminaries, to be more precise, it began early to surface in the adoption of new methods of interpretation of the Bible. Among many biblical scholars it was no longer assumed that the confessional traditions or the literal rendering of the text was enough to get at meaning. Historical consciousness required the historical-critical reading of the Bible as an ancient document, written in different social contexts and different times by different human authors. Many reacted violently to this new scholarship, branding it as heresy, as an attempt to undermine the authority of the Scriptures and take them away from common folk. The fundamentalist movement was born in reaction. It had felt the old, comforting, simple world slipping away. It deemed that it was necessary to provide a way for common folk to read the Bible that would keep the old world intact, and at the same time speak to some of the difficulties that the new breed of scholars had pointed out. An inductive reading of the texts and a dispensationalist hermeneutic were devised and promoted among the new "Bible-believing" churches, associations, denominations, and academies founded at this time. This response was intended to secure the "fundamentals" of the faith drawn up by the movement against "modernism."[35]

African Americans were not a significant part of the beginnings of the fundamentalist movement in America.[36] Only in recent decades have significant numbers come to embrace in a self-conscious manner fundamentalist ideology and white fundamentalist communities. This phenomenon seems to reflect a rejection of—or at least a relativizing of the importance of—racialist or culturalist perspectives insofar as they are associated with the African American heritage. The intentional attempt to embrace Christian traditions, specifically the attempt to interpret the Bible, without respect for the historical experiences of persons of African descent in this country radically marks this reading and this period from others.

The growth of fundamentalism among African Americans is evident both in the different orientations of African American churches and in the increase in the number of African Americans who actually join white fundamentalist churches, and send their children to white fundamentalist academies. Those African Americans who actually join white fundamentalist communities find themselves for the most part having to relativize race and culture as factors in religious faith and piety, and having to argue for the universal nature of the fundamentalist perspective. At the seventeenth annual meeting of the National Black Evangelical As-

---

35. Ibid., 113–14.
36. George M. Marsden, *Fundamentalism and American Culture: The Shaping of Twentieth Century Evangelicalism: 1870–1925* (New York: Oxford University Press, 1980), 228.

sociation in 1980 controversy broke out over resignations in leadership provoked by differences of opinion about the theological perspective that should characterize the organization. Although this organization has the reputation for being relatively moderate on theological, social, and political issues, it could not escape having to address the tension between race and culture, on the one hand, and "pure" doctrine, on the other hand. Two divergent views emerged: one maintained that covenant theology, understood as emphasizing God's work in the black community through history, should be embraced by the association; the other maintained that a strict premillennial and dispensationalist stance was essential. A spokesperson for the second position argued that the association "must rest on the Word, be unified in theology, not culture, color, or history."[37]

Perhaps, very much like the whites who in earlier decades had experienced a crisis situation with the onslaught of modernism, some African Americans have embraced fundamentalism because they are experiencing a crisis. Their crisis has to do with their perception of the inadequacy of culturalist religion—African American religion—to vouchsafe, or guarantee, the traditions that are "Christian." Buttressing this perception is the assumption that anything distinctively black is inadequate in the dominant white world. Of course, this latter assumption has always been held by some African Americans. In the last few decades, however, many events—especially the failures of the African American leadership itself—have confirmed the assumption in the eyes of many. That this is the case even in the churches, traditionally the place where black self-confidence and pride were concentrated, is most significant. This lack of confidence is leading some African Americans to abandon their churches, to attempt to transform them into fundamentalist camps, and even to consider debating the question whether culture and color should inform a reading of the Bible or the quest to know God.

Summary

This essay has sought to provide only an outline of an interpretative history of African Americans as they have spoken about themselves and the worlds in which they have lived through their readings of the Bible. It is hoped that sufficient problems have been posed, questions raised, and arguments provoked to justify serious discussion and further research. The story is still being told because the Bible is still being read "in divers places and at sundry times."

---

37. Anthony T. Evans, quoted in Jimmy Locklear, "Theology–Culture Rift Surfaces among Black Evangelicals," *Christianity Today* 24 (May 23, 1980): 44.

— 5 —

"An Ante-bellum Sermon": A Resource for an African American Hermeneutic

David T. Shannon

Introduction

According to current folklore, a young boy was once told about the many conquests of hunters over the lion. This story intrigued the little boy; he was puzzled and inquired: "If the lion is supposed to be the king of the jungle, why is it that the hunter always wins?" The father responded: "The hunter will always win until the lion writes his own story!" The same may be said about African Americans, who have also been victimized by having their story told by others. As long as this tendency persists the real story of African Americans will not have been told. Fortunately, this is now changing. African American scholars have researched slave testimonies to insure that the nobility of their people and culture is acknowledged, recognized, and celebrated. John W. Blassingame, noted researcher on the slave narrative, states, "If scholars want to know the hearts and secret thoughts of Blacks they must study the testimony of Blacks."[1] As I hope to show, the African American slave sermon can be one such testimony.[2]

---

1. John W. Blassingame, *Slave Testimony* (Baton Rouge: Louisiana State University Press, 1977), lxv.
2. This study is informed by the perceptions of Keneth Kinnamon and others who argue that African American literature from its earliest time to the present has been

The primary focus of this study is a sermon in verse by Paul Laurence Dunbar entitled "An Ante-bellum Sermon."[3] The purpose of this study is to examine the sermon's hermeneutic (i.e., its interpretative principle) in order to determine how African Americans have sought in times past to tell their own story.

In the preceding chapter Vincent L. Wimbush discusses how African Americans through their history have used and interpreted the Bible to tell their own story. He rightly affirms the necessity of a critical study of African American songs and sermons as original sources for African American life. The same concern has been issued by William L. Andrews in his book *To Tell a Free Story: The First Century of Afro-American Autobiography, 1760–1865;* by Bernard W. Bell in his critical study entitled *The Afro-American Novel and Its Tradition;* and by Henry Louis Gates, Jr., in his book *The Signifying Monkey: A Theory of Afro-American Literary Criticism.*[4] Such endeavors represent an appropriate task; however, that task is difficult because we have to depend more on oral tradition rather than literary records. There are rare instances of published African American sermons, but most reflect editorial tampering that undermines their reliability as accurate representations of the folk tradition of African American oral delivery. One exception is the extensive collection of the sermons of Alexander Crummell.[5] In addition, many of the sermons are cited in speeches and essays.[6]

---

collectivistic and political. This is in contrast to Anglo-European literature, which has been individualistic and intuitive. African American writers who have lived in a condition of alienation and oppression have articulated this predicament and have protested the condition of African American people through their autobiographies, oratory, public letters, and other belletristic forms. Included in this list of writers are Maya Angelou, James Baldwin, Toni Cade Bambara, Benjamin Banneker, Imaru Amiri Baraka, William Wells Brown, Charles W. Chestnutt, Frederick Douglass, W. E. B. Du Bois, Paul Laurence Dunbar, Ralph Ellison, Olaudah Equiano, Henry Highland Garnet, Nikki Giovanni, Lorraine Hansberry, Langston Hughes, Kristin Hunter, Zora Neale Hurston, Claude McKay, Toni Morrison, Sonia Sanchez, Nat Turner, Alice Walker, David Walker, Margaret Walker, and Richard Wright. See Keneth Kinnamon, "Political Dimension of Afro-American Literature," *Soundings* 58 (Spring 1975): 130–44.

3. Paul Laurence Dunbar, *Lyrics of Lowly Life* (New York: Dodd, Mead and Company, 1901), 26–30.

4. William L. Andrews, *To Tell a Free Story: The First Century of Afro-American Autobiography, 1760–1865* (Chicago: University of Chicago Press, 1986); Bernard W. Bell, *The Afro-American Novel and Its Tradition* (Amherst: University of Massachusetts, 1987); Henry Louis Gates, Jr., *The Signifying Monkey: A Theory of Afro-American Literary Criticism* (New York: Oxford University Press, 1988).

5. Work Projects Administration, comp., *Calendar of the Manuscripts in the Schomburg Collection of Negro Literature* (New York: Andronicus Publishing Co., Inc., 1943), 92–132.

6. See Carter G. Woodson, *Negro Orators and Their Orations* (Washington, D.C.: Associated Publishers, Inc., 1925); Newbell Puckett, *Folk Beliefs of the Southern Negro* (Chapel Hill: University of North Carolina Press, 1926); William H. Pipes, *Say Amen, Brother* (Westport, Conn.: Negro Universities Press, 1970); Bruce A. Rosenberg, *The Art of the American Folk Preacher* (New York: Oxford University Press, 1970); Philip S. Foner, *The Voice of Black America* (New York: Capricorn Books, 1975); Henry Mitchell, *Black Preaching* (San Francisco: Harper and Row, 1979); Mechal Sobel, *Trabelin' On* (Westport, Conn.: Green-

However, the majority of the material on African American preaching comes from oral accounts. One of the best-known accounts drawn from folk/oral tradition is the collection of sermons by James Weldon Johnson entitled *God's Trombones*.[7] These sermons are classic examples of the style and the language of the preacher. The use of the Bible is taken for granted and hermeneutical principles seem apparent as Bible stories are treated dramatically. Johnson presents the subject matter of the stories rhetorically rather than analytically. An example of these stories is "The Creation."[8] The interpretative principle that is found in this collection is analogical rather than dialectical. By this I mean that the author compares the divine creative acts with human activities rather than engaging in logical argumentative discourse.

Another study that presents the oral African American sermon in a poetic form is Zora Neale Hurston's *The Sanctified Church*.[9] Hurston reports on a sermon by Reverend C. C. Lovelace at Eau Gallie, Florida, on May 3, 1929. Hurston presents this sermon in the context of her description and analysis of the sanctified church. Lovelace's sermon is described in the context of the congregation's response (call-and-response) to his flowery language and imaginative descriptions. The emphasis is thereby on the sermon's evocative nature rather than on its possible hermeneutical principles. Nevertheless, this sermon uses the Bible as its primary source. At the beginning of the sermon Zechariah 13:6 is referred to: "Our theme this morning is the wounds of Jesus. When the Father shall ask 'What are these wounds in thine hand?' He shall answer, 'Those are they with which I was wounded in the house of my friends.'"[10] The sermon continues: "We read in the 53rd chapter of Isaiah where He was wounded for our transgressions and bruised for our iniquities."[11] The underlying theme is God's deliverance of sinful humankind through the sacrificial death of Jesus Christ upon the cross and his resurrection from the dead. Listen to the cadence of this sermon in the idiom of the period:

> When God said, ha!
> Let us make man
> And the elders upon the altar cried, ha!
> If you make man, ha!
> He will sin....
> And Jesus said, ha!
> And if he sin,

wood Press, 1979); Cheryl Sanders, "Slavery and Conversion: An Analysis of Ex-slave Testimony" (Ph.D. diss., Harvard University, 1985).

7. James Weldon Johnson, *God's Trombones; Seven Negro Sermons in Verse* (New York: Viking Press, 1927).

8. Ibid., 17–20.

9. Zora Neale Hurston, *The Sanctified Church* (Berkeley, Calif.: Turtle Island, 1983).

10. Ibid., 95.

11. Ibid.

I'll go his bond before yo mighty throne. . . .
If he sin, I will redeem him
I'll break de chasm of hell
Where de fire's never quenched
I'll go into de grave
Where de worm never dies, Ah![12]

Lovelace's sermon emphasizes the significance of creation and redemption. It highlights the meaning of the inscription of the antislavery medal that was designed by the English Committee for Effecting the Abolishment of the Slave Trade: "Am I not a man and a brother?"[13] The hermeneutical principle is that the Afro-American is a part of God's creation and is included in God's act of redemption through Jesus Christ. The sermon affirms the unity of the African American with all humankind, both in creation and in redemption. Thus the sermon was remembered as being content-laden as well as evocative. Hurston's rendition of the sermon illustrates the lasting impression sermons made upon the hearers.

Similarly, Ned Walker of South Carolina remembered an African American sermon that made a powerful impression on its hearers.[14] Walker gives his recollection of the scene and of the words of the preacher at the funeral of a person called Uncle Wash.

Uncle Pompey took his text 'bout Paul and Silas layin' in jail and dat it was no 'ternally against a church member to go to jail. Him dwell on de life of labor and bravery, in tacklin' kickin' hosses and mules. How him sharpen de dull plow points and make de corn and cotton grow, to feed and clothe de hungry and naked. He look up thru de pine tree tops and say: "I see Jacob's ladder. Brother Wash is climbin' dat ladder. Him is half way up. Ah! Brudders and sisters, pray, while I preach dat he enter in them pearly gates. I see them gates open. Brother Wash done reach de topmost rung in dat ladder. Let us sing wid a shout, dat blessed hymn, 'Dere is a Fountain Filled Wid Blood.'" Wid de first verse de women got to hollerin' and wid de second, Uncle Pompey say: "De dyin' thief [mentioned in the second stanza] I see him dere to welcome Brother Wash in paradise. Thank God! Brother Wash done washed as white as snow and landed safe forever more." Dat Attorney General turn up his coat in de November wind and say: "I'll be damn!" Marse William smile and 'low: "Oh Tom! Don't be too hard on them. Member He will have mercy on them, dat have mercy on others."[15]

Walker commented that the attorney general, who was in attendance at the funeral, was also tremendously impressed by such a moving sermon.

12. Ibid., 96–97.
13. Andrews, *To Tell a Free Story*, 1.
14. Henry H. Mitchell, *Black Belief: Folk Beliefs of Blacks in America and West Africa* (New York: Harper and Row, 1975), 131.
15. Ibid.

Also, the early African American sermons influenced the genre of early African American autobiography.

> The unity of black autobiography in the antebellum era is most apparent in the pervasive use of journey or quest motifs that symbolize multiple layers of spiritual evolution. In black spiritual autobiography the protagonist wishes to escape sinfulness and ignorance in order to achieve righteousness and a knowledge of the saving grace of God. In the slave narrative the quest is toward freedom from physical bondage and the enlightenment that literacy can offer to the restricted self- and social consciousness of the slave. Both the fugitive slave narrator and the black spiritual autobiographer trace their freedom back to an awakening of their awareness of their fundamental identity with and rightful participation in *logos*, whether understood as reason and its expression in speech or as divine spirit. The climax of the quests of both kinds of autobiographer usually comes when they seize the opportunity to proclaim what are clearly complementary gospels of freedom. Before the fugitive slave narrator could have success in restoring political and economic freedom to Afro-Americans, the black spiritual autobiographer had to lay the necessary intellectual groundwork by proving that black people were as much chosen by God for eternal salvation as whites.[16]

In addition, the African American sermon had significant influence upon African American writers, both early and contemporary. For example, Ralph Ellison's classic novel, *The Invisible Man*, includes the "Let My People Go Sermon" and the "Train Sermon"; James Baldwin includes his "Uncleanness Sermon" in *Go Tell It on the Mountain*; and Richard Wright presents a parody of Ellison's "Train Sermon" in *Lawd Today*.

Even though we do not have written records of many of the early African American sermons, we do have access to the oral tradition of biblical exposition and interpretation through such works as those of James Weldon Johnson, Zora Neale Hurston, Ned Walker, Paul Laurence Dunbar, Ralph Ellison, Richard Wright, and James Baldwin. I contend that the traditional categories of hermeneutics—i.e., allegorical, christological, typological, and *sensus plenior* hermeneutics[17]—do not fully explain the interpretive principle or the hermeneutics of the early African American preacher.

However, there is a sense in which the African American preacher used one or more of these categories. Dunbar's "Ante-bellum Sermon" includes these at different points. In that sermon the allegorical category is used throughout in relation to Pharaoh as the personification of evil and God as the Redeemer. The typological dimension is used in reference

---

16. Andrews, *To Tell a Free Story*, 7.
17. See Robert Bennett, "Biblical Hermeneutics for the Black Preacher," *Journal of the Interdenominational Theological Center* 1 (Spring 1974): 38–53.

to Israel and the African American slaves. Israel represents the type of people who endured slavery and were redeemed. For the African American preacher, the slaves will also be freed.

> Their voices rise in constant warnings to whites to beware of the inevitable judgment of God for the sin of slavery. In this kind of jeremiad, blacks also revealed a concept of themselves as a chosen people whose covenant with God paralleled that between Jehovah and the Jews and whose history was also typified by that of the Israelites of the Old Testament. Black autobiographers in America were early participants in and developers of several motifs in the black jeremiad. African-born Olaudah Equiano . . . identified his people, the Ibo, with the Hebrews before they reached the promised land, thus establishing in the late eighteenth century a tradition on which many subsequent slave narrators drew.[18]

The christological focus is a basic principle informing the African American hermeneutic. Although this is not fully explicit in Dunbar's sermon, the emphasis upon the role of Christ as the liberator transcends the allegorical and typological approaches to the interpretation of Scripture. Christology undergirds the hope for both spiritual and political liberation. However, the sermon by Lovelace, quoted above, reflects this christological hermeneutic even more than Dunbar's re-creation in "An Ante-bellum Sermon."

The African American sermon as illustrated by Dunbar and Lovelace is a significant part of the testimony of black Americans. It contributes to the discussion of African American hermeneutics in several ways. First, the folk preacher (in the following case one Brother Belden) was pictured as a gifted man:

> He was blessed or gifted with a stentorian pair of lungs, a very active and original imagination, and could read the Bible with the lids closed, with as much satisfaction to himself as he could when open, because Brother Belden could not read at all. He had, however, been called to preach and . . . he responded. . . . They were all equally deprived, both the called and the uncalled. . . . In him [they] confided; him they honored; in him they saw the messenger of the Lord bearing the only consolation, which was like balm to their deepest sufferings.[19]

The style and content of the sermon are also informative for understanding the message of the preacher and the response of the congregation. In this call-and-response format we can see the African roots of the African American worship experience.[20]

These folk preachers employed a system of rhetoric and interpretation that enhanced the African oral narratives built on double entendres.

---

18. Andrews, *To Tell a Free Story*, 14. See also Bell, *The Afro-American Novel*, 3–36.
19. Bell, *The Afro-American Novel*, 31.
20. See Mitchell, *Black Preaching*, 58–94.

When employing this device, the preacher would say one thing but would mean something entirely different. Given the oppressive social situation of the preachers and their congregations, it was often necessary to use this method to convey significant messages.

In addition, the sermons contributed to the origins of the oral myths and speculative stories that formed the basis of the African American tradition and folklore. Bernard Bell states:

> The two principal myth-legends that inform the early novel are a messianic delivery from oppression and an eschatological overthrow of white supremacy, rewritten from the oral tradition and the King James Bible. Mainly self-educated and missionary school trained preachers and teachers fired with a passion for justice and social reform, the first generation of black novelists were frequently concerned with how sanctification and sin, virtue and vice, in this world related to the ultimate destiny of man.[21]

Clearly, the African American sermon has had a wide-ranging influence on African American life and literature. An examination of Paul Dunbar's re-creation of an antebellum sermon can help us to understand the message and meaning of the early African American sermons and can enable us to see these sermons as sources of an African American hermeneutic. What follows, then, is a detailed treatment of Dunbar's poem. The focus will be upon the poem's use of double entendre[22] and its use of the Bible to give immediate comfort to the hearers by affirming liberation from slavery. I hope this analysis will show that the African American sermon, whether passed on through literary forms or oral tradition, is a resource for an African American hermeneutic.

Following my treatment of Dunbar's poem, I will conclude with some reflections upon the significance of the sermon for the development of an African American hermeneutic.

"An Ante-bellum Sermon"

In the poem "An Ante-bellum Sermon," Dunbar, an elevator boy who became one of the most celebrated American poets, presents a sermon from the pre–Civil War period that exhibits the principles of interpretation for that critical period. It also forms a basis for analysis and synthesis of African American social and political thought in that period.

The sermon, which is composed of eighty-eight lines, can be divided into the following sections:

---

21. Bell, *The Afro-American Novel*, 23.
22. See Miles M. Fisher, *Negro Slave Songs in the United States* (Secaucus, N.J.: Citadel Press, 1978).

Breaking the poem into seventeen sections helps us to follow the thought of this great poet as he demonstrates the genius of the antebellum preacher. It also helps us to observe the way in which an African American slave functioned in the context of worship. I will explicate the different sections and seek to show how they form a principle of interpretation for the first hearers in the "howlin' wildaness" and thereby provide a hermeneutic for us today.

A. Setting for the Sermon (Lines 1–2)

> We is gathahed hyeah, my brothahs,
> In dis howlin' wildaness,

These lines set the context for the sermon. They have a double meaning. There is a sense in which the lines describe the physical setting, the brush arbor[23] where the slaves met for worship.

---

23. An arbor made of brushwood, especially as a place for a camp meeting. See *Webster's Third New International Dictionary of the English Language Unabridged*, s.v. "brush arbor."

At the same time the second line has a symbolic meaning. The "howlin' wildaness" is a metaphoric representation of slavery. It was a condition of uncertainty, unpredictability, and danger. Slavery was a context of denial, restriction, and pain. Slavery could be described as a "howlin' wildaness" in many ways. This has been graphically described by Arna Bontemps in his book *Great Slave Narratives*.

> One way or another, the considerable body of writing in the New World known as *slave narratives*, an influential contribution to American cultural history of the nineteenth century, has been allowed to languish. Only one title in a form that may have produced several hundred, by some estimates, was in print when the Supreme Court decision of 1954 made authentic the upsurge of feeling that produced the Civil Rights Revolution, and that title had escaped oblivion by disguising itself as something other than part of the genre in which it was first presented.
>
> The Negro's suffering in his private hell of oppression was the point at which the narratives invariably began. Enduring this ordeal until he became desperate, or until he otherwise engaged the reader's interest or sympathy, the slave was eventually impelled to attempt the perils of escape. The stratagems used differed with the individuals, and the journeys varied as did the roads followed. A promised land and a chance to make a new life as a free man was always the goal, even though sometimes the realization fell short of the expectation. The recorded memoirs of the questing slaves were felt by many readers of the nineteenth century to epitomize the condition of man on the earth as it documented the personal history of the individual to whom bondage was real and freedom was more than a dream.[24]

B. Purpose of Meeting (Lines 3–4)

> Fu' to speak some words of comfo't
> To each othah in distress.

The next text focuses upon the purpose of their meeting together. The author sees the meeting as a communal affair. They did not gather just to hear the preacher. On the contrary, they affirmed the Protestant principle of the priesthood of all believers. Mutual comfort is a significant theme in the gathering of these slaves. They were able to share their problems and project their hope. Two words are placed in juxtaposition—*comfo't* and *distress*.

Slavery was a state of constant distress. Those who described this deplorable state as a "peculiar institution" recognized the horrible reality of slavery. Worship provided a temporary respite from such horrors. This respite was enriched by words and actions of comfort. The slaves were able to receive pats on the back, words of encouragement, and smiles

---

24. Arna Bontemps, *Great Slave Narratives* (Boston: Beacon Press, 1969), vii.

of support. The preacher stated clearly the purpose for their meeting; it was to comfort each other.

Christian language is not used explicitly, but the gathering by nature was a Christian worship. Therefore, it can be assumed that the power of the gospel was recognized, acknowledged, and celebrated. "For where two or three are gathered in my name, there am I in the midst of them" (Matt. 18:20). It is reasonable to surmise that these slaves had heard the message of the gospel. The good news of the gospel comforts and empowers.

This word of comfort for each other constituted a source of strength. The slaves were very clear why they were worshiping together. They were a support community in a common quest. "The historical quest of black Americans, their principal canonical story, in short, is for life, liberty, and wholeness—the full development and unity of self and black community—as a biracial, bicultural people, as Americans of African descent."[25]

C. Subject and Text (Lines 5–8)

> An' we chooses fu' ouah subjic'
> Dis—we'll 'splain it by an' by;
> "An' de Lawd said, 'Moses, Moses,'
> An' de man said, 'Hyeah am I.'"

As his subject the preacher chooses Exodus 3:4: "God called, . . . 'Moses, Moses!' And he said, 'Here am I.'" This is an ingenious use of the biblical text. The call of Moses is one of the classic texts in the Old Testament. Not only do we have the significance of the role of Moses in Hebrew history but we also have the context in which the mighty God delivered Israel from slavery in Egypt. The foundation of Israel's faith was that it was brought out of Egypt (see Num. 23:22-24; 8; 2 Sam. 7:23; 1 Sam. 4:8; Judg. 6:13; and Exod. 20:2). Thus, the deliverance from Egypt became the heart of Israel's confession of faith.

Wherever it occurs, the phrase "Jahweh delivered his people from Egypt" is confessional in character. Indeed, so frequent is it in the Old Testament, meeting us not only in every age (down to Dan. ix. 15), but also in the most varied contexts, that it has in fact been designated as Israel's original confession. In the deliverance from Egypt Israel saw the guarantee for all the future, the absolute surety for Jahweh's will to save, something like a warrant to which faith could appeal in times of trial (Ps. lxxiv. 2). In its oldest form this confession glorifies an act of Jahweh's unaccompanied by any divine utterance. And Israel too, the object of this event, is silent. But when the tellers of the story come to describe it, they introduce a plethora

---

25. Bell, *The Afro-American Novel*, 12.

of words, some allegedly spoken by Jahweh and some by Israel. Important as these are, the event which took place still remains the basic thing that happened. This datum ancient Israel never spiritualized.[26]

The preacher's "subjic'"—i.e, Exodus 3:4—contains the central theme of the sermon. God took the initiative to call Moses to lead Israel out of bondage. The theme is introduced through the subject. God called a man who responded to God's call—Moses. He answered, "Here am I."

D. Biblical Background (Lines 9–22)

> Now ole Pher'oh, down in Egypt,
> Was de wuss man evah bo'n,
> An' he had de Hebrew chillun
> Down dah wukin' in his co'n;
> 'T well de Lawd got tiahed o' his foolin',
> An' sez he: "I'll let him know—
> Look hyeah, Moses, go tell Pher'oh
> Fu' to let dem chillun go."
>
> "An' ef he refuse to do it,
> I will make him rue de houah,
> Fu' I'll empty down on Egypt
> All de vials of my powah."
> Yes he did—an' Pher'oh's ahmy
> Was n't wuth a ha'f a dime;

This section, which the author uses to prepare for the main point of the poem, can be divided into the five parts mentioned earlier:

1. Pharaoh's Evil Deed in Holding Israel in Bondage

2. God's Reaction to Pharaoh's Evil

3. Call of Moses

4. Consequences upon Pharaoh If He Refuses to Let the People Go

5. God's Act of Deliverance

1. Pharaoh's Evil Deed in Holding Israel in Bondage. The sermon recounts the Old Testament story of the bondage of the Hebrews in Egypt. Pharaoh is described as an evil man, the "wuss man evah bo'n." Pharaoh's character is manifested in his evil deeds. He was a slavemaster. He had the Hebrews working his corn, toiling and laboring as "hewers of wood and drawers of water," making brick without straw.

---

26. Gerhard von Rad, *Old Testament Theology* (New York: Harper and Row, 1962), 1:175–76.

And Pharaoh said, "Behold, the people of the land are now many and you make them rest from their burdens!" The same day Pharaoh commanded the task masters of the people and their foremen, "You shall no longer give the people straw to make bricks, as heretofore; let them go and gather straw for themselves. But the number of bricks which they made heretofore you shall lay upon them, you shall by no means lessen it; for they are idle; therefore they cry, 'Let us go and offer sacrifice to our God.' Let heavier work be laid upon the men that they may labor at it and pay no regard to lying words" [Exod. 5:5-9; see also Exod. 5:12-19].

2. God's Reaction to Pharaoh's Evil. The sermon continues with a description of God's response to Israel's predicament. Lines 13–16 retell God's command to Moses.

"And now, behold, the cry of the people of Israel has come to me, and I have seen the oppression with which the Egyptians oppress them. Come, I will send you to Pharaoh that you may bring forth my people, the sons of Israel, out of Egypt." But Moses said to God, "Who am I that I should go to Pharaoh, and bring the sons of Israel out of Egypt?" He said, "But I will be with you; and this shall be the sign for you, that I have sent you: when you have brought forth the people out of Egypt, you shall serve God upon this mountain" [Exod. 3:9-12].

3. Call of Moses. God uses Moses as an instrument to tell Pharaoh to let God's people go. Dunbar's text echoes the words of the spiritual, "Go Down Moses, way down in Egypt's land. Tell ole Pharaoh, let my people go."

4. Consequences upon Pharaoh If He Refuses to Let the People Go. Lines 17 and 18 of the sermon predict what will happen to Pharaoh. This anticipates the plagues. This will make him "rue de houah," regret the hour, he was born.

In lines 19 and 20 the author identifies the consequences upon Pharaoh if he refuses to let the Hebrews go. These plagues ("vials of my powah") are described in Exodus 7:8—11:10 (see also Pss. 78:44-51; 105:28-36). These include: (1) pollution of the Nile causing it to turn to blood (Exod. 7:17-18); (2) a plague of frogs (Exod. 7:25—8:15); (3) a plague of gnats (Exod. 8:16-18); (4) a plague of flies (Exod. 8:20-32); (5) a plague upon cattle, probably anthrax (Exod. 9:1-7); (6) boils (Exod. 9:8-12); (7) hail and thunderstorms (Exod. 9:13-35); (8) a plague of locusts (Exod. 10:1-20); (9) thick darkness (Exod. 10:21-29); (10) death of firstborn (Exod. 12:29-32); the spoliation of the Egyptians (see Exod. 3:21-22; 12:35-36).

5. God's Act of Deliverance. God did deliver Israel because Pharaoh refused to let Israel go.

> Yes he did—an' Pher'oh's ahmy
> Was n't wuth a ha'f a dime";

The genius of this preacher is that he uses graphic language to describe God's spoliation of the Egyptians. He uses the story to dramatize how God deals with slavemasters. What God did with Pharaoh and the Egyptians is a case in point. Pharaoh and his army were no match for God.

E. Theme: Trust in God, for God Will Send a Liberator (Lines 23–36)

> Fu' de Lawd will he'p his chillun,
> You kin trust him evah time.
>
> An' yo' enemies may 'sail you
> In de back an' in de front;
> But de Lawd is all aroun' you,
> Fu' to ba' de battle's brunt.
> Dey kin fo'ge yo' chains an' shackles
> F'om de mountains to de sea;
> But de Lawd will sen' some Moses
> Fu' to set his chillun free.
>
> An' de lan' shall hyeah his thundah,
> Lak a blas' f 'om Gab'el's ho'n,
> Fu' de Lawd of hosts is mighty
> When he girds his ahmor on.

The author ties together the synchronic (simultaneous) and diachronic (historical) meanings of the text. The slave preacher displays interpretive skills in tying together the liberation theme in past and present tenses. He interprets the full meaning and significance of the text for both the Hebrews and the slaves. The slaves were reminded what God did at the time of Israel's bondage.

The historic meaning is stressed in these thirteen lines. The theme is that God delivers those who trust in the divine. Lines 23 and 24 are the crux of the interpretation of the sermon. God is the liberator. Just as God delivered Israel, God will deliver those who trust and obey.

The language of these lines is clear and precise. Three insights emerge from this treatment by this great preacher. First, the preacher identifies the God of the Hebrews. He uses the term *the Lawd* to identify the Hebrew God who delivered the people.

Then Moses said to God, "If I come to the people of Israel and say to them, 'The God of your fathers has sent me to you,' and they ask me, 'What is his name?' what shall I say to them?" God said to Moses, "I AM WHO I AM." And he said, "Say this to the people of Israel, 'The Lord, the God of your fathers, the God of Abraham, the God of Isaac, and the God of Jacob, has sent me to you': this is my name for ever, and thus I am to be remembered throughout all generations" [Exod. 3:13-15].

Second, the preacher uses the terms of family relationship; he says God will "he'p his chillun." Slaves and all persons are children of God. Masters do not occupy a special place before God. On the contrary, they are under divine wrath for holding humans as slaves. The use of such familial terms shows that slavery did not destroy the sense of kinship with God.

Third, the preacher stresses trust. God is known by those who trust, who have faith, who realize that the sovereign God acts in history on behalf of those who call for divine help.

Lines 25–32, which affirm that God acts no matter how difficult things may be, should be read with Psalm 46. Enemies can attack from all sides, "in de back an' in de front" (line 26). The preacher affirms God's presence "all aroun' you" (line 27). God protects the people from the enemy, for God "ba' de battle's brunt" (line 28). Lines 29–30 declare that chains and shackles and slavery itself could not destroy God's abiding and providential care.

Lines 31–32 declare that God will liberate the oppressed, no matter what the condition. A human liberator will be sent. Not only will the oppressed recognize God's might; the whole world will know of God's power.

The preacher celebrates that God is the Lord of Hosts, one of the Hebrew titles for God. God is described in military language. The term that is translated *host* literally means armies. God has legions to fight for the oppressed. When God is ready for battle, "he girds his ahmor on."

F. Disclaimer That Speaker Is Not Addressing Contemporary Situation (Lines 37–40)

> But fu' feah some one mistakes me,
> I will pause right hyeah to say,
> Dat I'm still a-preachin' ancient,
> I ain't talkin' 'bout to-day.

The preacher, having clearly established the premise that God is the great liberator, makes his first of three disclaimers. This technique is significant because it underscores the fact that the speaker does indeed want his hearers to connect the past and the present. However, this was a device to keep the slavemaster and any informers off guard. They could not accuse the preacher of "talkin' 'bout to-day." The slave preacher was aware that his message could create trouble for him and the listeners; therefore, he utilized double entendre when there was a feeling that informers were present.

The folk preacher was always aware that there was a thin line between telling the Bible story and making application of this message in reference to liberation. The masters had interpreted Paul's letters as approving of slavery, but the African American slave preacher was forbidden to use the Bible in reference to liberation. Therefore, the folk preacher used these disclaimers to protect himself from detection. At the same time these disclaimers had the power of reminding the hearers to make the connection between the Bible story and their situation.

G. Theme: God's Power of Deliverance Was Not Limited to Israel (Lines 41–46)

> But I tell you, fellah christuns,
> Things 'll happen mighty strange;
> Now, de Lawd done dis fu' Isrul,
> An' his ways don't nevah change,
> An' de love he showed to Isrul
> Was n't all on Isrul spent;

Following the disclaimers, the preacher makes the connection between the past and present. He calls attention to the fact that God will act in strange ways. His words affirm the biblical view of God as majestic, powerful, and mysterious. "Remember this and consider, recall it to mind, you transgressors, remember the former things of old; for I am God, and there is no other; I am God, and there is none like me" (Isa. 46:8-9). Although the preacher does not mention these powerful words, he expresses faith in God who would deliver those who are oppressed. He does not claim knowledge of how or when this would happen. His message is a word of hope that it would happen. He believes that God works in strange and mysterious ways.

This recognition of God's strange ways leads him to affirm that the way God acted with Israel is consistent with divine activity. The preacher engages in a kind of parallelism, perhaps akin to ancient Hebrew poetry. The thoughts in lines 43 and 44 are parallel to those in lines 45 and 46.

> A43—Now the Lord did this for Israel.
> B44—And his ways don't ever change.
> A45—And the love he showed to Israel
> B46—Was not all on Israel spent.

Line A43 parallels A45; line B44 parallels B46. The thought is that God is the liberator. The liberation of Israel is evidence of God's lordship of the world. The author argues that God did not expend all of God's love on Israel. Therefore, the same God who delivered Israel from bondage would also free the slaves in America.

The preacher moves from the particular to the universal. Although he does not make any special reference to the specific context of slavery, he makes it clear that God's love extends to all. This is the basis of his faith and hope.

H. Repeat of Disclaimer (Lines 47–48)

> Now don't run an' tell yo' mastahs
> Dat I's preachin' discontent.

This powerful restatement of his theme in lines 41–46 echoes his introduction of his thesis in lines 23–36. Since he had to issue a disclaimer at the end of that section, he felt it necessary to utter a second disclaimer. These disclaimers help to frame the sections that stress his theme of liberation.

In lines 47 and 48 his disclaimer clarifies the earlier statement. Earlier he had said that he wanted everyone to understand that he was "still a-preachin' ancient"; now he clarifies that by telling the informers that he does not want them to accuse him of "preachin' discontent." He is aware that if he really communicated his message, the people would not be satisfied with words; they would be stirred to revolt. He is aware of the power of his message. The recognition that God is deliverer is a potent discovery. Caution was necessary.

However, this second disclaimer has another function. It is to make the people aware that the liberation will come from God. God will send the deliverer. Thus, they should not misinterpret his message. It is not a message of rebellion but an affirmation of deliverance through one whom God would choose; it is God who would decide the way in which liberation would take place. The slave preacher was not preaching discontent; he was declaring God's care and concern for the people. God's role was that of divine liberator of those who were oppressed.

I. Theme: God Created All Persons Free (Lines 49–56)

> 'Cause I is n't; I'se a-judgin'
> Bible people by deir ac's;
> I'se a-givin' you de Scriptuah,
> I'se a-handin' you de fac's.
> Cose ole Pher'oh b'lieved in slav'ry,
> But de Lawd he let him see,
> Dat de people he put bref in,—
> Evah mothah's son was free.

The preacher is clarifying his thesis. This is an amplification of the theme in lines 23–36 and 41–46. In the former instance, the *particular* is stressed. God destroyed Pharaoh's army. In the latter, the *universal* is emphasized. God did not spend all divine love on Israel. Now the preacher explicates the particular by assessing the character of the slaveholder. Pharaoh is the object of his attack. The thesis is affirmed in lines 55–56.

Freedom is not a gift to any one person or group of persons. It is a gift of God to all. Therefore, no one has a right to take it from anyone.

The preacher becomes bold and declares judgment upon Pharaoh. The preacher uses the example of Pharaoh's holding Israel in slavery as the criterion of the judgment: "Cose ole Pher'oh b'lieved in slav'ry." The preacher pronounces judgment on those who follow Pharaoh. God, in destroying Pharaoh's army, declared judgment upon him and upon all who believe and act in favor of human bondage.

The dialectic is clear. Human belief in slavery is contrary to the divine creation of freedom; slavery is antithetical to freedom. In this struggle, the victor is clear. God demonstrated to Pharaoh what happens to those who enslave others. This message will be repeated again. All will recognize what God intends in creation: "Evah mothah's son was free."

J. Attack upon Detractors (Lines 57–64)

> An' dahs othahs thinks lak Pher'oh,
> But dey calls de Scriptuah liar,
> Fu' de Bible says "a servant
> Is a-worthy of his hire."
> An' you cain't git roun' nor thoo dat,
> An' you cain't git ovah it,
> Fu' whatevah place you git in,
> Dis hyeah Bible too 'll fit.

The affirmation that God created all persons free leads the preacher to continue his argument. He moves from the ancient reference of Pharaoh to the current situation. He dares to move from the attack on Pharaoh for his belief in and practice of slavery to an attack upon those who do not believe the Bible.

The argument is sharp and forceful. Having established that the defense of freedom is based upon divine creation, the preacher argues that those who defend slavery are opposed to the Bible. The argument runs as follows: The believers in slavery do not believe in the Bible because they deny the biblical principle that people who work should receive compensation for their work.

The preacher uses the Bible as the basis for the attack on slavery. He rests his case on what "de Bible sez." He argues the Bible must be dealt with as a moral force. It is a force that cannot be avoided and is relevant even to those who reject its message, like Pharaoh. Lines 61 and 62 refer to the Bible's breadth, height, and depth, and lines 63 and 64 refer to its relevance.

K. Reiteration of Theme That God Created All Persons Free (Lines 65–68)

> So you see de Lawd's intention,
> Evah sence de worl' began,

Was dat his almighty freedom
Should belong to evah man,

The preacher returns to the themes of freedom and liberation. He suggests that just as liberation is integral to the *being* and *action* of God (see lines 44 and 23), liberation is also integral to the thought and intention of God. Freedom was not an afterthought. God intended for humans to be free. The preacher echoes the thought of the biblical writers in Genesis.

> Then God said, "Let us make man in our image, after our likeness; and let them have dominion over the fish of the sea, and over the birds of the air, and over the cattle, and over all the earth, and over every creeping thing that creeps upon the earth." So God created man in his own image, in the image of God he created him; male and female he created them. . . . The Lord God took the man and put him in the garden of Eden to till it and keep it. And the Lord God commanded the man, saying, "You may freely eat of every tree of the garden; but of the tree of the knowledge of good and evil you shall not eat, for in the day that you eat of it you shall die." Then the Lord God said, "It is not good that the man should be alone; I will make him a helper fit for him." So out of the ground the Lord God formed every beast of the field and every bird of the air, and brought them to the man to see what he would call them; and whatever the man called every living creature, that was its name [Gen. 1:26-27; 2:15-19].

In both of these passages the purpose of God in creation is clear. Humans are to be in partnership with God and with each other. They are to image God by sharing sovereignty over the creatures God made. There is no indication that humans are to exercise dominion over other human beings. The African American slave preacher proclaims this biblical understanding in this antebellum sermon. The profundity of this preacher's thought derives from the way he intuits the basic meaning of the biblical text. He is able to read the *full meaning* of the text and share it with his hearers. His interpretation rests upon a universal rather than a particularistic application.

L. Repeat of Disclaimer (Lines 69–72)

But I think it would be bettah,
Ef I'd pause agin to say,
Dat I'm talkin' 'bout ouah freedom
In a Bibleistic way.

As has been the case in two other occasions in the sermon, wherever the preacher makes a strong affirmation of his theme, he makes a disclaimer. In these lines he admits that he is talking about freedom but suggests that he is using the Bible as his norm. In a way, this is not a disclaimer but a qualification of the previous disclaimers.

The genius of the preacher is that he is using this qualification to underscore his interpretation of the Bible as source of liberation. The phrase "in a Bibleistic way" indicates that the Bible is its own interpreter. He appeals to a higher authority. His reasoning is based upon the Bible and its treatment of freedom. His authority for proclaiming that freedom is a divine thought and act is rooted in the Holy Scripture. In this sermon, no particular text is used to prove this point. The biblical thought rather than the particular text is used. The approach to the biblical text is indicative of the preacher's ability to handle and interpret the Bible. He is able to distill the principle meaning of the biblical concept and is not enslaved by a particular word or phrase. Thus, he is able to restate his theme.

M. Reiteration of Theme That God Will Send a Liberator (Lines 73–76)

> But de Moses is a-comin',
> An' he's comin', suah and fas'
> We kin hyeah his feet a-trompin',
> We kin hyeah his trumpit blas'.

The preacher continues his theme of liberation by discussing the agent of liberation. Earlier he had made the following points about that agent: (1) God has demonstrated that God is the liberator who will help God's children (line 23); (2) what God did for Israel God will do for all (line 46); (3) God has created all persons free (line 56); (4) the freedom of all people was God's intention from the beginning (lines 65–68). Now the preacher focuses upon the agent of liberation.

He reiterates a notion that he mentioned in lines 31–32: The Lord will send a new Moses to set God's children free. The message takes on a clearer focus: If God is the liberator, has liberated Israel, has created all persons free, and has always intended for all to be free, then why were the slaves still in bondage? The preacher speaks to their context in assuring them that God is faithful and would send a deliverer. This is the word that they needed to hear as a source for hope and consolation. This word empowered them to face the horrors of slavery.

He speaks in terms of certainty and assurance: He says the liberator is coming sure and fast. This strong affirmation is followed by poetic language that suggests the immediacy of God's coming deliverer: The people can hear the liberator's feet "a-trompin'" and can hear his trumpet blast. This language echoes another biblical scene in which God is described as liberator. It is graphically narrated in the biblical account:

> But on the seventh day they rose at dawn and marched seven times round the city in the same way; that was the only day on which they marched round seven times. The seventh time the priests blew the trumpets and Joshua said to the army, "Shout! The Lord has given you the city" [Josh. 6:15-16, NEB].

This scene is alluded to by the preacher to firm up the people's hope.

N. Interlude: Warning to be Humble, to be Patient (Lines 77–80)

> But I want to wa'n you people,
> Don't you git too brigity;
> An' don't you git to braggin'
> 'Bout dese things, you wait an' see.

The preacher warns the people to be humble. At the same time he wants them to be faithful. His assurance has been so powerful that he cautions them against arrogance. He has promised liberation a number of times and has assured the people that God will send a deliverer. This has created the context in which a false piety could be developed. He wants them to be prepared for God's action but to respond in a godly way.

This warning against overconfidence and braggadocio reveals the preacher's sensitivity to the effect of his word. He wants the people to remember that the agent of God's liberation would be God's action. Therefore, their behavior should reflect God's liberation. They should act in a way appropriate to those called children of God.

O. Reiteration of Theme That God Will Send a Liberator (Lines 81–82)

> But when Moses wif his powah
> Comes an' sets us chillun free,

The preacher returns to the assurance of a deliverer. He describes the role of the deliverer: He will come with "powah" and will set God's children free. He begins this stanza with the word of proclamation. Three points are worth noting. First, the preacher uses a word that indicates assurance: "But *when* Moses . . . comes." The preacher does not hesitate to give assurance—he does not use the word *if*; he uses the word *when*. This word indicates the tone of the preacher's message. It expresses the preacher's faith.

The coming Moses will be empowered by God. This agent of liberation will have power to represent God. The coming agent will have God's presence; that is the source of his power.

Also, the preacher proclaims the purpose of the liberator: to set "us chillun free." The messenger proclaims that the new Moses will satisfy the longings of the people's hearts. Their shackles and their chains will fall off. The new liberator will bring in the day of jubilee.

P. Celebration of Liberation (Lines 83–87)

> We will praise de gracious Mastah
> Dat has gin us liberty;

An' we'll shout ouah halleluyahs,
On dat mighty reck'nin' day,
When we'se reco'nised ez citiz'—

The preacher projects what will be the response to liberation. The flow of this part of the sermon shows the theological sophistication of the preacher. The reaction to the new Moses will be God-centered. "We will praise de gracious Mastah" and "we'll shout ouah halleluyahs" (note the parallelism in the two clauses) are ways of affirming God's liberty. The word *hallelujah* means praise God. Thus, the preacher focuses upon God's role in salvation and projects praise to God for God's marvelous acts. Also, line 84 (stating that the people will be given liberty) is synonymous with line 87 (stating that the people will be recognized as citizens).

These lines in the final stanza begin to bring the poem to a close on a note of praise and of anticipation of the day when the slaves will be free.

As one reads this sermon one notes the this-worldly (here and now) rather than the otherworldly (by and by) tone of the sermon. This is seen especially in the last stanza. The anticipation of the new Moses is clearly this-worldly. The preacher uses the Hebrew experience of the Exodus to frame his message. Therefore, it is clear that he expects liberation in his own lifetime.

The preacher makes the meaning of liberty clear. It is to be recognized as citizens. The clause "we'se reco'nised ez citiz'" points to the content of freedom. This is not an abstract concept of being free. It is the specific notion of being citizens, having the rights guaranteed by the Constitution. Being recognized as free meant the abolition of slavery but also the implementation of the Fourteenth and Fifteenth Amendments. Freedom would mean the full right to the Jeffersonian ideals of life, liberty, and the pursuit of happiness.

Q. Call to Prayer (Line 88)

Huh uh! Chillun, let us pray!

The sermon ends with a call to prayer—a reflection of the preacher's piety. This prayer manifests the tone of the sermon in the celebration of the sovereignty of God, emphasizing that God is the center of the struggle for liberation. The preacher affirms that God, who delivered Israel, will set the slaves free. The call to prayer is indicative of the heart of the preacher's faith. The people are challenged to recognize that God is the source of their strength and their hope for liberation.

Hermeneutical Reflections

Paul Laurence Dunbar's "An Ante-bellum Sermon" represents a genre of the African American sermon that was content-laden. These sermons were remembered not only for their immediate effect, but also for their lasting value in empowering their hearers to live in the midst of the "howling wilderness" of oppression with faith and hope.

The early African American sermons, of which Dunbar's poetic rendition is a remarkable remembrance, make a significant contribution to the development of an African American hermeneutic in several ways. They address the issues of (1) *contextuality*, (2) *correlation*, (3) *confrontation*, and (4) *consolation*. These sermons affirm the full humanity of all persons in the sense of the Aristotelian notion of entelechy—that is, complete actuality as distinguished from potentiality. William L. Andrews raises this notion in reference to black autobiography, a genre similar to the black sermon.

> In a number of important black autobiographies . . . a quest more psycho-literary than spiritual can be discerned. It is spurred by many motives, perhaps the most important of which is the need of another to *declare* himself through various linguistic acts, thereby reifying his abstract unreality, his invisibility in the eyes of his readers, so that he can be recognized as someone to be reckoned with. Such declarative acts, as we shall see, include the reconstructing of one's past in a meaningful and instructive form, the appropriating of empowering myths and models of the self from any available resource, and the redefining of one's place in the scheme of things by redefining the language used to locate one in that scheme.[27]

In other words, the biblical faith led the slaves to affirm that God had already made them free in spite of the chains of slavery. This faith is expressed in the words of the spiritual, "Before I'll be a slave, I'll be buried in my grave and go home to my Lord and be free."

Contextuality

The early African American sermons demonstrate a clear awareness of the role of the context of oppression in the human predicament and in the spiritual condition of the hearers.

The African American sermon grew out of the context of the African American experience. It is impossible to study any of these sermons, whether in their oral or literary form, and fail to recognize the way in which oppression was a fundamental reality:

> Slave narratives and black autobiographies provide dramatic personal testimonies of the discovery of racism in the process of secondary accul-

---

27. Andrews, *To Tell a Free Story*, 7.

turation, a process that at some point frustrates individuals in their efforts to realize their potential wholeness, unity, or balance as black people and American citizens, compelling them to turn primarily to their ethnic group for protection and direction.[28]

This contextual approach parallels the situation of the prophet in Israel. John H. Hayes has stated, "Prophetic speech was addressed to a particular historical situation."[29] This is the situation of the African American sermon also. These sermons were addressed to the critical situation of slavery and oppression in America.

Basic to the treatment of Scripture was the fact that those who heard these sermons lived in a society that rejected, debased, and discriminated against them. This context informed what was said, how it was said, and what was expected as a result of the sermon. Although the early African American preachers were probably not influenced by modern critical scholarship, they did indeed use Scripture in its synchronic and diachronic dimensions. They were able to sense the meaning of the text for those who lived at the time the text was written (the synchronic dimension) and also to appropriate the meaning for those who have experienced similar situations across the centuries (the diachronic dimension). These sermons manifest the amazing ability of these preachers to correlate the biblical text with their current predicament of human servitude. One has to suspect that this stems from Africans' similar application of traditional proverbs to their lives and problems.[30]

Correlation

The sermons harmoniously correlate the ancient biblical stories and changing historical situations.

The African American sermons employ the principle of correlation: they bring together, into a mutual or reciprocal relationship, text and context, the synchronic and the diachronic dimensions of the text. These sermons were not burdened by either biblicism (literal interpretation of the Bible) or bibliolatry (worship of the Bible as literally interpreted). Biblicism enslaves the interpreter within the necessity of explicating according to the rigid letter, destitute of all awareness of the dynamics of language. Bibliolatry enslaves the preacher by demanding a worship or veneration of the text without any critical reflection. On the contrary, these sermons reflect a sense of freedom and openness that enables them to use figurative or metaphorical language as a way of explicating the

---

28. Bell, *The Afro-American Novel*, 9.

29. John H. Hayes, "Understanding Hosea" (lecture presented at Old Testament Consortium, September 12, 1988, at Emory University, Atlanta, Georgia).

30. Kofi A. Opoku, *Speak to the Winds: Proverbs from Africa* (New York: Lothrop, Lee and Shepard, 1975).

text. The focus of worship was God, the actor, rather than abstractions that attempt to interpret God's action.

This principle of correlation provided the context in which both the present hearers and the ancient hearers were joined together. Therefore, there was a mutuality between the ancient oppressed people, described in the Old Testament, and the African Americans who experienced slavery and oppression. The African Americans and the Israelites shared bondage, and since Israel was redeemed, it was hoped that the slaves would also experience divine redemption.

In this sense, the biblical text became a tool of liberation and comfort; it became a two-edged sword. The sermons addressed a word to the oppressor: "You are Pharaoh, let God's people go" (see Exod. 6:11). In addition, the oppressed were told: "Joshua fit the battle of Jericho, and de walls come tumblin' down" (see Josh. 6:1-27).

The principle of correlation is at the heart of the early African American preachers' approach to the Bible. The Bible not only describes what God did for Israel but assured the slaves of what God would do for them. Therefore, the principle of correlation became the basis for the use of the Bible as a means of confrontation.

Confrontation

In their presentation of the biblical message the preachers used double entendre and humor as methods of confrontation.

I accept Keneth Kinnamon's assertion that whereas modern white writers have, for the most part, been individualistic, intuitive, and often escapist, most African American writers have been collective and political. One of their main impulses has been protest against racism and affirmation of black values. This collective sense of black values and protest against oppression is the heart of an African American hermeneutic. In part, Dunbar's "An Ante-bellum Sermon" communicates this affirmation and protest through double entendre and humor.

Double entendre, as I stated earlier, is a linguistic device that at the same time disguises the truth from some and reveals it to others. The use of biblical narrative was central to African American preachers' employment of rhetorical double entendre. The one variable that distinguished the early African American sermon was the use of the Bible in conjunction with double entendre and humor. The purpose of this combination was to confront both master and slave with the biblical message. The core of this message included the following pronouncements: (1) God created humankind free. (2) Slavery and any kind of human bondage are against the divine will. (3) God is present in history as redeemer and Lord. (4) God will destroy all forms of evil and redeem those who have faith.

These sermons declare that the battle is not between the slave and the master, and it is not between the system of oppression and the system of liberation. The battle is between God and evil. Both the Bible and these sermons proclaim that God will win. Evil will be destroyed. This is the basis of the message of hope and comfort that permeates these sermons.

Consolation

The sermons present the basic biblical theme of divine presence in the midst of oppression and suffering as a basis for hope.

The sermons under discussion addressed two main goals, one immediate and the other long-term. As to the immediate goal, the sermons were basically pastoral in that they sought to empower the hearers to deal with the daily insults, humiliations, and other abuses related to slavery. Their focus was upon bringing the word of good news to those in distress. Their goal was to empower the slaves by focusing upon the deeds of God in history. This was the basis of their hope and consolation.

The sermons brought comfort, condolence, encouragement, sympathy, and cheer from the lips of one who shared the slaves' predicament. The sermons grew out of a situation in which the wounded was speaking to the wounded. In the terms of Henri Nouwen, we have a case of the "wounded healer," the one who heals in spite of his or her own infirmity.[31] This atmosphere of consolation echoes the words of the prophet Ezekiel, who went to the exiles by the river Chebar and exclaimed, "I sat... among them" (Ezek. 3:15).

The suffering of the African Americans was immeasurably oppressive, but they overcame the temptation to succumb to defeatism and escapism. They overcame such challenges and persisted in hope. This was their long-term strategy. Ultimate liberation would have been useless without psychic and physical survival.

This hope is expressed by the exilic prophet who spoke to the people of Israel who were in exile, and declared that their state of oppression was over. Although they had lost their land, temple, and leaders, he assured them that God had not forgotten them and that a new day was dawning.

Comfort, comfort my people, says your God. Speak tenderly to Jerusalem, and cry to her that her warfare is ended, that her iniquity is pardoned, that she has received from the Lord's hand double for all her sins. A voice cries: "In the wilderness prepare the way of the Lord, make straight in the desert a highway for our God. Every valley shall be lifted up, and every mountain and hill be made low; the uneven ground shall become level, and the rough places a plain. And the glory of the Lord shall be revealed, and all flesh shall see it together, for the mouth of the Lord has spoken" [Isa. 40:1-5].

31. See Henri Nouwen, *The Wounded Healer* (Garden City, N.Y.: Doubleday, 1972).

The words of this prophet were reflected in the tone of the early African American preachers whose sermons I have discussed in this essay.

In addressing the issues of *contextuality, correlation, confrontation,* and *consolation,* the African American sermon as presented in Paul Laurence Dunbar's classic poem "An Ante-bellum Sermon" is a resource for African American hermeneutics.

This sermon is one example of the African Americans telling their own story. It reflects the way in which one of the major African American writers viewed the style, content, and significance of the slave preacher.

The language, method, and scope of the sermon provide a way of understanding the hermeneutical principles that the African American slave preacher utilized in providing empowerment, hope, and consolation to the slaves who were faced with the daily and life-long struggles of chattel slavery.

The African American preacher used the rhetorical device of double entendre to communicate to the slaves without undue danger to the preacher or to the listeners. The use of this device yielded a cunning style of interpretation of the Bible in its fullest sense.

The African American preacher used the biblical text as a source to address the context of human slavery. The preacher drew a correlation (i.e., established the crossing point) between the Hebrew slaves and the African American slaves. Confrontation grew out of the relevance of the biblical Word in terms of divine creation and human liberation. The intent was to provide consolation, to empower the slaves to deal with their daily insults and burdens, and to give them hope for ultimate deliverance.

PART III

Race and Ancient Black Africa in the Bible

— 6 —

Race, Racism, and the Biblical Narratives

Cain Hope Felder

The aim of this chapter is to discuss the questions of race and ethnic identity in the diverse biblical narratives. I hope to clarify, for modern readers, the profound differences in racial attitudes between those in the biblical world and in the subsequent history of Eurocentric interpretation. In antiquity, we do not have any elaborate definitions of or theories about race. This means that we must reckon with certain methodological problems in attempting to examine racial motifs as contained in the Bible. Ancient authors of biblical texts did have a color consciousness (awareness of certain physiological differences), but this consciousness of color/race, as we shall show, was by no means a political or ideological basis for enslaving, oppressing, or in any way demeaning other peoples.[1] In fact, the Bible contains no narratives in which the original intent was to negate the full humanity of black people or view blacks in an unfavorable way.[2] Such negative attitudes about black people are entirely postbiblical. In this regard, the following observation by Cornel West is most instructive:

---

1. See Frank Snowden, *Before Color Prejudice: The Ancient View of Blacks* (Cambridge: Harvard University Press, 1983), 14–17, 43–46; and Nicholas F. Gier, "The Color of Sin/The Color of Skin: Ancient Color Blindness and the Philosophical Origins of Modern Racism," *Journal of Religious Thought* 46, no. 1 (Summer-Fall 1989): 42–52.

2. See Charles B. Copher, "3,000 Years of Biblical Interpretation with Reference to Black Peoples," *The Journal of the Interdenominational Theological Center* 30, no. 2 (Spring 1986): 225–46; see also his "The Black Presence in the Old Testament," included as chapter 7 in this volume.

The very category of "race"—denoting primarily skin color—was first employed as a means of classifying human bodies by François Bernier, a French physician, in 1684. The first authoritative racial division of humankind is found in the influential *Natural System* (1735) of the preeminent naturalist Carolus Linnaeus.[3]

Indeed, theories that claim to provide a "scientific" basis for white racism are peculiar post-Enlightenment by-products of modern civilization.

The specific racial type of the biblical Hebrews is itself quite difficult to determine.[4] Scholars today generally recognize that the biblical Hebrews probably emerged as an amalgamation of races rather than from any pure racial stock. When they departed from Egypt, they may well have been Afro-Asiatics. To refer to the earliest Hebrews as "Semites" does not take us very far, inasmuch as the eighteenth-century term designates no race, but a family of languages, embracing Hebrew, Akkadian, Arabic, as well as Ethiopic (*Ge'ez*).[5] The language of the ancient Ethiopians ("burnt-face" Africans), for example, is as Semitic as the language of early Hebrews (Jahwists), or of the Arabs.[6] This reaffirms the contention that sophisticated theories about race and the phenomenon of racism are cultural trappings that appear well after the biblical period. Consequently the task at hand is to construct an interpretative framework for a range of biblical attitudes about race and to determine implications for the postbiblical problems of racism and ethnocentrism that continue to bedevil both church and society in many nations today, including those of the Third World. There is still too much sad evidence of the dominant classes within Third World nations imitating oppressive racial/ethnic patterns of their former European colonizers.

Although the Bible primarily presents socio-political entities that are differentiated as empires, nations, and tribes, there are important ways in which the subject of race acquires particular significance. This essay will examine the thesis that in the biblical corpus two broad processes related to racism may be operating. First, there is the phenomenon of *sacralization*. By this I mean the transposing of an ideological concept into a tenet of religious faith (or a theological justification) in order to serve

---

3. Cornel West, *Prophetic Fragments* (Grand Rapids, Mich.: William B. Eerdmans Publishing Company, 1988), 100.

4. G. Johannes Botterweck and Helmer Ringgren, eds., *Theological Dictionary of the Old Testament* (hereafter TDOT), 6 vols. (Grand Rapids, Mich.: William B. Eerdmans Publishing Co., 1974–84), 2:426–29, s.v. "*gôy.*"

5. D. Goitein, *Jews and Arabs: Their Contacts through the Ages* (New York: Schocken Books, 1964), 19–21.

6. *Aithiops* (burnt-face) is the most frequent translation of CUSH found in the Septuagint; usually it designates Africans of dark pigmentation and Negroid features. It was used as early as Homer (*Odyssey* 19.246ff.). While *Aithiops* in ancient biblical and classical texts refers specifically to Ethiopians, the term also identifies Africans, regardless of race (see Frank M. Snowden, Jr., *Blacks in Antiquity: Ethiopians in the Greco-Roman Experience* [Cambridge: Belknap Press of Harvard University, 1970], 118–19).

the vested interest of a particular ethnic/racial group. Second, there is the process of *secularization:* the weakening of a powerful religious concept under the weighty influence of what today we call "secular" (i.e., socio-political and ideological) pressures.[7] In this second process ideas are wrenched from their original religious moorings due to the weighty influence of nationalistic ideologies and cultural understandings. This is not to say that the process of sacralization or secularization was a conscious design on the part of ancient biblical writers. On the contrary, I only suggest that the process was circumstantial and subtle. It becomes problematic when the meaning of ancient texts assumes a normative character centuries later. The phenomena of sacralization and secularization often cultivate patterns of ethnocentrism and even racism that in turn can have harmful effects on certain racial and ethnic groups who are inevitably scorned and marginalized.

Race and Sacralization in the Old Testament

Several Old Testament passages are quite suitable as illustrations of sacralization and as such require a new kind of critical engagement. First, I shall consider the so-called curse of Ham (Gen. 9:18-27), which rabbis of the early Talmudic periods and the church fathers, at times, used to demean black people. Later Europeans adopted the so-called curse of Ham as a justification for slavery and stereotypical aspersions about blacks. Second, I will focus on the Old Testament genealogies that contributed to the Israelites' and ancient Jews' perception that they implicitly constituted a most divinely favored people ("race"). Third, I shall discuss the fascinating narrative about Miriam and Aaron, who objected to Moses' Ethiopian wife (Num. 12:1-16). Fourth, I shall take up the explicit biblical doctrine of election (i.e., of a chosen people) as it developed as a theme in the Old Testament; my discussion of that theme will conclude with a brief comparison of the Old Testament's and New Testament's handling of the doctrine.

The Curse of Ham

My first example of sacralization occurs in some of the earliest Jahwist (J) traditions of the Old Testament. Genesis 9:18-27 has achieved notoriety in many quarters because it contains the so-called curse of Ham. The passage technically should follow directly upon the J passage that concludes the flood narrative (Gen. 8:20-22) since critical investigations

---

7. G. E. Mendenhall employs the term *secularization* in this sense in George A. Buttrick et al., eds., *The Interpreter's Dictionary of the Bible* (hereafter IDB), 4 vols. (New York: Abingdon, 1962), 2:77, s.v. "election."

have shown that Genesis 9:1-17 and verses 28-29 represent the much later Priestly (P) exilic tradition.[8] The great significance of Genesis 9:18-27 is not that it contains the so-called curse of Ham (which technically does not take place at all); rather, it is that these verses make it clear that to the mind of the ancient Israelite author "the whole post-diluvial humanity stems from Noah's three sons."[9] On Genesis 9:19, Claus Westermann remarks as follows:

> The whole of humankind takes its origin from them [Shem, Ham, Japheth].
> ... Humanity is conceived here as a unity, in a way different from the creation; humanity in all its variety across the earth, takes its origin from these three who survived the flood. The purpose of the contrast is to underscore the amazing fact that humanity scattered in all its variety throughout the world comes from the one family.[10]

Once the passage establishes the perception about this essential and fundamental aspect of human origin (vv. 18-19), it continues by providing what appears to be a primeval rationale for differences in the destinies or fortunes of certain groups of persons. Certainly, as one scholar notes, "from a form critical viewpoint Genesis 9:20-27 is an ethnological etiology concerned with the theology of culture and history."[11] This observation alerts us to the theological motives in verses 20-27 that have implications for definite construals of both culture and history. In my view, it is this development that most clearly attests to the process of sacralization wherein cultural and historical phenomena are recast as theological truths with vested interest for particular groups.

Prior to delineating some of the internal difficulties and other features of Genesis 9:18-27, a word may be said about the literary form of this narrative. The narrative passages of Genesis 1–11 generally concern the matter of "crime and punishment: this is particularly evident in the ('J') narratives."[12] Westermann informs us that these narratives have antecedents and parallels in ancient African myths: "It is beyond dispute that African myths about the primeval state and biblical stories of crime and punishment in J correspond both in their leading motifs and in their structure."[13] African and African American scholars have

---

8. Claus Westermann, *Genesis 1–11: A Commentary* (Minneapolis: Augsburg, 1984), 459. The Priestly tradition (P) may be dated 550–450 B.C.E., beginning in the exilic period (Babylonian captivity) but extending into the postexilic period where the redaction evidently continued.

9. Ibid., 482.

10. Ibid., 486.

11. Gene Rice, "The Curse That Never Was (Genesis 9:18–27)," *Journal of Religious Thought* 29 (1972): 13.

12. Westermann, *Genesis*, 47.

13. Ibid., 54.

reached similar conclusions.[14] With respect to Genesis 9:18-27, the crime is Ham's allowing himself to see the nakedness of his drunken father, Noah, without immediately covering him. In error, Ham leaves his father uncovered (according to Hebrew tradition, an act of great shamelessness and parental disrespect) while he goes to report on Noah's condition to Shem and Japheth, his brothers (v. 22). For their part, Ham's two brothers display proper respect in meticulous ways as they cover their father (v. 23). When Noah awakens (v. 24), the problems begin. Noah pronounces a curse not upon Ham, but upon Canaan, who has not been mentioned previously. Noah also blesses Shem and Japheth, presumably as a reward for their sense of paternal reverence as demanded in ancient Hebrew tradition.

If one attempts to argue for the unity of the passage, inconsistencies and other difficulties abound. To illustrate, Ham commits the shameless act in verse 22, but Canaan is cursed in verse 25. In Genesis 9:18, the list of Noah's sons refers to Ham as being second, but in verse 24 the text, presumably referring to Ham, uses the phrase Noah's "youngest son." Also, the mention of Canaan as cursed in verse 25 raises the possibility, albeit slightly untenable, that Noah had a fourth son so named. Then too, uncertainties about the precise nature of Ham's error have resulted in a fantastic variety of suggestions about the incident: it has been suggested that Ham possibly castrated his father, that he sexually assaulted his father, that he committed incest with his father's wife, and that he had sexual relations with his own wife while aboard the Ark.[15] As I have suggested, the matter was far less complicated, for Ham violated the sacred rule of respect for his father. Many of the difficulties within this passage find a solution once we allow the possibility that the original version of Genesis 9:18-27 referred only to Ham and his error and that a later version of the story, motivated by political developments in ancient Palestine, attempted to justify the subjugation of Canaanites by Shem's descendants (Israel) and those of Japheth (Philistines).[16]

While admitting the passage's contradiction that it is Ham who shows disrespect to Noah, but Canaan, Ham's son, who is cursed, Westermann asserts:

---

14. J. Oluminde Lucas, *The Religion of the Yorubas* (Lagos: C. M. S. Bookshop, 1948) (cited by Cheikh Anta Diop, *The African Origin of Civilization: Myth or Reality?* [New York: Lawrence Hill and Co., 1974], 184–99). See also Robert E. Hood, "Creation Myths in Nigeria," *Journal of Religious Thought* 45 (Winter-Spring 1989): 70–84.

15. Rice, "Curse," 11–12; Westermann, *Genesis*, 488–89; Ephraim Isaac, "Genesis, Judaism and the 'Sons of Ham'," *Slavery and Abolition: A Journal of Comparative Studies* 1, no. 1 (May 1980): 4–5.

16. Rice ("Curse," 7–8) suggests that the passage contains two parallel but different traditions—one universal (Gen. 9:18-19a; cf. 5:32; 6:10; 7:13; 10:1; 1 Chron. 1:4) and the other limited to Palestine and more parochial (Gen. 9:20-27; see also Gen. 10:21).

The same person who committed the outrage in verse 22 falls under the curse in verse 25. The Yahwist has preserved, together with the story of Ham's outrage, a curse over Canaan which could be resumed because of the genealogical proximity of Canaan to Ham. Those who heard the story knew the descendants of Ham as identical with those of Canaan.[17]

Thus, in Westermann's view, Ham, in effect, *was* cursed and presumably with him not just Canaan but all of the other descendants of Ham, that is, Cush, Egypt, and Put (Phut), as cited in Genesis 10:6. Although I disagree with Westermann's contention that Ham was, *in effect*, cursed in Genesis 9:18-27, Westermann does help us to see that the ambiguity of the text can lead Bible interpreters to justify their particular history, culture, and race by developing self-serving theological constructs. In one instance, the Canaanites "deserve" subjugation; in another instance, the Hamites "deserve" to be hewers of wood and drawers of water.

Whether or not sacralization was ever part of the original narrative of the error of Ham, we have much evidence of such sacralization in the Midrashim, for example in the fifth-century (C.E.) Midrash in which Noah says to Ham: "You have prevented me from doing something in the dark (cohabitation), therefore your seed will be ugly and dark-skinned."[18] Similarly, the Babylonian Talmud (sixth century C.E.) states that "the descendants of Ham are cursed by being Black and are sinful with a degenerate progeny."[19] Into the seventeenth century the idea persisted that the blackness of Africans was due to a curse, and that idea reinforced and sanctioned the enslavement of blacks.[20] Indeed, even today in such versions of Holy Scripture as *Dake's Annotated Reference Bible* one finds at Genesis 9:18-27 a so-called great racial prophecy with the following racist hermeneutic:

All colors and types of men came into existence after the flood. All men were white up to this point, for there was only one family line—that of Noah who was white and in the line of Christ, being mentioned in Luke 3:36 with his son Shem.... [There is a] prophecy that Shem would be a chosen race and have a peculiar relationship with God [v. 26]. All divine revelation since Shem has come through his line.... [There is a] prophecy that Japheth would be the father of the great and enlarged races [v. 27]. Government, Science and Art are mainly Japhethic.... His descendants constitute the leading nations of civilization.[21]

---

17. Westermann, *Genesis*, 484.
18. *Midrash Bereshith Rabbah* (London: 1939), 1:293 (cited by Rice, "Curse," 17, 25).
19. See Isaac, "Genesis," 19.
20. Rice, "Curse," 26n.116.
21. Finis Jennings Dake, *Dake's Annotated Reference Bible* (Lawrenceville, Ga.: Dake Bible Sales, Inc., 1981), 8, 9, 36, 40. One of my African seminarians, who had been given *Dake's Annotated* by fundamentalist American missionaries, innocently presented me with a gift copy for study and comment!

Old Testament Genealogies

Another instance of sacralization confronts us quite early in the Old Testament within the genealogies of the descendants of Noah. It is especially useful to consider the so-called Table of Nations (Gen. 10) in conjunction with the much later genealogical listing of 1 Chronicles 1:1—2:55. On the one hand, these listings purport to be comprehensive catalogues. All too often the general reader erroneously has taken these catalogues to be reliable sources of ancient ethnography. Critical study of these genealogies illuminates theological motives that inevitably yield an increasing tendency to arrange different groups in priority, thereby attaching the greatest significance to the Israelites as an ethnic and national entity, greater than all other peoples of the earth. I shall first examine the deceptive quality of these Old Testament genealogies and then— after discussing the narrative regarding Miriam and Aaron—will show how their evident sacralization parallels yet another instance of this phenomenon, namely, the whole notion of election (of a chosen people).

While at first glance Genesis 10 has the appearance of being a single listing of ancient nations, biblical criticism has for some time demonstrated that Genesis 10 represents a conflation of at least two different lists, i.e., the Jahwist (J) and the Priestly (P), separated by centuries.[22] In fact, the conflation of different traditions in Genesis 10 doubtlessly accounts for matters such as the discrepancies in identifying the land of Cush, discrepancies in determining the relationship between Cush and Sheba, and the differences between Seba and Sheba. For example, Genesis 10:7 mentions Seba (*sĕb'ā*) as a son of Cush, whereas Sheba (*šĕb'ā*) is a grandson of Cush according to Genesis 10:8. Here the text clearly is identifying the descendants of Ham (*ḥām*). Then in Genesis 10:28, the text introduces an anomaly, since, at this point, Sheba is mentioned as a direct descendant not of Ham but of Shem. Furthermore, since the initial Samech (*s*) of *sĕb'ā* is the equivalent of and interchangeable with the Hebrew Shin (*š*) in Old South Arabic,[23] one could argue that Genesis 10 offers us two persons named Sheba as descendants of Cush, but only one person by that name as a descendant of Shem. In any case, the Table of Nations as it stands does not delineate sharp racial differences between the ancient peoples of Africa, South Arabia, and Mesopotamia. The true motive lies elsewhere.

Rather than any objective historical account of genealogies, the Table of Nations in Genesis 10 presents us with a theologically motivated catalogue of people. The table not only ends with the descendants of

22. Martin Noth, *A History of Pentateuchal Traditions*, trans. Bernhard W. Anderson (Chico, Calif.: Scholars Press, 1981), 21–23, 28, and the translator's supplement on 262–63. See also Otto Eissfeldt, *The Old Testament: An Introduction* (New York: Harper and Row, 1965), 184.

23. IDB 4:311, s.v. "Sabeans."

Shem, but does so in a way consciously stylized to accentuate the importance of the descendants of Shem among the peoples of the earth.[24] About this, the author of the genealogy in 1 Chronicles 1:17-34 is most explicit, inasmuch as of all the descendants of the sons of Noah, those descended from Shem receive the most elaborate attention. Thus, the Jahwist listing of the nations is the most primitive; the list in Genesis 10 was composed centuries later and was edited theologically according to a postexilic Priestly tradition in order to establish the priority of the descendants of Shem; that list was followed by a further elaboration, centuries later, found in the genealogies of 1 Chronicles. In this long progression, the theological presuppositions of a particular ethnic group displace any concern for objective historiography and ethnography. The descendants of Noah apart from those of Shem are increasingly insignificant and gain access to the text only as they serve as foils to demonstrate the priority of Israelites.

The subtle process being described may consequently be called "sacralization" because it represents an attempt on the part of succeeding generations of one ethnic group to construe salvation history in terms distinctly favorable to it as opposed to others. Here, ethnic particularity evolves with a certain divine vindication, and inevitably the dangers of rank racism lie just beneath the surface. Gene Rice has noted rightly that the genealogies do not express negative attitudes about persons of African descent, but it is important to clarify an aspect of Rice's judgment in light of the way in which sacralization nevertheless expresses itself in these genealogies. Consider Rice's remarks:

> Genesis 10 has to do with all the peoples of the world known to ancient Israel and since this chapter immediately follows the episode of Noah's cursing and blessing, it would have been most appropriate to express here any prejudicial feelings toward African peoples. Not only are such feelings absent, but all peoples are consciously and deliberately related to each other as brothers. *No one, not even Israel, is elevated above anyone else and no disparaging remark is made about any people, not even the enemies of Israel.*[25]

It is necessary to qualify Rice's contention that the genealogies do not elevate even Israel above any other people. After all, Genesis 10:21-31 becomes the basis for amplifying in great detail the descendants of Shem and Judah (1 Chron. 2:1-55) as the distinctive *laos tou Theou* ("people of God," LXX). Thus these genealogies are construed theologically to

---

24. The postexilic Priestly (P) redaction accounts for the order Shem, Ham, Japheth (omitting Canaan) in Gen. 10:1 as well as for the inversion of this order in the subsequent verses: e.g., the sons of Japheth (Gen. 10:2), the sons of Ham (Gen. 10:6), and "To Shem also, the father of all the children of Eber (Hebrew)" (Gen. 10:21).

25. Rice, "Curse," 16; emphasis mine.

enhance the status of a particular people ("race"); and this is precisely the process that I am describing as sacralization.

The Narrative about Miriam and Aaron

Numbers 12:1-16 may also attest to a process of moving from ethnic particularity to a kind of sacralized ethnocentrism with certain class implications. In Numbers 12:1 Moses' brother (Aaron) and sister (Miriam) castigate him for having married a Cushite (i.e., "Ethiopian") woman (*hā'iŝā hacūŝit*). Several factors point to the probability that the offensive aspect of the marriage was the woman's black identity. In the first place, this is clearly the view expressed in the wording of the Septuagint: *heneken tēs gunaikos tēs Aithopisses* (on account of the Ethiopian woman).[26] Second, God visits leprosy upon Miriam as a punishment (v. 9), and it can hardly be accidental that Miriam is described as "leprous, as white as snow." Quite an intentional contrast is dramatized here, i.e., Moses' black wife, accursed by Miriam and Aaron, is now contrasted with Miriam, who suddenly becomes "as white as snow" in her punishment. The contrast is sharpened all the more since only Miriam is punished for an offense in which Aaron is equally guilty. The testimony of the Septuagint together with these exegetical considerations point strongly to the probability that more than arrogance is at issue in this text. Also involved is a rebuke to the prejudice characterized by the attitudes of Miriam and Aaron.

In the Numbers 12 narrative, God sternly rebukes Miriam and Aaron, but the central question is: Why? The ambiguities of this narrative abound. Is God's rebuke the result of the presumptions of Miriam and Aaron to question Moses' decision no matter whom he married? Is God's censure caused by the fact that the black wife of Moses is a foreigner (from Ethiopia/Nubia = present-day Sudan)? Or may it be the case, as Randall Bailey suggested in a recent conversation with me, that the black identity of Zipporah indeed may be pertinent, but not for the reasons that I offered in chapter 3 of *Troubling Biblical Waters?*[27] As a rejoinder to my published argument, Bailey surmised that not only did those in the ancient world regard black Africans favorably, but at times, they became the standard by which others judged themselves. In chapter 8, below, Bailey develops this idea of "valorization" in relation to ancient Israel's self-esteem and black Africans. In Bailey's line of reasoning, God's rebuke had more to do with attitudes of class in relation to race than with

---

26. Contra B. W. Anderson's note on Num. 12:1 in *The New Oxford Annotated Bible* (New York: Oxford University Press, 1977), 179: "The term Cushite apparently includes Midianites and other Arabic peoples (Hab. 3:7)."

27. Cain Hope Felder, "Racial Motifs in the Biblical Narratives," in *Troubling Biblical Waters: Race, Class, and Family* (Maryknoll, N.Y.: Orbis Books, 1989), 42.

matters of religion. The jealousy of Moses' relatives stemmed from his marriage to a woman of *higher* social standing than the Hebrews themselves, who were of mixed Afro-Asiatic stock. If Bailey is correct, his idea of class bias would thereby account for the anomaly of having only this text in the Bible exhibiting some bias *against* a black, as I had earlier intimated. This is a perennial reminder that the racial values of the Bible are progressive in comparison to later hostile racial attitudes in the medieval and modern periods.[28] The Numbers 12 narrative exposes the contrast between the biblical world before color prejudice and our postbiblical Western history of translation and interpretation that have marginalized blacks in antiquity while sacralizing other groups.

The process of sacralization in the Old Testament inescapably involves certain racial ambiguities. For example, Eurocentric Bible translators and interpreters over the years routinely have considered the mixed stock of ancient Afro-Asiatics as somehow "nonblack." This academic "sleight of hand" becomes most apparent when one then finds that in places such as the United States of America the racial classification of a person as black is made on the basis of the most miniscule amount of traceable African descent. Thus, we arrive at the utter absurdity where in the United States mulattos/coloreds are considered Negro/black; whereas in South Africa or Brazil, the same racially mixed peoples attain, as nonblacks, a higher social standing than those who have more pronounced traditionally black African features. By contrast, when we turn to the Hebrew Scriptures, the ancient authors there tend to distinguish ethnic identity solely on the basis of tribes or nationality. The distinction that the Old Testament makes is not racial. Through the process of sacralization a principle of exclusion or prioritization is indeed present—all who do not meet the criteria for salvation as defined in the Old Testament are relegated to an inferior status. However, that exclusion is not based upon race but rather upon not being a part of the ethnic or national "in-group." This is the reason that black people are not only frequently mentioned in numerous Old Testament texts but are also mentioned in ways that are most favorable in terms of acknowledging their actual and potential role in the salvation history of Israel. By no means are black people excluded from the particularity of Israel's story as long as they claim it, however secondarily, and do not proclaim their own story apart from the activity of Israel's God.

Extensive lists of Old Testament passages that make favorable reference to black people are readily accessible.[29] There are many illustrations

---

28. Isaac, "Genesis," 3–17.

29. Sergew Hable Sellassie, *Ancient and Medieval Ethiopian History to 1270* (Addis Ababa: United Printers, 1972), 96; R. A. Morrisey, *Colored People and Bible History* (Hammond, Ind.: W. B. Conkey Company, 1925), esp. chaps. 1 and 2; Edward Ullendorf, *Ethiopia and the Bible* (London: Oxford University Press, 1968), 6–8.

of such provocative texts. Isaiah 37:9 and 2 Kings 19:9 refer to Tirhakah, king of the Ethiopians. This ancient black Pharaoh was actually the third member of the twenty-fifth Egyptian dynasty, which ruled all of Egypt (689–64 B.C.E.).[30] According to the biblical texts, Tirhakah was the object of the desperate hopes of Israel; in the days of Hezekiah, Israel hoped desperately that Tirhakah's armies would intervene and thus stave off an impending Assyrian assault by Sennacherib. More than a half-century later, another text could refer to "the mighty men of Ethiopia and Put who handle the shield" (Jer. 46:9). Indeed the Old Testament indicates that black people were part of the Hebrew army (2 Sam. 18:21-32) and even part of the royal court. The 'Ebed-melek takes action to save Jeremiah's life (Jer. 38:7-13) and thereby becomes the beneficiary of a singular divine blessing (Jer. 39:15-18). The dominant portrait of the Ethiopians in the Old Testament is that of wealthy people (Job 28:19; Isa. 45:14) who would soon experience conversion (Ps. 68:31; Isa. 11:11; 18:7; Zeph. 3:10). The reference to "Zephaniah, son of Cush" (Zeph. 1) may indicate that one of the books of the Old Testament was authored by a black African.[31]

The Doctrine of Election

Israel's particularity, as considered in the foregoing discussions of race and sacralization, loses much of its subtlety as the dubious concept of its election (bāḥar) begins to gain a firm footing in the Old Testament. Certainly, traces of the idea of Israel's chosenness and special relationship with its deity were present in "the pre-Jahwistic cult of the ancestors," but the explicit concept of Jahweh's loving preference for the people of Israel develops relatively late.[32] The theologically elaborated belief that Jahweh specifically chose Israel above all other nations does not become a matter of religious ideology and hence an instance of sacralization until the period of Deuteronomistic history toward the end of the seventh century B.C.E. (Deut. 7:6-8; 10:15; Jer. 2:3; cf. Isa. 43:20; 65:9).[33]

Regardless of the theological structure that attempts to support the Deuteronomistic concept of Israel's election, ambiguities almost immediately engulf the concept. Horst Seebass, for example, insists that even among the Deuteronomistic writers, Israel's election "only rarely stands at the center of what is meant by election."[34] According to him, bāḥar, as a technical term for Israel's election, always functions as a symbol

30. Snowden, Blacks in Antiquity, 115–17; Diop, African Origin, 220–21; Alan Gardiner, Egypt of the Pharaohs (New York: Oxford University Press, 1974).

31. Copher, "3,000 Years."

32. Gerhard von Rad, Old Testament Theology, trans. D. M. G. Stalker, 2 vols. (New York: Harper and Row, 1962), 1:7; 2:322.

33. Ibid., 1:118, 178; TDOT 2:78, s.v. "bāchar"; IDB 2:76, s.v "election."

34. TDOT 2:82, s.v. "bāchar."

of universalism; that is, it represents Israel in the role of "service to the whole."[35] Seebass is representative of those who want to de-emphasize the distinctive ethnic or racial significance of the concept in Israel's self-understanding in the Deuteronomistic period.[36]

The ethnic and racial ambiguities involved in the concept of Israel's election seem to persist, albeit with many rationales to the contrary. The ambiguity does not so much result from the fact that a universalistic history is presupposed by the biblical writers who advance the Old Testament concept of Israel's election; rather, the ambiguities stem from the nature of the so-called universalism that is presupposed. Gerhard von Rad points out that in the Deuteronomistic circles, the chosenness of Israel attains a radical form and its universal aspect is at best paradoxical.[37] I would further suggest that perhaps the real paradox resides in the notion that Israel's election in a universal divine scheme seems to lead inevitably to sacralization, with the people of Israel as an ethnic group at the center. Certainly, the Deuteronomistic authors struggled to demonstrate Jahweh's singular affirmation of the Davidic monarchy and, more importantly, Jahweh's selection of Jerusalem as the center of any continuing redemptive activity.[38] Again, it seems quite paradoxical that, although the people of Israel exhibit few extraordinary attributes or values by which they objectively merit Jahweh's election, there develops, particularly in postexilic Judaism, an elaborate doctrine of merit by which those who know and follow the Torah within Israel as an ethnic group attempt to prove their worthiness as the chosen people.

Despite the absence of any inherent superiority of the people of Israel in their lengthy biblical documentary of their own sin and instances of faithlessness, the concept of election becomes inextricably bound up with ethnic particularity. Accordingly, the people of Israel arrogate to themselves the status of being preeminently chosen and thereby claim to possess the Law and the covenant and a continuing promise of the land and the city. At the same time, all who stand outside the community or apart from the supporting religious ideology of election are relegated to the margins of Israel's "universal" saving history. In this progression, as we have seen, other races and ethnic groups may, of course, subscribe to Israel's religious ideology and derive the commensurate benefits, but always the criteria for such subscription seem to be mediated through the predilections of an ethnic group reinforced by elaborate genealogies and the transmission of particular legal religious traditions.

---

35. TDOT 2:83, s.v. "*bāchar.*"
36. So IDB 2:79, s.v. "election"; George F. Moore, *Judaism* (Cambridge: Harvard University Press, 1932), 2:95. But cf. M. Rosenbaum and A. M. Silverman, *Pentateuch with Targum Onkelos, Haphtaroth and Rashi's Commentary: Genesis, Deuteronomy* (New York: Hebrew Publishing Co., n.d.), 56, 195.
37. Von Rad, *Old Testament Theology*, 1:178, 223.
38. TDOT 2:78, s.v. "*bāchar.*"

This development typifies what I have called the process of sacralization, and it is striking to see the different way that New Testament authors treat the doctrine of election. The Old Testament scholar George Foot Moore provides us with a glimpse of the different conception that one encounters in the New Testament; he asserts that, for the Old Testament idea of national election, "Paul and the church substituted an individual election to eternal life, without regard to race or station."[39] Rudolf Bultmann provides us with a more helpful understanding of the New Testament in this regard. He argues that, in the New Testament, the Christian church becomes "the true people of God"; in Bultmann's view, the New Testament no longer concerns itself with a preeminent ethnic group, i.e., *Israēl kata sarka* (1 Cor. 10:18), but with the Israel of God (Gal. 6:16) without any exclusive ethnic or racial coordinates.[40]

In contrast to the Deuteronomistic usage of *bāḥar*, the New Testament never presents the term *eklegomai* or its nominal derivatives *eklektos* (chosen) and *eklogē* (election) in an ethnically or racially restrictive or exclusive sense. Paul wants to maintain a certain continuity with aspects of Israel's election in the Old Testament, but that continuity is neither ethnic not cultic (Rom. 9:11; 11:2, 11, 28-29). For Paul, corporate election can include some Jews, but it must also embrace Gentiles (Rom. 11:25; Gal. 3:28; 1 Cor. 12:13); being "in" and "with" Christ becomes the new *crux interpretum*. In Paul's view, God chose (*exelexato*) the foolish, weak, and low (1 Cor. 1:27-28). For James, God chose (*exelexato*) the poor who are rich in faith (James 2:5); for Matthew, God calls many, but chooses only the few (Matt. 22:14). The new universalism and unity to be found in the Christian church express themselves further in the new sequence of thoughts found in Galatians 3:28 ("There is neither Jew nor Greek, there is neither slave nor free, there is neither male nor female; for you are all one in Christ Jesus"); 1 Corinthians 12:13 ("For by one Spirit we were all baptized into one body—Jews or Greeks, slaves or free—and all were made to drink of one Spirit"); and Colossians 3:11-12 ("Here there cannot be Greek and Jew, circumcised and uncircumcised, barbarian, Scythian, slave, free man, but Christ is all, and in all").

The only New Testament text that refers to Christians as a chosen race (*genos eklekton*) is 1 Peter 2:9. Yet, in the text of 1 Peter, the phrase is manifestly metaphorical. The text depends very heavily on the wording found in Isaiah 43:20-21 (LXX), but the ethnic particularity implied in the Old Testament text has fallen away entirely in 1 Peter.[41] Thus, in Christian literature throughout the New Testament period (which extends well into the second century), the elect become the church, which

---

39. Moore, *Judaism*, 95.
40. Rudolf Bultmann, *Theology and the New Testament* (London: SCM Press, Ltd., 1965), 1:97.
41. Isa. 43:20 (LXX), *to genos mou to eklekton* = M.T., *'ammi beḥiri.*

is the new Israel. Matthew is even more specific because for him the elect represent the faithful few in the church who accept the call to the higher righteousness and the doing of the will of God. In either case, these New Testament perspectives eliminate all ethnic or racial criteria for determining the elect.[42]

Secularization in the New Testament

Ambiguities with regard to race in the New Testament do not appear within the context of what I have defined as sacralization. Accordingly, I have tried to show that the New Testament disapproves of an ethnically focused idea of corporate election (or "Israel according to the flesh"). In fact, the New Testament offers no grand genealogies designed to sacralize the myth of any inherent and divinely sanctioned superiority of Greeks and Romans in any manner comparable to the Table of Nations found in Genesis 10. Further, many Palestinian Jews of Jesus' time could be easily classified as Afro-Asiatics, despite the fact that European artists and American mass media have routinely depicted such persons as Anglo-Saxons. Indeed, Matthew, Mark, and Luke report that an African helped Jesus to carry his cross (Matt. 27:32; Mark 15:21; Luke 23:26; contra John 19:17).

Consequently, if one is to explore the subject of racialist tendencies in the New Testament narratives, one must turn to a different phenomenon, namely, the process of secularization. The question now becomes: How did the expanding church, in its attempt to survive without the temporary protection it derived by being confused with Judaism, begin to succumb to the dominant symbols and ideologies of the Greco-Roman world? We will want to see how, in this development, the universalism of the New Testament circumstantially diminishes as Athens and Rome become substituted for Jerusalem of the Old Testament, as, in effect, the new centers for God's redemptive activity.

The conceptualization of the world by early Christian authors of New Testament times scarcely included Sub-Saharan Africa and did not at all include the Americas or the Far East. These early Christian writers referred to Spain as "the limits of the West" (1 Clem. 5:7; Rom. 15:28); they envisioned the perimeters of the world as the outer reaches of the Roman Empire.[43] For New Testament authors, Roman socio-political realities as

---

42. W. Bauer, *A Greek-English Lexicon of the New Testament*, trans. and ed. W. E. Arnot and F. W. Gingrich (Chicago: University of Chicago Press, 1957), 242, s.v. *"eklektos."*

43. In 1 Clem. 7, "the limits of the west" (*epi to terma tēs duseōs*) designates Spain (i.e., Spain is at the western limits of Rome) (see *Apostolic Fathers*, Loeb Classical Library [Cambridge: Harvard University Press, 1975], 1:16). See Rom. 15:28 and the analysis of it in Ernst Käsemann, *Commentary on Romans*, trans. and ed. Geoffrey W. Bromiley (Grand Rapids, Mich.: William B. Eerdmans Publishing Company, 1980), 402.

well as the language and culture of Hellenism often arbitrated the ways in which God was seen as acting in Jesus Christ. Just as Jerusalem in the Old Testament had come to represent the preeminent holy city of the God of Israel (Zion), New Testament authors attached a preeminent status to Rome, the capital city of the world in which an increasingly Gentile church was emerging.[44]

It is no coincidence that Mark, probably the earliest composer of the extant passion narratives, goes to such great lengths to show that the confession of the Roman centurion (only here the Latinism *kentyrion* [*centurio*] in the Synoptic passages) brings his whole gospel narrative to its climax.[45] For his part, Luke expends considerable effort to specify the positive qualities of his various centurions (*hekatontarches*).[46] There is even a sense in which their official titles symbolize Rome as the capital of the Gentile world, for their incipient acts of faith or confessions, according to Luke, find their dénouement in the Acts 28 portrait of Paul who proclaims relentlessly the kerygma in Rome. The immediate significance of this New Testament tendency to focus upon Rome instead of Jerusalem is that the darker races outside the Roman orbit are circumstantially marginalized by New Testament authors.

For lack of more descriptive terminology, this process by which the darker races are marginalized in the New Testament may be called secularization. Here, socio-political realities of the secular framework tend to dilute the New Testament vision of racial inclusiveness and universalism. In order to expose this process one must examine early traditions and show how they were adapted at later stages in such a way as to be slanted to the detriment of the darker races. Perhaps one of the most cogent illustrations of this process of secularization is Luke's narrative about the baptism and conversion of the Ethiopian official in Acts 8:26-40.

On the surface, Acts 8:26-40 is a highly problematic text. One wonders immediately if the Ethiopian finance minister of the *kandakē* (the queen of Nubia/biblical Ethiopia with her capital at Meroë) is a Jew or Gentile. One also wonders about the efficacy of the finance minister's baptism and whether it constituted or led to a full conversion to Christianity. Probably the best survey of the several problems posed by this

---

44. Luke's Acts of the Apostles outlines this scheme quite decidedly: Jerusalem (Acts 2), Antioch (Acts 12), Athens (Acts 17), and Rome (Acts 28). See Werner Georg Kümmel, *Introduction to the New Testament*, trans. Howard C. Kee, rev. ed. (Nashville: Abingdon Press, 1975), 164f.

45. Vincent Taylor, *The Gospel according to St. Mark* (New York: St. Martin's Press, 1966), 598; Werner H. Kelber, ed., *The Passion of Mark* (Philadelphia: Fortress Press, 1976), 120n., 155, 166.

46. The good reputations of the centurion in Luke 7:2ff. and Cornelius the centurion in Acts 10:1, 22 are intentional designs by Luke (see F. J. Foakes-Jackson and Kirsopp Lake, eds., *The Acts of the Apostles* [Grand Rapids, Mich.: Baker Book House, 1979], 4:112; and Ernst Haenchen, *The Acts of the Apostles: A Commentary* [Philadelphia: Westminster Press, 1971], 346, 349).

pericope is that by Ernst Haenchen, who entitles the pericope "Philip Converts a Chamberlain."[47] According to Haenchen, Luke is intentionally ambiguous about the Ethiopian's identity as a Gentile or Jew—Luke merely appeals to this conversion story in order to suggest "that with this new convert the mission has taken a step beyond the conversion of Jews and Samaritans."[48] The story itself derives from Hellenistic circles and represents for Luke, in Haenchen's view, a parallel and rival to Luke's own account of Cornelius as the first Gentile convert under the auspices of Peter.[49] Haenchen detects no particularly significant racial difficulties posed by Acts 8:26-40. For him, Luke merely edits this Hellenistic tradition to conform to his own theological design.

Today there are those who tend to exclude black people from any role in the Christian origins, and they need to be reminded that quite possibly a Nubian was the first Gentile convert.[50] Nonetheless, Luke's awkward use of this story seems to have certain racial implications. Notice that in Acts 8:37, the Ethiopian says, "See, here is some water! What is to prevent me from being baptized?" A variant reading immediately follows in some ancient manuscripts of the text (i.e., "And Philip said, 'If you believe with all your heart, you may [be baptized].' And he [the Ethiopian] replied, 'I believe that Jesus Christ is the Son of God' ").[51] Whether or not one accepts this variant reading as an authentic part of the text, it is clear that the Ethiopian's baptism takes place in the water without reference to a prior or simultaneous descent of the Holy Spirit (cf. John 3:5; 1 John 5:6-8). By contrast, Luke provides an elaborate narrative about Cornelius's conversion and baptism (Acts 10:1-48), at the end of which the Holy Spirit descends and the baptism by water follows. Furthermore, Peter's speech (Acts 10:34-43) indicates a new development in which Gentiles are unambiguously eligible for conversion and baptism. Given the importance of the Holy Spirit's role throughout Luke-Acts as a theological motif, Luke's narrative about Cornelius's baptism un-

---

47. Haenchen, *Acts of the Apostles*, 309.

48. Ibid., 314.

49. Ibid., 315. Similarly, Martin Hengel, *Acts and the History of the Earliest Christianity* (Philadelphia: Fortress Press, 1980), 79.

50. Irenaeus (C.E. 120–202) reports that the Ethiopian became a missionary "to the regions of Ethiopia"; and Epiphanius (C.E. 315–403) says that he preached in Arabia Felix and on the coasts of the Red Sea. Unfortunately, there are no records of Ethiopian Christianity until the fourth century (see Foakes-Jackson and Lake, eds., *Acts*, 4:98).

51. Irenaeus cites the text as if the variant reading is part of the text (*Adv. Haer.* 3.12.8) (see Alexander Roberts and James Donaldson, eds., *The Ante-Nicene Fathers* [Grand Rapids, Mich.: Wm. B. Eerdmans Publishing Co., 1981], 1:433; see also *The Western Text, The Antiochian Text*, and *Textus Receptus*; the English A.V. includes verse 37). Foakes-Jackson and Lake (eds., *Acts*, 4:98) suggest that the principal significance of verse 37 is that it is "perhaps the earliest form of the baptismal creed. It is also remarkable that it is an expansion of the baptismal formula 'in the name of Jesus Christ,' not of the trinitarian formula."

wittingly gives the distinct impression that Cornelius's baptism is more legitimate than that of the Ethiopian.

I, by no means, want to suggest that Luke had a negative attitude toward black people. On the contrary, one need only consider the list of the Antiochene church leadership that Luke presents in Acts 13:1 to dispel such notions. There Luke mentions one "Simeon who is called the black man" (*Symeon ho kaloumenos Niger*). The Latinism here (i.e., *Niger*) probably reinforces the idea that Simeon was a dark-skinned person, probably an African.[52] Luke's vision was one of racial pluralism in the leadership of the nascent Christian church at Antioch (Acts 11:26). Furthermore, I hasten to add that in no way do I think it important or useful to dwell on the point that the first Gentile convert was quite possibly a Nubian as opposed to an Italian. This would be absurd, of course, given the confessional nature of the entire Luke-Acts corpus, which does not come to us as objective history. The racial implication that I do wish to highlight is that Luke's editorializing results in a circumstantial de-emphasis of a Nubian (African) in favor of an Italian (European) and enables Europeans thereby to claim that the text of Acts demonstrates some divine preference for Europeans.

Beyond this merely circumstantial de-emphasis of that which is African, it seems that Luke's literary scheme in the Acts of the Apostles falls prey to secular ideologies. His possible apologetics for a Roman provincial official (Theophilus) as well as the great significance that he attaches to Rome as the center of the world contribute to this (see Luke 1:3; Acts 1:1).[53] In the last third of the first century, the church generally struggled to survive in an increasingly hostile political environment. Luke, not unlike other New Testament writers of this period and after,[54] seeks perhaps to assuage Rome by allowing his theological framework to be determined by the assumption of a Roman-centered world.[55] In this process of secularization, the Lukan vision of universalism is undermined by this seeming theological emphasis upon Europe. Of course, we must remember that the New Testament's final vision of the holy

---

52. "Simeon the 'black' may have come from Africa and may possibly be Simon of Cyrene" (C. S. C. Williams, *The Acts of the Apostles* [New York: Harper and Row, 1957], 154). Haenchen (*Acts of the Apostles*, 395n.2) reminds us that 1 Cor. 12:28f. lists first apostles, prophets, and teachers as persons endowed with charismata, and these constituted a charismatic office in Pauline churches.

53. See Hans Conzelmann, *The Theology of St. Luke*, trans. Geoffrey Buswell (New York: Harper and Row, 1960), 138–41; and Richard J. Cassidy, *Jesus, Politics, and Society* (Maryknoll, N.Y.: Orbis Books, 1978), 128–30.

54. Notably the pastorals (1 and 2 Timothy and Titus) and 1 Peter; cf. Rom. 13:1-5.

55. It should be noted, however, that the extent of the political-apologetic element in Luke-Acts continues to be at the storm center of New Testament debate. See Cassidy, *Jesus, Politics, and Society*; idem, *Society and Politics in the Acts of the Apostles* (Maryknoll N.Y.: Orbis Books, 1987); Donald Juel, *Luke-Acts: The Promise of History* (Atlanta: John Knox Press, 1983); Jack T. Sanders, *The Jews in Luke-Acts* (Philadelphia: Fortress Press, 1987).

remnant (Rev. 7:9) is consistent with Luke's notion of racial pluralism as shown in Acts 13:1. In Acts, two Africans are mentioned as part of the leadership team of the Church of Antioch, namely Simeon, who was called *Niger* (Latin: the black man), and Lucius of Cyrene (a province or a city in Africa). Both Revelation 7 and Acts 13 indicate that persons of all nations and races constitute the people of God in the history of salvation.

Another instance of secularization in the New Testament has to do with the Eurocentric bias that has accentuated the movement of the gospel geographically from Jerusalem to points north. This geographical progression is then translated into modern maps of New Testament lands that de-Africanize the entire New Testament. The result is that New Testament scholarship limits itself to focusing upon the Greco-Roman world. Hence, modern readers of the Bible take it for granted that maps of New Testament lands appropriately eliminate the continent of Africa. Even the modern creation of the so-called Middle East can only be seen as an extension of this Western tendency to de-Africanize this section of the world. Thus it has trivialized the ancient contribution of Africa in the shaping of the peoples and cultures of the entire region. Clearly, we are dealing with a modern ideological set of hermeneutical assumptions that suggests that nothing good has ever come out of Africa. What we must remember is that this thinking constitutes nothing short of fraudulent historiography on the part of Eurocentric Bible scholars. This in fact is another form of secularization because modern Eurocentric translators and interpreters of the New Testament have tended to allow secular ideological presuppositions to govern their exegesis and interpretation. The post-Enlightenment, systematic theories of race and thus racism have been tacitly affirmed and strengthened by the acquiescence of Eurocentric Bible scholars who ignore or trivialize ancient black culture as reflected in the Bible.

Finally, I want to stress once again that the biblical world predated any systematic notion of races and theories of racism. In this chapter I have tried to examine authors of ancient biblical narratives in order to reveal surprises that constitute a basis for interrogating modern-day mainline churches and synagogues afresh on their "readings" and subjective modernist "applications" of Scripture. Secularization in the New Testament is a process that needs much fuller exploration in terms of its racial dimensions. At one level, it highlights the continuing ambiguity of race in the New Testament. At another level, it confronts us today with a challenge to search for more adequate modes of hermeneutics that can be used to demonstrate that the New Testament—even as it stands locked into the socio-religious framework of the Greco-Roman world—is relevant to blacks and other marginalized peoples. Of all the mandates that confront the church in the world today, the mandate of world community predicated on a renewed commitment to pluralism and the attendant acknowledgment of the integrity of all racial groups constitutes an urgent agenda for Bible scholars and the laity alike. It is an agenda far too long neglected in the vast array of Eurocentric theological and ecclesial traditions that continue to marginalize people of color throughout the world.

— 7 —

The Black Presence in the Old Testament

Charles B. Copher

It is extremely difficult to deal with the subject of a black presence in the Old Testament. It is complicated by the fact that it is impossible to arrive at a conclusion that comes anywhere near universal acceptability. Among the difficulties, at points overlapping ones, confronting the investigator into this subject the following are to be noted: (1) a traditional view (influenced by ancient rabbinical interpretations of some biblical texts) often seems to have precedence over what is in the texts themselves; (2) there are differences between ancient and modern concepts of what constitutes black when as a color term it is applied to peoples; (3) confusions have arisen in the use of the terms *black* and *Negro* by different persons in modern times; (4) there are differences and confusions between socio-legal definitions of black/Negro on one hand and anthropological/physiological definitions on the other; (5) disagreements have arisen among scholars with respect to the relative significance of color terms in the biblical texts.

Any approach that would adequately deal with the difficulties encountered in determining a black presence in the Old Testament must take into account at least the following interrelated entities: (1) the significance of the color attributed to the Hamites and Elamites in the Table of Nations (Gen. 10:6-14; 1 Chron. 1:8-16); (2) the confused and contradictory modern Euro-American definitions of black/Negro that result in defining people as "literally black," "Negroid in physical appearance," and "socio-legal black/Negro"; these definitions are based upon

146

percentage of African Negro blood, and some take into consideration even one drop of such blood; (3) the testimonies of ancient Hebrew, Greco-Roman, and early Christian writers with respect to the color of the ancient Egyptians and Ethiopians; (4) the evaluation and application of some Hebrew words indicative of color; and (5) the views of some modern critical scholars with regard to the subject. Such an approach is employed in this essay.

Before engaging in this approach, however, I will review some four views that have been and are still held in various quarters with respect to a black presence in the Old Testament. I will then discuss several Hebrew terms, adjectives and proper nouns, indicative of color in the Old Testament. Finally, I will take the above five points into account and will address them according to the successive periods in Old Testament history.

Apart from the biblical text itself, and yet related to it in varying degrees, three or even four basic views of the subject at hand have arisen through the years since the Old Testament reached its final form, around C.E. 100. The first and most prevailing of these over the centuries is that set forth by the ancient rabbis and adopted by later interpreters including not only Jews but also Christians. This is the "Old Hamite view," which is to be distinguished from the "New Hamite view," which arose in the nineteenth century. The former is based upon the curse of Canaan recorded in Genesis 9:24-27, interpreted in instances also as a curse upon Ham, whose descendants are listed in the Table of Nations in Genesis 10:1-14 and 1 Chronicles 1:8-16. According to this view, which proliferated into several versions,[1] Ham and/or Canaan, more often Ham, was turned black as a result of Noah's curse, and his descendants were doomed to bear the same color.

In the Babylonian Talmud it is stated: "Our Rabbis taught: 'Three copulated in the ark, and they were all punished—the dog, the raven, and Ham. The dog was doomed to be tied, the raven expectorates [his seed into his mate's mouth], and Ham was smitten in his skin.'"[2]

This passage in the Babylonian Talmud, related to other sources such as *Tanhuma Noah* 13, 15, is used by Graves and Patai to produce the following narrative:

---

1. T. Peterson, "The Myth of Ham among White Antebellum Southerners" (Ph.D. diss., Stanford University, 1975), 146, isolates four versions of the Ham myth among white Southern Americans. See also this dissertation in book form under the title *Ham and Japheth: The Mythic World of Whites in the Antebellum South* (Metuchen, N.J., and London: The Scarecrow Press, Inc., and The American Theological Library Association, 1978).

2. I. Epstein, ed., *Hebrew-English Edition of the Babylonian Talmud*, trans. Jacob Shacter and H. Freedman, rev. ed. (London: The Soncino Press, 1969), *Sanhedrin* 108b. The explanatory footnote states, "i.e., from him descended Cush (the negro) who is black-skinned."

Moreover because you twisted your head around to see my nakedness, your grandchildren's hair shall be twisted into kinks, and their eyes red; again, because your lips jested at my misfortune, theirs shall swell; and because you neglected my nakedness, they shall go naked, and their male members shall be shamefully elongated. Men of this race are called Negroes.[3]

Midrash Rabbah, Genesis, reads, in part:

R. Huna said in R. Joseph's name (Noah declared), "you have prevented me from begetting a fourth son, therefore I curse your fourth son." R. Huna also said in R. Joseph's name: "you have prevented me from doing something in the dark (... co-habitation), therefore your seed will be ugly and dark-skinned." R. Hiyya said: "Ham and the dog copulated in the Ark, therefore Ham came forth black-skinned while the dog publicly exposes his copulation."[4]

Thus, with the curse of blackness resting upon Ham and his descendants, all four of them—the Cushites (Ethiopians), Mizraimites (Egyptians), Phutites, and Canaanites—are regarded as black, and wherever these peoples or individuals of them, along with the lands associated with them, appear in the Old Testament, there the black presence is found.

A second view is based upon the story of Cain (Gen. 4:1-16); this view is distinct from—and yet in some instances tied to—the various views concerning Ham/Canaan. According to this view Cain was turned black and became the ancestor of black peoples, or black peoples came into the world through the loins of Cain. Various and several reasons are given for Cain's having turned black. The ancient rabbis declared that he was turned black in connection with his having offered an unacceptable sacrifice: The smoke from his sacrifice blew back upon his face, blackening him. *Midrash Rabbah, Genesis* 22:6 reads: "And Cain was very wroth [*wayyihar*] and his countenance fell: [His face] became like a firebrand [blackened]."[5] Other sources say that Cain's face was blackened by hail:

And the Lord was wroth with Cain, and as a handful of dust is carried away of the wind, so he scattered all his harvest of corn and destroyed all his riches, so that not even an ear of corn could be found. He beat Cain's

---

3. Robert Graves and Raphael Patai, *Hebrew Myths: The Book of Genesis* (New York: Greenwich House, 1983), 121. *Tanhuma Noah* 13f. are also cited in C. G. Montefiore and H. Loewe, eds. and trans., *A Rabbinic Anthology* (1938; reprint, New York: Schocken Books, 1974), 56. See also Louis Ginzberg, *Bible Times and Characters from the Creation to Jacob*, vol. 1 of *The Legends of the Jews*, trans. Henrietta Szold (Philadelphia: The Jewish Publication Society of America, 1913), 168f.

4. H. Freedman and Maurice Simon, eds., *Midrash Rabbah, Genesis* (London: The Soncino Press, 1939), chap. 36, also pp. 7–8, 293.

5. Ibid., 184.

face with hail, which blackened like coal, and thus he remained with a black face.[6]

In addition to these reasons, Cain's blackness has been attributed either to a curse pronounced upon him, or to the mark placed upon him by God, or even both. These views can be traced back among Europeans at least to the twelfth century, and perhaps even to the tale of Beowulf, in which Cain's descendants are depicted as black.[7] At any rate, Cain as black and Negroid entered European thought and theology, and became a permanent element with respect to black peoples.[8] In instances the view of Cain's blackness has been united with the Ham/Canaan story by having Ham marry a daughter of Cain, thus bridging the gap between Cain's descendants—all of whom supposedly were destroyed in the flood—and the continuation of life after the flood through Noah's family, which included Ham/Canaan.[9] Thus, again, wherever in the Old Testament reference is made not only to the descendants of Ham/Canaan but also to those of Cain, there the black presence is found.

Closely related at points to the story of Cain as ancestor of black peoples is the pre-Adamite view. According to it, blacks, particularly so-called Negroes, are not descendants of Adam. Rather, they belong to a black race created before Adam and from among whom Cain found his wife, and thus in this way Cain became the progenitor of black peoples.[10] Originating as a result of European discovery of new worlds and peoples

---

6. Quoted by Ruth Mellinkoff, *The Mark of Cain* (Los Angeles: University of California Press, 1981), 77.

7. See ibid.

8. Although the belief that Cain was the ancestor of Negroes was common among Euro-Americans, the Mormons made it into a basic doctrine. Primary references to the blackness of the Canaanites and Cain appear in Joseph Smith's *The Holy Scriptures: Inspired Version* (Gen. 7:10, 29) and *The Book of Moses* (7:8, 22). For other primary source materials and for secondary discussions of the Mormon views, see Fawn M. Brodie, *No Man Knows My History: The Life of Joseph Smith*, 2d ed., rev. and enlarged (New York: Alfred A. Knopf, 1978); Newell G. Bringhurst, *Saints, Slaves, and Blacks: The Changing Place of Black People within Mormonism* (Westport, Conn.: Greenwood Press, 1981); Mellinkoff, *The Mark of Cain*, 78; Jerald Tanner and Sandra Tanner, *Mormonism: Shadow or Reality*, enlarged ed. (Salt Lake City, Utah: Modern Microfilm Company, 1972); Wallace Turner, *The Mormon Establishment* (Boston: Houghton Mifflin Co., 1966); William J. Whalen, *The Latter Day Saints in the Modern Day World*, rev. ed. (Notre Dame, Ind.: University of Notre Dame Press, 1967); Naomi Felicia Woodbury, "A Legacy of Intolerance: Nineteenth Century Pro-Slavery Propaganda and the Mormon Church Today" (M.A. thesis, University of California, Los Angeles, 1966).

9. The Mormon literature aptly illustrates this view, and it appears over and over again in anti-Negro literature elsewhere up to the present time.

10. The pre-Adamite view appears to have had its origins in the works of such authors as Paracelsus (1520), Bruno (1591), Vanini (1619), and Peyrère (1655), as indicated by Thomas F. Gossett, *Race: The History of an Idea in America* (New York: Schocken Books, 1965), 14f. It reached a high level of sophistication with the nineteenth-century scholar Alexander Winchell, who relied heavily on Peyrère. See Winchell's book *Preadamites: Or a Demonstration of the Existence of Men before Adam*, 2d ed. (Chicago: S. O. Griggs and Company, 1880).

during the fifteenth and sixteenth centuries, this view took on accretions and ramifications that regard the "Negro" as the beast of the field in Genesis 3:1ff., and even the tempter of Eve in the Garden of Eden.[11]

In the course of the nineteenth century there developed still another view in regard to a black presence in the Old Testament. Over against the Old Hamite/Canaan view it may be called the New Hamite view, based upon the fact that it too is related to Ham and his descendants as represented in the Table of Nations. Just the opposite of the older view, it holds that the Hamites were all white rather than black.[12] An exception may occur in the case of Cush who, according to some adherents, even if black in color, must be regarded as white, that is, as Caucasoid-black— because Negroes allegedly were not within the purview of the biblical writers.

With particular reference to biblical studies, over against social and physical scientific pursuits, subscribers to the New Hamite view include even modern biblical scholars whose views are reflected in some recent versions of the Bible in English. One such scholar in discussing the Table of Nations writes:

> This list, however, is not exhaustive. No reference is made to the Indians, Negroes, Mongolians, Malayans, Chinese, Japanese, etc. The author names only the peoples within his own sphere of knowledge.[13]

Another states:

> All known ancient races in the region [the biblical world] which concerns us here belonged to the so-called "white" or "Caucasian" race, with the

---

11. Mixed and confused accounts that combine the pre-Adamite view, Cain's marriage to a pre-Adamite Negro, and Eve's tempter having been a Negro beast are to be found in the writings of Josiah Priest (friend of Joseph Smith), *Slavery as It Relates to the Negro, or African Race . . .* (Albany: C. Van Benthuysen and Co., 1843), and idem, *Bible Defense of Slavery or the Origin, History, and Fortunes of the Negro Race* (Louisville: J. F. Brennan, 1851); Ariel [Buchner H. Payne], *The Negro: What Is His Ethnological Status?* (Cincinnati: Proprietor, 1872); G. G. H. Hasskarl, *"The Missing Link" or the Negro's Ethnological Status* (borrowed mostly from Ariel) (1898; reprint, New York: AMS Press, Inc., 1972); and Charles Carroll, *"The Negro a Beast" or "In the Image of God"* (1900; reprint, Miami: Mnemosyne Publishing Co., Inc., 1969). See also I. A. Newby, *Jim Crow's Defense: Anti-Negro Thought in America, 1900–1930* (Baton Rouge: Louisiana State University Press, 1965). Carroll's views have been continued by such publishers as Destiny Publishers, *In the Image of God*, rev. ed. (Merrimac, Mass.: 1984). Additionally, see George M. Fredrickson, *The Black Image in the White Mind: The Debate on Afro-American Character and Destiny, 1817–1914* (New York: Harper and Row, 1972).

12. For a discussion of the development of the New Hamite view, see Edith R. Sanders, "The Hamites in Anthropology and History: A Preliminary Study" (M.A. thesis, Columbia University, n.d.); see also her article "The Hamite Hypothesis: Its Origin and Function in Time Perspective," *Journal of African History* 10, no. 4 (1969): 521–32.

13. Paul Heinisch, *History of the Old Testament*, trans. William G. Heidt (Collegeville, Minn.: The Order of St. Benedict, Inc., 1952), 32.

exception of the Cushites ("Ethiopians") who were strongly Negroid in type, as we know from many Egyptian paintings.[14]

Still another scholar claims that the ancient Egyptians incorrectly depicted the Nubians as Negroes, and criticizes them for doing so. He says:

> The Egyptians frequently portrayed Negroes. The Egyptians also portrayed the people living along the Nile south of Egypt in a generalized and certainly incorrect manner, with typical Negro faces, beardless, and with large earrings, especially in the stereotyped lists of conquests in foreign lands, by incorrectly classifying the Nubians as Negroes. The Nubians were at most very slightly related to the Negro tribes bordering them on the south.[15]

Thus, according to the New Hamite view, there is no black, especially Negro, presence in the Old Testament. Or, if there is any such presence, it is only that slight bit that may be attributable to the Cushites or Nubians—terminology differing according to particular scholars.

Turning from views with regard to the color significance of the Table of Nations to the biblical text itself, there are several terms, adjectives and proper names, that are indicative of color. Among these are *Sāḥor*, *ḥūm (ḥām)*, *Qēdār*, *Pīneḥᵃs*, and *Kūš*, with cognates.[16] I shall discuss each of these. *Sāḥor*, and its derivatives, is a term used with reference to color of skin or complexion (Song of Songs 1:5, 6). Traditionally it has been translated "black"; but in most modern versions of the Bible in English it is translated "swarthy," "tawny," or "very dark." The word *ḥām* occurs as the name of one of Noah's sons, as the name of a location in Canaan (Gen. 14), and poetically as the name of Egypt, which is referred to as the tents or land of Ham (Pss. 78:51; 105:23, 27; 106:21f.). The closest approximation to it as a color term is the word *ḥūm*, translated "darkened," "dark brown," or "black," and applied only to the color of sheep (Gen. 30:32ff.). As an adjective *ḥām* is translated "warm" or "hot" and generally is taken to be related to the verb *ḥāmām*—"to be or become warm."

Although the attribution of the name Ham to one of Noah's sons as indicative of a black color is inconsistent with his having been turned black, and although the term is translated "warm/hot," it appears that it has connotations of blackness in the biblical text, including the Table

---

14. William F. Albright, "The Old Testament World," in George Arthur Buttrick, ed., *The Interpreter's Bible* (New York: Abingdon-Cokesbury Press, 1952), 1:233–77.

15. Martin Noth, *The Old Testament World*, trans. Victor I. Gruhn (Philadelphia: Fortress Press, 1966), 236.

16. For definitions see standard dictionaries; for names other than Phinehas, see especially Athalya Brenner, *Colour Terms in the Old Testament*, Journal for the Study of the Old Testament Supplement Series, no. 21 (Sheffield, Eng.: JSOT Press, Department of Biblical Studies, The University of Sheffield, 1982).

of Nations. In the table, the Hamites are southerners not only in Africa but also in Asia. Moreover, there would seem to have been some historical reality underlying the locations of a land of Ham in Canaan; the designations of Egypt as the tents and land of Ham; and the rabbinical attribution of black color to Ham.

Translations of the word *Qēdār* and its derivatives range from "to be dark" and "swarthy" to "very black," "dark-skinned," and "dusky." As a proper name it is that of one of the sons of Ishmael (Gen. 25:13), and appears as the name of a powerful Arabian tribe in several biblical texts, especially in the books of Isaiah, Jeremiah, and Ezekiel. On the other hand, *Pīneḥ*ᵃ*s*, from the Egyptian *Pa-Nehsi*, means the Negro or Nubian, depending upon a given translator. It is the name given to a grandson of Aaron, to one of the sons of Eli, and to others among the Jews into postexilic times. As the name of a grandson of Aaron it has great significance as indicative of a black presence in the family of Moses, as will be noted further.

By far the most common term that designates a black color when reference is to a person, people, or land is *Kūš* (Cush), with its cognates. These appear some fifty-eight times in the King James Version of the Old Testament. And in the Table of Nations *Kūš* is listed as the eldest son of Ham.

When dealing with a black presence in the Old Testament, however, and *apart from Ham's sons, Canaan and Phut, in the Table of Nations,* Egypt must be included, along with Cush. Whatever modern scholars may argue pro and con about the black color of the ancient Egyptians, the testimony of ancient Hebrew, Greek, and Roman writers is that, at least in their eyes, the Egyptians as well as the Ethiopians were both black and Negroid. Thus James Cowles Prichard, after an investigation of ancient Greco-Roman writers, concludes: "The national configuration prevailing in the most ancient times was nearly the Negro form, with wooly hair. . . . The general complexion was black or at least a very dusky hue."[17]

As with the Egyptians, so also with the Elamites, who in the Table of Nations are listed among the sons of Shem (Gen. 10:22). Modern archaeologists, historians, and others, upon the basis of archaeological discoveries and personal observations, have concluded that the ancient

---

17. James Cowles Prichard, *Researches into the Physical History of Man,* ed. and with an introductory essay by George W. Stocking, Jr. (Chicago: The University of Chicago Press, 1973), 388. More recently, Cheikh Anta Diop, "Origin of the Ancient Egyptians," in *Ancient Civilizations of Africa,* vol. 2 of *General History of Africa* (Berkeley, Calif.: University of California Press, 1981), 27–58, has given an extensive discussion of the views of classical authors of antiquity. The editors of *Ancient Civilizations of Africa* do well in the introduction to observe that "like the Ancients, we come back to determining 'black' by the nature of the hair and the color of the skin" (14).

Elamites, as well as other peoples of southern and western Asia, were black, or at least included a large black element in their populations.[18] The black presence in the Old Testament may thus be established on several grounds: (1) references to the Hamites and Elamites in the Table of Nations; (2) the confused modern Euro-American definitions of black/Negro; (3) ancient Hebrew, Greco-Roman, and early Christian views with respect to the Ethiopians and Egyptians; (4) Hebrew terms such as *Ṣāḥor; ḥūm (ḥām); Qēdār; Pīnᵉḥᵃs;* and excepting *Pīnᵉḥᵃs,* early translations of the Hebrew terms into Greek and Latin; and (5) some modern scholarly opinion.

With such guides to the black presence in the Old Testament, I shall now amplify my discussion according to the successive periods of Old Testament history as follows: (1) the prepatriarchal period; (2) the patriarchal period; (3) the period of the enslavement, Exodus, and wilderness wandering; (4) the period of the judges; (5) the period of the United Monarchy; (6) the period of the two kingdoms—Israel and Judah; (7) the period of the one kingdom—Judah; and (8) the period of the exile and restoration.

The Prepatriarchal Period

A black presence prior to the Hebrew patriarchs' arrival on the scene appears in the person of Nimrod, son of Cush. He is depicted as the founder of civilization in the region of Mesopotamia (Gen. 10:8-12) and

---

18. On black peoples in various Asian countries, see the following modern scholars and popular writers: Emmanuel Anati, *Palestine before the Hebrews: A History, from Earliest Arrival of Man to the Conquest of Canaan* (New York: Alfred A. Knopf, 1963), 322; James E. Brunson, *Black Jade: The African Presence in the Ancient East and Other Essays* (Dekalb, Ill.: James E. Brunson and KARA Publishing Co., 1985); V. Gordon Childe, *The Most Ancient East: The Oriental Prelude to European History* (New York: Alfred A. Knopf, 1929), 144f., 215; Marcel Dieulafoy, *L'Acropole de Suse d'après les fouilles executées en 1884, 1885, 1886 sous les auspices du Musée du Louvre* (Paris: Libraire Hachette et Cie, 1890); Cheikh Anta Diop, *The African Origin of Civilization: Myth or Reality?* trans. Mercer Cook (New York: Lawrence Hill and Company, 1974), 103ff.; W. E. B. Du Bois, *The World and Africa: An Inquiry into the Part Which Africa Has Played in World History,* enlarged ed. (New York: International Publishers, 1965), 176ff.; J. A. de Gobineau, *The World of the Persians* (Geneva: Editions Minerva S.A., 1971), 94; Joseph E. Harris, ed., *Africa and Africans as Seen by Classical Writers,* The William Leo Hansberry African Notebook, vol. 2 (Washington, D.C.: Howard University Press, 1977), 6, 50ff.; Clarence Maloney, *Peoples of South Asia* (New York: Holt, Rinehart and Winston, Inc., 1974), 47; G. Maspero, *The Struggle of the Nations: Egypt, Syria and Assyria,* ed. A. H. Sayce, trans. M. L. McClure, 2d ed. (London: Society for Promoting Christian Knowledge, 1925), 32; A. T. Olmstead, *History of the Persian Empire* (Chicago: The University of Chicago Press, 1948), 238, 244; George Rawlinson, *The Five Great Monarchies of the Ancient World,* 2d ed. (New York: Scribner, Welford, and Co., 1871), chap. 3; Charles E. Silberman, *Crisis in Black and White* (New York: Random House, Inc., Vintage Books, 1964), 162–74; Ivan Van Sertima and Runoko Rashidi, eds., *African Presence in Early Asia,* rev. ed. (New Brunswick, N.J.: Transaction Books, 1988); H. G. Wells, rev. Raymond Postgate, *The Outline of History* (Garden City, N.Y.: Garden City Books, 1949).

as having a kingdom that embraced Shinar and Assyria. As noted earlier, the aborigines of southern and western Asia included blacks. And whatever else may be said, on the basis of the Nimrod story, an ancient Hebrew writer believed civilization in Mesopotamia to owe its origin to a son of Cush, the black one.

The Patriarchal Period

According to one tradition (Gen. 11:31; Neh. 9:7; Acts 7:2-4) the original home of Abraham was Ur of the Chaldeans—a land whose earliest inhabitants included blacks. Representative of the black presence were the Sumerians, who referred to themselves as the "black-headed ones," indicative of skin color rather than of mere color of the hair, as some would argue. The significance of the phrase is well stated by A. H. Sayce:

> As, however, M. Dieulafoy's excavations on the site of Susa have brought to light enamelled bricks of the Elamite period on which a black race of mankind is portrayed, it may mean that the primitive Sumerian population of Chaldea was really black-skinned.[19]

In view of the black presence in the region of Abraham's origins, then, there is reason to believe that black blood flowed in the veins of at least some of the original Hebrew inhabitants, who, many scholars have argued, were very mixed from the beginning. More certainty with respect to a black presence appears in the accounts of Abraham's experiences in the lands of Canaan and Egypt. Canaan's aborigines consisted in part of black peoples, as is attested by biblical texts such as Genesis 14, with its reference to Ham as a Canaanite location during the time of Abraham, and 1 Chronicles 4:40ff., in which the former inhabitants of a region in Canaan are stated to have been Hamites. Additionally, attestation comes in the form of archaeological findings, as noted. Further indications and representations of a black presence are in the accounts of Hagar, the Egyptian maid or slave of Sarah; Ishmael, son of Hagar; Ishmael's unnamed Egyptian wife obtained for him by his mother; and Ishmael's sons, especially Kedar (Gen. 16, 17, 21, 25). Kedar becomes the ancestor of the Kedarites, who appear in several texts as a powerful Arab tribe and kingdom. Reference is made to them especially in the prophetical books of Isaiah, Jeremiah, and Ezekiel, and in the Book of Nehemiah (Isa. 21:16; 42:11; 60:7; Jer. 2:10; 49:28; Ezek. 27:21; Neh. 2:19ff.; 6:6). In addition to Hagar and Ishmael's wife, who are Egyptian, there are

---

19. A. H. Sayce, *Lectures on the Origin and Growth of Religion as Illustrated by the Religion of the Ancient Babylonians* (The Hibbert Lectures, 1887), 2d ed. (London: Williams and Norgate, 1888), 99.

several other unnamed Egyptians who figure in Abraham's sojourn in Egypt.

The black presence during the patriarchal period appears still further in the accounts of Joseph's experiences in Egypt: his marriage to an Egyptian woman, Asenath, by whom he sired Ephraim and Manasseh, eponymous ancestors of the two most prominent among the northern tribes of Israel, and Joseph's relationships with the Pharaoh and the Egyptians as a whole.

The Period of the Enslavement, Exodus, and Wilderness Wandering

There appears to have been a black presence as part of the enslavement, Exodus, and wilderness wandering, even though naturally Hebrews are the main people in the biblical narratives. This black presence figures first with respect to the locale where events take place, then in the peoples, Hebrews and Egyptians, and lastly in individual persons who are named in the accounts. Egypt, "the land of Ham," is home for the Hebrews for a period of some four hundred years. It is the land of nativity for generations of Hebrews, the land wherein they are born, live, die, and are buried.

Further, the term *Hebrew* is not one that may be limited altogether to the descendants of Jacob. It is indicative of a social class inclusive of others.[20] With respect to individuals whose names are given there is, in addition to members of Moses' own family, Bithiah, a daughter of Pharaoh, and foster mother of Moses. According to one account she married an Israelite man, Mered (Exod. 2:5ff.; 1 Chron. 4:17ff.). And in regard to Moses' family, several members bear Egyptian names. Among these are Moses, Aaron, Hophni, Merari, Miriam, Putiel in its first part, and Phinehas. The last of these, Phinehas, as already observed, means the Nubian/Negro, and serves as a clue to the racial or color identification of Moses' family. Concerning this William Foxwell Albright writes: "The name Phinehas ... is interesting as providing an independent (and absolutely reliable) confirmation of the tradition that there was a Nubian element in the family of Moses (Num. 12:1)."[21]

---

20. On the significance of the term *Hebrew* see H. Jagersma, *A History of Israel in the Old Testament Period*, trans. John Bowden (Philadelphia: Fortress Press, 1983), 11ff.; J. Maxwell Miller and John H. Hayes, *A History of Ancient Israel and Judah* (Philadelphia: The Westminster Press, 1986), 67, 68; and Gerhard von Rad, *Genesis: A Commentary*, trans. John H. Marks (Philadelphia: The Westminster Press, 1961), 363.

21. William Foxwell Albright, *From the Stone Age to Christianity: Monotheism and the Historical Process* (Baltimore: The Johns Hopkins Press, 1946), 193f.; idem, *Yahweh and the Gods of Canaan: A Historical Analysis of Two Contrasting Faiths* (Garden City, N.Y.:

Interestingly, Moses is identified as an Egyptian by the daughters of Jethro (Exod. 2:19). And according to one tradition recorded in the Old Testament, and referred to by Albright, Moses married a Cushite woman (Num. 12:1). This woman undoubtedly was Zipporah, daughter of Jethro, and not the Ethiopian princess referred to by Josephus; nor, as numerous modern scholars would have it, a *nonblack* woman of Cushan in Arabia; nor even a "black slave girl" who might have been among the "mixed multitude," as another thinks.[22] *Cush existed in Asia as well as in Africa;* and the account in Numbers 12:1 is directly related to the events of the Exodus as recorded in Exodus 18. Zipporah was rejoined with Moses, and was a stranger to both Aaron and Miriam. Reasons for the antipathy toward her are somewhat speculative. Be that as it may, the issue was hardly one of black color, for all of them were black.[23]

Beyond the matter of the color of Moses' family is that of the "mixed multitude" that participated in the Exodus. And the presence of blacks/ Negroes among that multitude is asserted by some who admit of a Negroid element in the modern Jewish peoples, datable from the time of the Exodus. Closely related to this subject are accounts of mixed marriages between Hebrews and Egyptians in the books of Leviticus (24:10-16) and 1 Chronicles (2:34f.). In these two instances an Egyptian man is married to an Israelite woman, while in the case of Bithiah, previously mentioned, an Egyptian woman is the wife of an Israelite man.[24]

Doubleday and Company, Inc., 1968), 165. See also Merrill F. Unger, *Archeology and the Old Testament* (Grand Rapids, Mich.: Zondervan Publishing House, 1954), 136.

22. Flavius Josephus *Antiquities of the Jews* 2.9, trans. William Whiston, in *The Works of Flavius Josephus* (Hartford: S. S. Scranton Co., 1903), 77f.; W. O. E. Oesterly and G. H. Box, *A Short Survey of the Literature of Rabbinical and Medieval Judaism* (1920; reprint, New York: Burt Franklin, 1973), 76; Roland de Vaux, *The Early History of Israel*, trans. David Smith (Philadelphia: The Westminster Press, 1978), 33f.; James Hastings, ed., *A Dictionary of the Bible* (New York: Charles Scribner's Sons, 1911), s.v. "Ethiopian Woman" by D. S. Margoliouth.

23. The statement that all of them (Zipporah, Moses, Aaron, Miriam) were black is based on these factors: the three definitions of black/Negro; scholarly opinion that views Moses' family as of Nubian origin; and the existence of Cushites in Asia as well as in Africa.

24. See Isaac Landman, ed., *The Universal Jewish Encyclopedia* (New York: Ktav Publishing House, Inc., 1969), s.v. "Race, Jewish," by Fritz Kahn; Henry S. Noerdlinger, *Moses and Egypt: The Documentation to the Motion Picture, "The Ten Commandments"* (Los Angeles: University of Southern California Press, 1956), 33; Nahum M. Sarna, *Understanding Genesis* (New York: Schocken Books, 1970), vi; Louis L. Snyder, *The Idea of Racialism: Its Meaning and History* (Princeton, N.J.: D. Van Nostrand Company, Inc., 1962), 76ff.; Juan Comas, *Racial Myths* (1951; reprint, Westport, Conn.: Greenwood Press, 1976), 27ff., and in UNESCO, *The Race Question in Modern Science: Race and Science* (New York: Columbia University Press, 1961), 13–55. In this latter volume, see Harry L. Shapiro, "The Jewish People: A Biological History" (107–78).

The Period of the Judges

The black presence during the time of the judges, roughly 1200–1000 B.C.E., appears as a distinct entity in three accounts. The first of these is that of Cushan-rishathaim, a Mesopotamian ruler, who is said to have oppressed the Hebrews for a period of eight years (Judg. 3:7-10). Here again, there is no need, as much modern scholarship has done, to dissociate this person from a black person in Asia. To speculate that he might have been someone from Cushan in Arabia does not eliminate his blackness for, as stated above, blacks were among the populations of Asia as well as of Africa. The ruler is simply called the "Cushite of Double Infamy." Also, there is the overall account of Eli and his two wicked, priestly sons, Hophni and Phinehas. Each son bears an old Egyptian name characteristic of Moses' family. And they are continuators of the Aaronic priesthood during the period. Finally, there is the account of Sheshan, who gives one of his daughters in marriage to his Egyptian slave, Jarha (1 Chron. 2:34ff.).

The Period of the United Monarchy

There are four references that indicate a black presence during the period of the United Monarchy, apart from any consideration of members of the family of Jesse, David's father. These are: (1) the account of Ha-Cushi (the Cushite) in 2 Samuel 18; (2) the accounts concerning Solomon's Egyptian wife in 1 Kings 1:1-4, 15, and 2 Chronicles 8:11; (3) the texts with reference to the color of the maiden in the Song of Songs (1:5f.; 6:13); and (4) the account of the Queen of Sheba in 1 Kings 10:1-13 and 2 Chronicles 9:1-12.

"The Cushite" appears as the designation for one of two messengers chosen to carry the news of Absalom's death to King David. Commentators readily see him as a Negro, but also as a slave. Henry Preserved Smith goes so far as to say "naturally" a slave, as if a black person even in ancient times could only have been a slave.[25] The truth of the matter, however, is that in the ancient biblical world, most slaves would have been what today are called Caucasians rather than Negroes.[26] Moreover, where Negroes do appear they do so either as mercenaries in the armies of the Egyptians, Ethiopians, Persians, and Greeks, or as being among the leading peoples. Some few commentators do refer to the Cushite as being possibly a mercenary, and this is the greater possibility. David's

---

25. Henry Preserved Smith, *A Critical and Exegetical Commentary on the Books of Samuel*, The International Critical Commentary (New York: Charles Scribner's Sons, 1899), 359.

26. Keith Crim, gen. ed., *The Interpreter's Dictionary of the Bible*, sup. vol. (Nashville: Abingdon, 1976), s.v. "Slavery in the New Testament" by W. G. Rollins.

private army, of which the Cushite was a member, was composed partially of Philistines who had come from Crete; and blacks from Ethiopia and Egypt were among the Cretan population, some as soldiers, from early times.[27]

Whether one regards Solomon's favorite wife, the Egyptian princess, as the daughter of a Libyan Pharaoh or not, in the eyes of the ancients she was black. Some identified her with the black maiden in the Song of Songs, and thought that Solomon had written the Song with reference to her. According to Robert M. Grant, Theodore of Mopsuestia (C.E. 350–420) regarded the historical occasion of the Song to have been the wedding of Solomon with the princess, arranged for political stability of Israel rather than for pleasure. Grant states that "since the princess was black and therefore not especially attractive to the court of Solomon, he built a palace for her and composed this song—so that she would not be irritated and so that enmity would not arise between him and Pharaoh."[28]

The Song of Songs has been variously interpreted, and so has the identity of the maiden in the Song, "the black and/but beautiful one." Some associated her with Moses' Cushite wife; others with Abishag the Shunammite maiden obtained to comfort David in his old age and inherited by Solomon (1 Kings 1:2-4; 2:13-25); still others, like Theodore, with the Egyptian princess. Whatever her identity, however, in the eyes of the ancient writers she too was black.[29]

With respect to the Queen of Sheba, she has been regarded as reigning over regions embracing lands from India to Ethiopia. Most modern writers view her, to the extent that she was an actual historical personality, as ruler in southwest Arabia. Interestingly, Josephus saw her as Queen of Egypt and Ethiopia.[30] Most probably, her domain included territory in both southwest Asia and Africa. Whatever her location, however, she must be included in the black presence. And she was regarded as such, by way of example, by Origen. In commenting upon Origen's view, Frank M. Snowden, Jr., writes:

> The Queen of Sheba, according to Origen's interpretation of the passage from 1 Kings, by her visit to Solomon provides an important parallel to

27. On blacks as inhabitants of Crete and as Cretan soldiers, see Brunson, *Black Jade*, 121–42; Du Bois, *The World and Africa*, 122; Gustave Glatz, *The Aegean Civilization*, The History of Civilization, ed. C. K. Ogden (New York: Barnes and Noble, Inc., 1968), 209, 214; Harris, *Africa and Africans*, 2:32ff.; Frank M. Snowden, Jr., *Blacks in Antiquity: Ethiopians in the Greco-Roman Experience* (Cambridge: The Belknap Press of Harvard University Press, 1970), 121, 291.

28. Robert M. Grant, *The Bible in the Church: A Short History of Interpretation* (New York: Macmillan Co., 1948), 77f.

29. See H. H. Rowley, *The Servant of the Lord and Other Essays on the Old Testament*, 2d ed. rev. (Oxford: Basil Blackwell, 1965), 197–245.

30. Josephus *Antiquities* 8.6.252.

the person of the Church, who comes to Christ out of the Gentiles. In fulfillment of the type represented by the Queen of Sheba, an Ethiopian, the Church comes from the Gentiles to hear the wisdom of the true Solomon and the true lover of Peace.... When this black and beautiful Queen had seen all in the House of the King of Peace, she expressed her amazement. But Origen concludes, when she comes to the heavenly Jerusalem, she will see wonders more numerous and splendid.[31]

The Period of the Two Kingdoms—Israel and Judah

This period lasted roughly from 922 to 722 B.C.E. References to a specific black presence during these years are located in historical records within the books of 1 and 2 Kings, and in the prophetical books of Amos and Hosea. The references are to events and oracles that pertain to Egypt and Ethiopia, primarily.

In 1 Kings 14:25ff. and 2 Chronicles 12:2ff., there is a report of an invasion of Judah by Shishak, Pharaoh of Egypt. According to Chronicles, his army included Libyans, Sukkin, and Ethiopians. And, according to an account in 2 Chronicles 14:9ff., Judah was invaded during the reign of King Asa by one Zerah, the Ethiopian. Finding no other reference to an Ethiopian ruler with this name, scholars have identified him in various ways. Some speculate that he was an Arabian chieftain, king, or leader from Cushan in Arabia; others postulate that he was an army officer over an occupation force left in Canaan by Shishak; still another suggests he was a bona fide Ethiopian who was permitted by Pharaoh Osorkon I to pass through Egypt.

In Amos 9:7, the prophet compares the people of Israel with the Ethiopians, declaring that they are equal in the sight of Yahweh. Typical of much Euro-American biblical interpretation with respect to black people, many commentators give a pejorative interpretation to Amos's comparison, viewing the Ethiopians as a distant and despised people. Such an interpretation, however, as Hughell E. W. Fosbroke has shown, is entirely wrong.[32] It overlooks the fact that in the times during which Amos lived, and afterwards, the Ethiopians were known as a people of renown. Even Hosea, the prophet, criticizes Israel for depending upon Egypt as also upon Assyria; he refers frequently to past experiences of Israel in relation to Egypt and foresees Israel's return to Egypt (7:11ff.; 9:3ff.; 11:1; 12:9, 13; etc.).

The editors of 2 Kings 17:4 report that, during the period that Hosea prophesied, King Hoshea of Israel sent to So of Egypt for help. As in

---

31. Snowden, *Blacks in Antiquity*, 202f.

32. George Arthur Buttrick, ed., *The Interpreter's Bible* (New York: Abingdon Press, 1956), s.v. "The Book of Amos, Introduction and Exegesis" by Hughell E. W. Fosbroke, vol. 6, 848.

the instance of Zerah, the Ethiopian, scholarly opinion is greatly divided over the identity of So. Speculation ranges from identification with the city of Sais to identification with a minor ruler in the Egyptian Delta.

The Period of the One Kingdom—Judah

After the fall of Israel in 722–21 B.C.E., the kingdom of Judah continued until 587/586 B.C.E. The intervening years include the last quarter of the eighth century, the whole of the seventh century, and most of the first two decades of the sixth century. During the first of these periods, the prophet Isaiah continued his career, begun shortly before the end of the Northern Kingdom. At the same time, the Ethiopian dynasty of Ethiopia/Egypt entered upon its heyday and became a participant in the affairs of Judah, especially during the reign of King Hezekiah. The seventh century B.C.E. was to witness the appearance of the prophets Zephaniah, Jeremiah, and Nahum, all of whom were to say something with reference to a black presence. Jeremiah's ministry continued during the first years of the sixth century B.C.E.

The black presence appears conspicuously in the chapters of the Book of Isaiah assigned to Isaiah, son of Amoz, of the eighth century. Chapter 18 contains two distinct references. In the first (vv. 1-2), the Ethiopians are referred to as "a nation tall and smooth, a people feared near and far, a nation mighty and conquering, whose land the rivers divide." In the second (v. 7), it is prophesied that these same people will bring gifts to the Lord of Hosts, to Mount Zion. Chapter 19 is a veritable anthology of prophecies concerning Egypt that range from oracles of doom upon Egypt, through oracles of Egypt's restoration, to oracles that predict that the Egyptians will become worshipers of Israel's God, along with Israel and Assyria. Moreover, the countries at war during the prophet's times, Israel (Judah), Assyria, and Egypt, will be equals, and will be blessed by God.

Chapter 20, recounting events around 714–11 B.C.E., contains a report of a symbolic prophecy engaged in by the prophet over a period of three years—the prophet going about as a prisoner of war, naked and barefoot. Through his behavior he was foretelling the fate of the Ethiopians and Egyptians in whom Judah was placing trust in its fight against the Assyrians under Sargon II. Again, oracles appear in chapters 30 and 31 concerning Egypt during the period of Ethiopian rule. In these, the prophet castigates Judah for relying upon a militarily strong Egypt instead of upon Yahweh. A similar thought is expressed in the speech of the Assyrian Rabshakeh (Isa. 36:4ff. = 2 Kings 18:19ff.); in 37:9, which is parallel to 2 Kings 19:9, reference is made to the coming of Tirhakah, "King of Ethiopia," and to the assistance of Hezekiah during Sennacherib's siege of Jerusalem.

The book of the prophet Zephaniah presents possibilities for the black presence in a unique manner. This uniqueness appears in connection with the prophet's identity: his color and race; his nationality; and his possible relationship to Hezekiah, king of Judah. His genealogy, unlike that of any other prophet, is traced back over four generations from his father Cushi to one Hezekiah (1:1). Opinions include one that regards the name Cushi as a proper name, without color significance;[33] one that regards the extensive genealogy as a means of "avoiding the embarrassing misconception that Zephaniah's father, Cushi, was an Ethiopian and not a Judean";[34] another that holds the prophet to have been black through his mother, and related to King Hezekiah through his father;[35] and still another that regards the prophet as a native black Judahite related through his father to the king.[36] And there are others.

The opinion that regards the prophet as a black through his mother is well supported by its proponent, Gene Rice, who ably refutes those who would deny a black identity.[37] It falls short, however, in not being aware of black persons in the native Hebrew-Israelite-Judahite population from earliest times. Upon the basis of this latter fact, as demonstrated earlier, and upon the basis of the usual meaning of Cushi, and further still, upon the basis of the significance of linear genealogies in the Old Testament, one must conclude that Zephaniah was indeed a native Judahite, black in color, and related to none other than Hezekiah, king of Judah, of the house and lineage of David.[38] Thus, at least one of the Old Testament prophets was a black man.

Apart from the matter of Zephaniah's identity, there are his oracles concerning Ethiopia as well as other lands and peoples. These, it is to be noted, are of two kinds: one that pronounces doom upon the Ethiopians (2:12), who, in his day, still are an outstanding people; and another that predicts a time when worshipers of Yahweh will come from beyond the rivers of Ethiopia and bring offerings (3:9-10). The context of this latter prophecy indicates that these worshipers will be native Africans rather than Judahite exiles.

33. Gerald A. Larue, *Old Testament Life and Literature* (Los Angeles: University of Southern California Press; Boston: Allyn and Bacon, Inc., 1968), 237.

34. George Fohrer, *Introduction to the Old Testament*, trans. David E. Green, rev. ed. (Nashville: Abingdon Press, 1968), 456.

35. Gene Rice, "The African Roots of the Prophet Zephaniah," *The Journal of Religious Thought* 36, no. 1 (Spring–Summer 1979): 21–31.

36. This is my opinion.

37. Rice, "African Roots."

38. This is my own opinion, supported by the reasons given. With respect to the genealogy, see George Adam Smith, *The Book of the Twelve Prophets*, rev. ed. (New York: Harper and Brothers Publishers, n.d.), 46; and especially Robert R. Wilson, *Prophecy and Society in Ancient Israel* (Philadelphia: Fortress Press, 1980), 279–82.

In the Book of Nahum, the black presence appears in an oracle concerning the fall of the city of Nineveh. The prophet compares Nineveh's fall, which is at hand, to that of Thebes (No-Amon) in Egypt some fifty years before; and he states that the Egyptian city fell despite help provided by Ethiopia, Egypt, Put, and the Lubim (3:8f.).

For the times shortly after that of Nahum, the books of 2 Kings, 2 Chronicles, and Jeremiah contain historical and prophetical data with reference to the black presence. Second Kings 23:29—24:5 (duplicated and expanded in 2 Chron. 35:20—36:4) recounts Egypt's domination of Judah during the years 609–5 B.C.E. under Pharaoh Necho II, specifying Necho's defeat of King Josiah, the dethronement and deportation of King Jehoahaz to Egypt, and the Egyptian installation of Jehoiakim as king of Judah. During Jehoiakim's reign, according to Jeremiah 26:20-23, Uriah, a prophet who like Jeremiah had prophesied against Jerusalem and Judah, escaped to Egypt for safety only to be brought back and executed by the king.

As a book, Jeremiah is a treasure trove of references to the black experience. It contains sixty-two references to Egypt as a country, apart from references to specific localities within the country as well as references to Ethiopia and other African lands. In addition to records of historical events there are several oracles against Judah's seeking Egypt's help (2:16-18); oracles of doom upon Egypt (25:19; 43:11-13; 46:1-26a); oracles of doom upon Judahites, some of whom are in Judah while others are in Egypt (42:14-22; 44:1-14, 24-30), these oracles being delivered in Egypt; and one brief oracle favorably disposed toward Egypt (46:26b). Included also in Jeremiah are oracles of doom upon Kedar (25:24; 49:28f.) and upon Elam (25:25; 49:34-38) and one brief oracle predicting restoration of Elam (49:39).

Moreover, the book contains historical accounts about persons of both immediate and remote African descent. Included in the remote category is the person of Jehudi, greatgrandson of one Cushi, and obviously a court official, who read Jeremiah's scroll of prophecies in the presence of King Jehoiakim (36:14, 23). Similarly, there are the accounts about Ebed-Melech, the Ethiopian, another official in the Judahite court, who was instrumental in saving Jeremiah's life, and was afterwards blessed by the prophet (38:7-13; 39:15-18). Prior to these accounts is Jeremiah's impartial analogy between Judah's inability to alter its sinful ways and the Ethiopian's powerlessness to change the color of his skin (13:23). And in 40:1—43:8, an expansion of 2 Kings 25:26, there is an account of a group of Judahites who fled to Egypt, taking Jeremiah with them against his will, and taking up residence in Tahpanhes (Fort of the Negro), where the prophet proclaims some of his oracles (43:7-9).

The Period of the Exile and Restoration

Biblical passages that attest to the black presence during the period of the Babylonian exile (586–38 B.C.E.) and the restoration (538 B.C.E. onwards) appear in the books of Jeremiah, Ezekiel, Isaiah (40–66), Psalms, and Zechariah. References in Jeremiah to events after 586 B.C.E. are, of course, to be dated in the immediate period of the exile, as are the prophecies attributed to Ezekiel.

References in Ezekiel are second in number only to those in Jeremiah. It is to be observed that with the exception of three verses (Ezek. 29:13-16) that predict a restoration of Egypt, and Egypt's recognition of Yahweh as Lord, all of chapters 29–32 consist of prophecies that in one way or another are antagonistic toward Egypt. Even so, Ezekiel's anti-Egyptian oracles depict Egypt to be a proud, great, wealthy nation, ruler over nations among whom it stands as a lion, exerting great influence upon both Hebrew kingdoms—not only in times past but also in Ezekiel's own days—and over Judah almost a hundred years after the fall of Thebes in 663 B.C.E. It is not without historical interest to note that according to Ezekiel, Egypt's origins lay in the land of Pathros, Upper Egypt, and that it is there that it will be restored, albeit as a lowly kingdom. Egypt, however, is not to be alone in its forthcoming destruction: Its African allies, especially Ethiopia, then Put, Lud, and Libya, and Asiatic Arabia, are to go down with it (30:1-9). The greatness of Kedar and Elam are depicted in 27:21 and 32:24-25.

Dating from the period of restoration is Isaiah 27:12-13, in which a prophet foresees a return of exiles from Egypt and Assyria to Jerusalem in order to worship on the holy mountain. Much the same prophecy appears in Isaiah 11:11, in which the prophet predicts a return of exiles from lands that include Egypt, Pathros, Ethiopia, Elam, and Shinar.

Belonging also to the period of restoration, and providing data on the black presence, are passages in that portion of the Book of Isaiah that are called Second Isaiah (Deutero-Isaiah), chapters 40–55. Also indicative of that presence are Psalm 78:51, with its reference to the tents of Ham, and Psalms 105:23-27 and 106:21f., with their references to Egypt as the land of Ham, the two latter dating from after the fall of Jerusalem in 586 B.C.E., as their contents indicate. Perhaps Psalm 68 also belongs in the postexilic period, with its verse 31 that states that "princes shall come out of Egypt, and Ethiopia shall soon stretch out her hands unto God."

The data in Second Isaiah consist of 43:3 and 45:14. In speaking of Judah's restoration, the prophet asserts that Yahweh will ransom "Israel" by exchanging Egypt and Ethiopia for it, and that the wealth of Egypt and the merchandise of Ethiopia, along with the Sabeans, will become Israel's possessions, even slaves, and they will acknowledge Israel's God.

Of the five references to Egypt in the Book of Zechariah (dated be-tween 332–164 B.C.E.) one prophesies that Jewish exiles will be brought back to Palestine from the land of Egypt (10:10-11) while a second (14:18-19) states, strangely enough, that a plague will come upon the Egyptians if they fail to come up to Jerusalem in order to observe the Feast of Booths.

Conclusion

On the basis of (1) references to the Hamites and Elamites of the Table of Nations; (2) confused modern Euro-American definitions of black/Negro; (3) ancient Hebrew, Greco-Roman, and early Christian views with respect to the color of the ancient Egyptians and Ethiopi-ans; (4) some Hebrew words indicative of color; and (5) some modern scholarly opinion, a black presence in the Old Testament may be estab-lished. Such a presence is attested in many passages and in many ways, from earliest times to the period of restoration. It appears in literature from many periods of Old Testament history: in historical accounts and in prophetic oracles; in Psalms and in the literature of love, the Song of Songs.

From slaves to rulers, from court officials to authors who wrote parts of the Old Testament itself, from lawgivers to prophets, black peoples and their lands and individual black persons appear numerous times. In the veins of Hebrew-Israelite-Judahite-Jewish peoples flowed black blood.

— 8 —

Beyond Identification:
The Use of Africans
in Old Testament Poetry
and Narratives

Randall C. Bailey

Introduction

For so long the tendency in Old Testament scholarship has been to deny that African nations and individuals either play a role in the text of the Hebrew Canon or had an influence upon it. Sometimes the methods used to deny the presence of Africans within the text have been subtle. Other times they have been not so subtle.

One strategy for achieving this is seen in the fact that for the past century the thrust of biblical scholarship has been on Mesopotamian and ancient Near Eastern studies.[1] This is most dramatically seen as one peruses the various current introductions to the Old Testament and

I am indebted to the Interdenominational Theological Center for a faculty development grant that was supported through the Lilly Endowment. The grant assisted me greatly in the completion of the research for this project.

1. See Ronald E. Clements, *One Hundred Years of Old Testament Interpretation* (Philadelphia: Westminster, 1976); and Douglas A. Knight and Gene M. Tucker, eds., *The Hebrew Bible and Its Modern Interpreters* (Chico, Calif.: Scholars Press, 1985).

histories of Israel, especially the sections dealing with geography.[2] In so doing, one gets the impression that other than Syria-Palestine, the Arabian Peninsula, and Mesopotamia, there is no other part of the ancient world to be considered in relation to the history of ancient Israel. In reference to Egypt, there is usually only a token paragraph or two, and this is still in the section on the Near East, as opposed to Africa.

Similarly, when one looks at maps of the "Bible Lands" one confronts the same tendency of de-Africanization. In other words most maps either show only Syria-Palestine or that region and areas to the east. If there is any depiction of Africa it is usually restricted to Egypt. This was especially the case in the eighteenth and nineteenth centuries for maps that purported to depict "all the places named in the Bible" but that often omitted the African nations of Cush, Put, Cyrene, and the like.[3] On the other hand, there were maps that located Cush, ancient Ethiopia, outside of Africa, especially when depicting the so-called Garden of Eden.[4] In modern maps, the de-Africanization takes place in presenting a map labeled the "Near East"; these maps include African territories,

---

2. See, for example, Norman K. Gottwald, *The Hebrew Bible: A Socio-Literary Introduction* (Philadelphia: Fortress, 1985), 38–44; Siegfried Hermann, *A History of Israel in Old Testament Times*, 2d ed. (Philadelphia: Fortress, 1981), 4; Otto Kaiser, *Introduction to the Old Testament: A Presentation of Its Results and Problems* (Minneapolis: Augsburg, 1975), 15–18; J. Maxwell Miller and John H. Hayes, *A History of Ancient Israel and Judah* (Philadelphia: Westminster, 1986), 30–36; Martin Noth, *The History of Israel*, rev. ed. (New York: Harper and Row, 1960), 7–17. See also Edward P. Blair, *Abingdon Bible Handbook* (New York: Abingdon, 1975), 68–389.

3. See, for example, W. R. Annim, engraver, "Places Recorded in the Five Books of Moses," where there is nothing located east of Egypt, and on an insert "Cuth" is located in Persia; C. Wiltberger, "Map of the Countries Found in Sacred Classic and Ecclesiastical Writers in Their Ancient and Modern Names. Carefully Compiled from the Best Authorities," engraved by John and William W. Warr (Philadelphia, 1829); "Die Länder der heiligen Schrift," insert on R. v. Raumer and F. v. Stüpnagel, "Palestina nach den zuverlässigsten alten und neuen Quellen" (Gotha, bei J. Perthes, 1844). I examined these maps in the collection of the Library of Congress.

One would expect that identifying the African nations mentioned in the Hebrew Canon would be easy. All one would need to do is look at a map of the ancient world. The problem with such a strategy is that we do not currently possess maps that were drawn during biblical times. Rather we have maps that have resulted from examination of written documents. In other words, place names mentioned in the Bible are situated on a map as a result of the exegesis of the biblical text and the use of other sources, such as archaeological investigations and travel reports. See, for example, the explanation given in the foreword to *Oxford Bible Atlas*, ed. Herbert G. May, 2d ed. (New York: Oxford University Press, 1974), 5.

4. See, for example, Joseph Erwin Wilson, "Maps of the Rivers of Eden" (1877). Such maps are based upon the text of Gen. 2:10-14, which gives the "location" of the "garden" in relation to four rivers and four other geographical landmarks. The last two of these four are designated as being in an east-west relationship. Thus, one would suspect that the first two are in a north-south relationship. Therefore, Cush, the second place mentioned in the passage, must be functioning in this passage as the southern or African "border" of the "garden." It appears, however, that suggesting that Africa was a landmark for the ancient Israelites is unthinkable for some cartographers.

thereby suggesting that these are not to be considered part of the African continent, but rather part of the Near East.[5] With regard to the dictionaries of the Bible, one notes a similar tendency to exclude and minimize exploration of the subject of African influence. For example, while the treatment of Cush in *The Interpreter's Dictionary of the Bible*[6] has increased from one-eighth of a column to one and one-half columns in the *Supplementary Volume*,[7] the focus of the increase has been on arguing for two locations of Cush, one in Africa and the other in the Arabian Peninsula. Once this second location is established within the scholarly set, de-Africanization occurs. In other words, within commentaries the location of Cush is argued to be either ambiguous or in Arabia.[8] This latter option is particularly the case in exegeting units in which an individual from Cush plays an important, positive role in the narrative or is associated with a major character.[9]

The treatment of Egypt is another example of this tendency to minimize African influence on the Hebrew Canon. This has been achieved by a twofold strategy. On the one hand, there are those efforts to move Egypt out of Africa by arguing for a sharp distinction between Sub-Saharan Africa and Egypt. On the other hand, there are those efforts that argue that the Hamites were not Africans. Because the latter theme is taken up elsewhere in this volume,[10] here I will briefly focus upon the former.

One of the more graphic examples of attempting to remove Egypt from Africa is found in *The Image of the Black in Western Art*. Volume 1 begins with an article that discusses the portrayal of blacks in Egyptian art. It should immediately strike one as strange to see Egyptian art depicted as Western. This puzzlement is resolved by the writer maintaining throughout the article that there is a classic differentiation between Egypt and Africa. Thus, the message of the chapter is that ancient Egypt should be considered Western and that the existence of blacks (= Africans) there

---

5. See, for example, maps in *Oxford Bible Atlas*, 54–55, 92–93. The maps in that book are often used in study editions of Bibles and in histories of Israel. One exception to modern cartographic de-Africanization is the map found on the inside cover of Bernhard Anderson's *Understanding the Old Testament*, 4th ed. (Englewood Cliffs, N.J.: Prentice-Hall, 1986), which not only locates Cush in Africa but also labels the whole continent, including Egypt, as Africa.

6. G. A. Buttrick, ed., *Interpreter's Dictionary of the Bible* (hereafter IDB), 4 vols. (Nashville: Abingdon, 1962), 1:751, s.v. "Cush."

7. K. Crim, ed., *Interpreter's Dictionary of the Bible: Supplementary Volume* (Nashville: Abingdon, 1976), 200–201, s.v. "Cush."

8. In this regard it should be noted that the underlying assumption in such argumentation is that ancient "Arabia" was not populated by Africans but rather by the "forerunners of our modern-day Arabs"; ancient "Arabia" is thereby de-Africanized.

9. The treatment of the Cushite wife of Moses, mentioned in Num. 12:1, is an example of this argument that Cush was non-African.

10. See the discussion on the "New Hamite hypothesis" in Charles Copher's essay in this volume.

was unusual.[11] Another example of this minimizing tendency is seen in Hubert Huffmon's article on Egypt in the *Harper's Bible Dictionary*. In it Huffmon admits that Egypt is in Africa but then goes on to claim that "Egyptian cultural influence on Palestine was modest."[12]

This bias in modern scholarship to either remove ancient Egypt from Africa or to suggest a minimal influence of Africa on ancient Israelite culture and religion is also noticeable in the work of church historians and theologians. For example, most treat the Alexandrian and other north African churches as a subunit of the Western church.[13] Similarly the whole basis of the idea of the Fertile Crescent as the cradle of civilization that extends from Egypt around through Syria-Palestine and on to the Tigris River appears to be an attempt to claim that Egypt is not part of Africa but rather part of the West.

The Purpose of This Study

Due to the aforementioned tendency within scholarship to deny or dilute African influence on the biblical text (i.e., to de-Africanize), the subject before us is one of immense importance, primarily in terms of the future development of and redirection for the biblical field. It is also important in terms of challenging and correcting previous distortions and omissions in scholarship. There have already been several exciting and provocative studies on the presence of Africans within the Hebrew Canon.[14] The objective for the current investigation is to take these stud-

---

11. Jean Vercoutter, "The Iconography of the Black in Ancient Egypt: From the Beginnings to the Twenty-fifth Dynasty," in Ladislas Bugner, gen. ed., *The Image of the Black in Western Art, From the Pharaohs to the Fall of the Roman Empire* (Cambridge: Harvard University Press, 1976), 1:33–88.

12. *Harper's Bible Dictionary* (New York: Harper and Row, 1986), 248, s.v. "Egypt." While this argument has been emphasized primarily in modern scholarship, there had been a tendency to accomplish the same objective in Midrashic and Talmudic literature (see Charles Copher, "Three Thousand Years of Biblical Interpretation," *Journal of the Interdenominational Theological Center* 13 [1986]: 225–46). Similarly the Midrashic treatment of Egyptian words within the Hebrew Canon was to shift the emphasis away from Egyptian to Greek explanations of these terms (see G. Vermes, "Bible and Midrash: Early Old Testament Exegesis," in *The Cambridge History of the Bible*, vol. 1, *From the Beginnings to Jerome*, ed. Peter R. Ackroyd and C. F. Evans [Cambridge: Cambridge University Press, 1970], 203–5).

13. E.g., Justo L. Gonzalez, *A History of Christian Thought* (Nashville: Abingdon, 1970), 175; Paul Tillich, *A History of Christian Thought frcm Its Judaic and Hellenistic Origins to Existentialism*, ed. Carl E. Braaten (New York: Simon and Schuster, 1969), 55f.; and Williston Walker, *A History of the Christian Church*, 4th ed. (New York: Scribner's, 1985), 87–89.

14. See, for example, David Tuesday Adamo, "The Place of Africa and Africans in the Old Testament and Its Environment" (Ph.D. diss., Baylor University, 1986); Robert A. Bennett, Jr., "Africa and the Biblical Period," *Harvard Theological Review* 64 (1971): 501–24; Charles B. Copher, "The Black Man in the Bîblical World," *The Journal of the Interdenominational Theological Center* 1 (1974): 7–16; Cheikh Anta Diop, *The African Origin of*

ies the next step, namely to examine the significance of the presence of African individuals and nations within the text. The current investigation, therefore, considers two very crucial questions. The first is: What do the references to ancient African nations and individuals tell us about how ancient Israel perceived these people? The second is: How do these perceptions help us to understand better the intention of the writers of the Hebrew Canon in utilizing these people?

I shall begin this study by identifying the particular African nations in question. Next I shall examine poetic passages in the prophetic, psalmic, and wisdom literatures that mention these African nations. This will lead to a grouping of characteristics of ancient Israel's perceptions of ancient Africa.[15] The study will then move to narratives in which individual Africans appear, with a focus on their function(s) within the particular narrative. Integral to this investigation, therefore, will be an examination of the values undergirding the story/narrative—that is, those foundational human values that help the narrative make sense. In this regard I will demonstrate how the principles and characteristics of ancient Israel's view of ancient Africa, which are discovered in the poetic sections, are operative in the roles performed by and ascribed to these individuals within the narratives.[16]

In examining these narratives I will first focus upon those in which the significance of the character is readily apparent by virtue of the narrator's comments. Next, I will direct attention to those passages where narrative clues are absent. My task will be to provide fresh insights into such texts.[17]

Civilization: Myth or Reality? (Westport, Conn.: Lawrence Hill, 1974); Alfred G. Dunston, *The Black Man in the Old Testament and Its World* (Philadelphia: Dorrace, 1974); Chancellor Williams, *The Destruction of Black Civilization: Great Issues of a Race from 4500 B.C. to 2000 A.D.* (Chicago: Third World, 1976).

15. Many of the prophetic statements regarding the subject appear either in the "accusations" segments of judgment speeches or in oracles against the foreign nations. On first reading one might get the impression that the view of ancient Africa was solely negative, as depicted in these units. However, the assumption in reading these passages must be that that which the prophets decry has its basis in the actions of the people. Thus, in many instances it will be necessary to reinterpret these statements in terms of what they imply about Israel's normative behavior and perceptions of ancient African nations.

16. In many respects this work is similar to the method advocated and performed by Phyllis Trible in her seminal article, "Depatriarchalizing in Biblical Interpretation," *Journal of the American Academy of Religion* 41 (1973): 30–48; also relevant is Trible's concept of "clues in the text," discussed in her *God and the Rhetoric of Sexuality*, Overtures to Biblical Theology, vol. 2 (Philadelphia: Fortress, 1978). In fact there are many similarities between the work of reclaiming African influence and the tasks undertaken by women in "reclaiming the text" from interpretation fostered by Eurocentric male interests. By the same token we are drawn to some of the same passages. In these instances there is the chance for complementarity in the assault upon racist, classist, and sexist oppression.

17. It should be noted at the outset that many of these poetic and narrative passages have a history of interpretation that appears to be grounded more in modern Western racial views than in Israel's perception of ancient Africans. These interpretations will be challenged on the basis of the evidence provided by this study.

Identification of the African Nations

I will begin by focusing upon those African nations with which ancient Israel came into contact. In this study the term *African* refers to
those nations that are located on the continent of Africa and that ancient Israelites designated as related to them. In order to make the study
manageable, therefore, the major nations to be considered are Egypt,
Cush, and Sheba.[18]

Genesis 10 is the major starting point for the identification of ancient
African nations that had a relationship to ancient Israel. In using Genesis 10, however, the reader must keep in mind that this chapter is a
composite of at least two different sources, J and P.[19]

The J passages are generally designated as 10:8-19, 24-30. The P
passages are generally designated as 10:1-7, 20-23, and 31-33.[20] On the
one hand, one sees from this breakdown that the chapter begins and ends
with P, while the J passages are interpolated into the P passages. On the
other hand, if one examines the differences in the formulaic ways the J (X
became the father of Y, who built . . .) and P (the sons of X) passages speak
of these nations, it becomes clear that the writers had different intentions
in their listings. The picture is further complicated in that Egypt and Cush
appear in both the J and P passages, but the relationship of Egypt and
Cush to each other is different in the two sources.

According to J, Egypt,[21] Cush,[22] and Canaan hold major influence
over various nations/city-states throughout Asia Minor, the Mediterranean, and on into Africa. This is seen by the formula "X was the father

---

18. See the studies listed in note 13, above.

19. Standard source-critical investigations of the composition of the Pentateuch argue
that at least four writers or schools of thought are represented. J, or the Jahwist (usually
dated in the mid–tenth century B.C.E. and viewed as a polemicist for the monarchy during
the time of Solomon), and P, the Priestly Writer (usually dated in the fifth century B.C.E.
and viewed as a polemicist for the theocracy in postexilic times), are found in Genesis 10.

20. See George W. Coats, *Genesis with an Introduction to Narrative*, Forms of the Old
Testament Literature, vol. 1 (Grand Rapids, Mich.: Eerdmans, 1983), 89–93; and Gordon J.
Wenham, *Genesis 1–15*, Word Biblical Commentary, vol. 1 (Waco, Tex.: Word, 1987), 210–
32. For additional works on this topic, see chap. 6 of this volume, especially the footnotes
accompanying the section entitled "Old Testament Genealogies."

21. In the listing in 10:13-14 there is reference to Egypt having "influence" over Euro-
pean territories. This is consistent with other ancient migration theories (see Martin Bernal,
Black Athena: The Afro-Asiatic Roots of Classical Civilization [New Brunswick, N.J.: Rutgers
University, 1987]).

22. The J passage on Cush in Gen. 10:8-12 is used to argue for a second Cush in
Arabia or Mesopotamia, since Cush is listed as having relationship with Babel, Accad,
and Nineveh. It should first be noted that the passage states that Cush begat Nimrod, a
mighty warrior who built these locations. By the same token the passage does not say Cush
was in these places. Thus, it appears that the writer is speaking more of an economic and
political influence of Cush on Mesopotamia. For further discussion of this African influence
see Modupe Oduyoye, *The Sons of the Gods and the Daughters of Men: An Afro-Asiatic
Interpretation of Genesis 1–11* (Maryknoll, N.Y.: Orbis, 1987), 24–27.

of Y," with Y being various city-states of little influence in the tenth century B.C.E. It thus appears that J is bespeaking the extent of the political and economic influence of these nations within these territories. This is in line with what J does in arguing for the foundations of cities and territories in Genesis 4 and 11. This also fits Solomonic times when these are the major nations on the scene.[23]

It is widely recognized that the P passage of the Table of Nations lists Egypt as one of the "sons of Ham" along with Cush, Put, and Canaan (vv. 6-7). This is buttressed by the Psalmists' designation of Egypt as being in the "land/tents of Ham" (Pss. 78:51 and 105:23). Unlike in J, however, these African nations are not the major nations; rather they are depicted only as elements within one branch of humanity, that of Ham. In addition, while the J passages in Genesis 10 bespeak political influence, the P passages seem only to list genealogical relationships. Thus, while J presents a picture of primary African influence within the world, P depicts a world in which African influence is diminished, which would be the case under Persian rule.

These observations are important for two reasons. First, they demonstrate that throughout ancient Israel's history the writers had to depict the African nations' influence upon and relationship to Israel. Second, they show us that Israel always viewed Egypt and Cush as African nations, and never viewed them as other than that. What the ancient writers differed on was the amount of importance these nations had in the overall scheme of things, which admittedly varied through the centuries.

Finally, the location of Sheba is much in dispute. Most geographers place it in the Arabian Peninsula because it is mentioned in the records of Tiglath-Pileser IV and because of similarities between the names Sheba and Sabeans.[24] A case can be made for locating it in Africa on several grounds. It should first be noted that in Genesis 10 Sheba appears in both J and P (vv. 7 and 28). In the first notation it is listed as Hamite. In the second it is under Eber, which P secondarily connects with the line of Shem. Even there, however, it is listed next to Ophir, which many have speculated to be in Africa and which is also mentioned in 1 Kings 10 as a distant land with which Solomon traded from Ezion-geber.[25]

Second, Psalm 72:10 notes Sheba in connection with Seba. This is significant for two reasons. First, both locations are in parallelism with Tarshish, giving the sense of expanse from Europe on the north to Africa on the south.[26] Second, Seba is mentioned in Isaiah 43:3 as being in the

---

23. Note that 10:14 assigns the Philistines to the Egyptian sphere of influence.

24. IDB, 4:311–12, s.v. "Sheba, Queen of."

25. IDB, 3:605–6, s.v. "Ophir."

26. This understanding of the reference to Sheba in Ps. 72 is in contrast to that of A. A. Anderson, *Psalms 1–72*, New Century Bible Commentary (Grand Rapids, Mich.: Eerdmans,

area of Cush and Egypt. We can conclude that Sheba in several contexts is associated with the Hamite line and/or other nations within Africa.

Thus it appears that the designation of Egypt, Cush, and Sheba as African nations holds. The attempts to argue for Arabian Peninsula locations for the latter two can be understood as instances of the de-Africanization tendency.

African Nations in the Poetry of the Hebrew Canon

I now take up the investigation of how Egypt, Cush, and Sheba are utilized in the poetic passages of the Hebrew Canon. The first way in which they are used is to designate the *farthest places to the south*. This appears to be the intention of the writer of Esther 1:1, which lists the extent of Ahasuerus's territory as being from "India to Ethiopia."

We also find these African nations in the list of the places where the Israelites and Judeans in the diaspora are found. Such is the case in Isaiah 11:11, which states, "On that day the Lord will extend his hand yet a second time to recover the remnant which is left of his people, from Assyria, from Egypt, from Pathros, from Cush." By the same token Zephaniah 3:10 states,

> From beyond the rivers of Ethiopia
> my suppliants, the daughter of my dispersed ones,
> shall bring my offering.

In both of the above instances it appears that the writers refer to distant points in Africa as a way of depicting the full extent of the return.[27] In other words, the return from the south is going to be not just from Egypt, but from Pathros, which Jeremiah 44 suggests is in southern Egypt, and also from Cush, which is below Pathros.

There is an interesting twist, or double-sidedness, to this first characteristic usage of these African nations. On the one hand, for Israel they represent the southernmost borders of the "world." On the other hand, their usage in this way, when related to the return from exile, suggests that the deity's power goes all the way to the "ends of the earth." In other words, the ancient hearer/reader of these words would have been immediately struck by how far-ranging was this power of return.

1972), 1:523, and Mitchell Dahood, *Psalms II:51–100*, Anchor Bible Series, vol. 17 (Garden City: Doubleday, 1968), 182. The above interpretation of "from Europe to Africa" fits more the sense of the psalm that is arguing for the spread of the "kingdom" (see Arthur Weiser, *Psalms*, Old Testament Library [Philadelphia: Westminster, 1962], 504).

27. Again we see the pattern of north, south, east, and west, which was noted above. See Otto Kaiser, *Isaiah 1–12*, Old Testament Library (Philadelphia: Westminster, 1972), 165; John D. N. Watts, *Isaiah 1–33*, Word Biblical Commentary, vol. 24 (Waco, Tex.: Word, 1985).

Second, Egypt is depicted as a political *hope for military assistance and protection* for both Israel and Judah. This is seen in passages such as the following:

Ephraim is like a dove,
   silly and without sense,
   calling to Egypt [Hos. 7:11].

"Woe to the rebellious children," says the Lord,
"who carry out a plan, but not mine; . . .
who set out to go down to Egypt,
   without asking for my counsel,
to take refuge in the protection of Pharaoh,
   and to seek shelter in the shadow of Egypt" [Isa. 30:1-2].

Woe to those who go down to Egypt for help
   and rely on horses,
who trust in chariots because they are many
   and in horsemen because they are very strong. . . .
The Egyptians are men, and not God [Isa. 31:1, 3; italics mine].

And [Egypt] shall never again be *the reliance of the house of Israel* [Ezek. 29:16; italics mine].

Similarly, Ezekiel 30:13-19, another "oracle against a foreign nation," not only uses the destruction of the Egyptian military and political might as the main metaphor for destruction, but it also couples this with the divine self-revelation formula, "Then they will know that I am Yahweh!" As these citations suggest, this Israelite trust in and respect for Egyptian political might were conditions that lasted over the centuries from preexilic times on through exilic times. This reliance was based upon Egypt's ability to withstand external invasion and its long history of independence.

The vehemence of these objections to Israel's dependence on the Egyptians bespeaks the extent to which these prophets felt they had to struggle against this tendency. Most scholarly attention given to these diatribes against trusting on Egypt for military and political support has been in the direction of establishing the historical background of the judgment speeches.[28] Scholars tend to ignore the implications this

---

28. See Robert P. Carroll, *Jeremiah*, Old Testament Library (Philadelphia: Westminster, 1986), 139–40; Ernest W. Nicholson, *Jeremiah 1–25*, Cambridge Bible Commentary (Cambridge: Cambridge University Press, 1973), 40; J. A. Thompson, *The Book of Jeremiah*, New International Commentary on the Old Testament, no. 2 (Grand Rapids, Mich.: Eerdmans, 1980), 186; James L. Mays, *Hosea*, Old Testament Library (Philadelphia: Westminster, 1969), 107–9; Gerhard von Rad, *The Message of the Prophets* (New York: Harper and Row, 1965), 114–15; John H. Hayes and Stuart Irvine, *Isaiah: His Times and His Preaching* (Nashville: Abingdon, 1987), 340–44; Watts, *Isaiah 1–33*, 395–96; Walther Zimmerli, *Ezekiel 2*, Hermenia (Philadelphia: Fortress, 1983), 102–5.

reliance has for highlighting the role of Africa in the history of Israel. Jeremiah calls the Egyptians "those in whom you trust" (2:37),
and Ezekiel refers to Egypt as "the reliance of the house of Israel"
(29:16); these epithets suggest the high regard that Israel had for African
nations.[29]

A third way in which these poetic passages refer to the African
nations is in terms of their *wealth*. Such statements appear from several different centuries. Often these statements come as instances of
simile, metaphor, or contrast, in order for the writer to make a point
about another matter. In the eighth century Isaiah made note of
the economic state of Egypt by referring to its "workers in combed
flax... weavers of white cotton" (19:5).[30] During the exile Ezekiel observed that Egypt was a place of "fine embroidered linen" (27:7),[31] while
Deutero-Isaiah, a contemporary of Ezekiel, remarked on the "wealth of
Egypt and the merchandise of Ethiopia and the Sabeans, men of stature"
(45:14).[32]

During the postexilic period the writer of one of the discourses of
Job, in attempting to demonstrate the importance and value of wisdom,
noted that "the topaz of Ethiopia cannot compare with it" (28:19).[33] Even
during Maccabean times the writer of Daniel referred to the "treasures of
gold and of silver, and all the precious things of Egypt and the Libyans
and the Ethiopians" (11:43).[34]

The Psalmist also makes reference to African wealth. Psalm 68:28-
35 speaks of foreign nations bringing tribute and worshiping Yahweh in

---

29. The prophetic fight against this Israelite reliance upon Egypt and Cush for military
protection could also explain the extremism and bizarre quality of some of the prophets'
actions and speeches against Egypt. For example, the symbolic act of Isaiah mentioned
in chapter 20, when he is reported to have walked nude for three years, and the use of
sexual innuendo by Ezekiel in referring to the Egyptians in chapter 16 could have been
necessitated by the prophets' attempt to combat a well-entrenched attitude of the people.

30. Watts, *Isaiah 1–33*, 253–54.

31. Walther Eichrodt calls this the best type of sailing gear (*Ezekiel*, Old Testament
Library [Philadelphia: Westminster, 1970], 383). Zimmerli observes that such luxury was
characteristic of the New Kingdom (*Ezekiel 2*, 58).

32. While there is disagreement as to how this unit relates to its context, there is total
agreement as to the description being one of opulence. See John McKenzie, *Second Isaiah*,
Anchor Bible Series, no. 20 (Garden City, N.Y.: Doubleday, 1968), 83; Claus Westermann,
Isaiah 40–66, Old Testament Library (Philadelphia: Westminster, 1969), 169–70; and R. N.
Whybray, *Isaiah 40–66*, New Century Bible (Greenwood, S.C.: Attic, 1975), 109.

33. Given ancient Israel's high regard for African wisdom (see below) this comparison is full of symbolism. Interestingly, while Norman Habel points out that the "source"
(*maqom*) of gold and silver referred to in 28:1 is to be understood as Ophir and Sheba, he
neither connects these with Africa nor mentions the irony in the metaphor of verse 19. See
Habel's *The Book of Job*, Cambridge Bible Commentary (Cambridge: Cambridge University Press, 1975), 146–49; idem, *Job*, Old Testament Library (Philadelphia: Westminster,
1985), 395–98. So also Gustavo Gutiérrez, *On Job: God-Talk and the Suffering of the Innocent*
(Maryknoll, N.Y.: Orbis, 1987), 38.

34. See Norman Porteous, *Daniel*, Old Testament Library (Philadelphia: Westminster,
1965), 165–68.

the Jerusalem sanctuary. In depicting this, however, only two nations are listed: Egypt is to bring bronze[35] and Cush is to "stretch out her hands," in other words bring its possessions (v. 31).[36] Since there are only these two nations mentioned as bringing tribute to Yahweh, the Psalmist must be implying that the mention of these two bringing "wealth" would suffice in making the point of how far-reaching (geographically) and how rich (economically) will be this universal appeal of Yahwism. Thus, the people of that day must have viewed these nations as wealthy.

Along with their wealth, these African nations were respected for their *wisdom*, which is a fourth type of reference to these nations. As Isaiah 19:11-15, one of the "oracles against Egypt," attests in the section announcing the punishment:

> The princes of Zo'an are utterly foolish;
>> the wise counselors of Pharaoh give stupid counsel....
> Where then are your wise men?
>> Let them tell you and make known
>> what the LORD of hosts has purposed against Egypt.
> The princes of Zo'an have become fools,
>> and the princes of Memphis are deluded.

Thus, the sign that destruction will come on Egypt is given in terms of the confounding of the wise. In other words, the prophet appeals to the aspect of this nation that Israel holds in high esteem, wisdom, to portray graphically how great the devastation will be.

One reason for these references to African wisdom as a paradigm for destruction/punishment could be the heavy reliance of ancient Israel upon ancient African wisdom. Scholars have long pointed out the strong similarities between Israelite wisdom literature and that of Egypt.[37] Thus, it could very well be that again the intensity of the prophetic attack upon this dimension of the life and culture of Egypt could be in direct proportion to its esteem in ancient Israel.[38]

---

35. Anderson (*Psalms 1-72*, 497) notes that bronze was usually imported into Egypt; thus the reference here must not be to the natural resources of the area. Rather it speaks to the materials that were held high and that the rich were able to buy.

36. So Dahood, *Psalms II*, 229; and Anderson, *Psalms*, 498. It should be noted that this text has a long history of interpretation within the African American religious community, most especially in antebellum preaching, although not usually in the sense of African wealth.

37. See for example James L. Crenshaw, *Old Testament Wisdom: An Introduction* (Atlanta: John Knox, 1981), 212–36; William McKane, *Proverbs: A New Approach* (Philadelphia: Westminster, 1977), 51f.; Roland E. Murphy, *Wisdom Literature: Job, Proverbs, Ruth, Canticles, Ecclesiastes and Esther* (Grand Rapids, Mich.: Eerdmans, 1981), 9–10; Gerhard von Rad, *Wisdom in Israel* (New York: Abingdon, 1978), 15, 26; and R. B. Y. Scott, *The Way of Wisdom in the Old Testament* (New York: Macmillan, 1971), 23–47, 58–63.

38. As has been noted above, this line of argumentation is based upon the understanding that the function of the details found in the announcement of punishment within the various judgment speeches in the prophetic literature is to depict in the most graphic

A fifth way in which these poetic passages speak about these African nations is in terms of their being the *norm for valuation*. One of the earlier such statements is found in Amos 9:7, in which Yahweh states, "Are you not to me like the Cushites, O Israel?" There has been much argument as to the intention of this statement, namely whether it reflects positively or negatively upon the Cushites. Most scholars have argued that it is negative as regards the Cushites.[39] Gene Rice has shown that these arguments seem to be based more in the exegetes' own negative view of Africans than in the sense of the text. He has also argued convincingly that the statement is to be taken as reflecting positively upon the Cushites.[40]

Further, Regina Smith has argued that, on the basis of a historical reconstruction of the eighth century, Cush was in control of Egypt and one of the major political and military forces of Amos's day. Thus, this statement must be understood as a positive reference to Cush.[41]

Similarly, Jeremiah's famous set of rhetorical questions in 13:23,

> Would[42] the Cushite change his skin, or the leopard his spots?
> So also you who have learned to do evil could[43] do good!
> [translation mine]

has been the subject of much debate as to their positive or negative intention.[44] Most of the negative interpretations of this passage appear to stress the use of *ykl*, "to be able, can," in the concluding part of the

---

terms possible the nature of the destruction. In order to accomplish this task, the prophets appeal to the image that is the most potent in the life of the people. For a further discussion of this characterization of the use of motifs in the announcement of punishment in prophetic judgment speeches, see P. Riemann, "Desert and Return to Desert in the Pre-Exilic Prophets" (Ph.D. diss., Harvard University, 1964).

39. The treatment by James L. Mays is characteristic. He states, "Precisely why Amos chose the Cushites for comparison with Israel must unfortunately remain somewhat obscure.... On the evidence one can say no more than that the Cushites were a distant, different folk whom Israelites *knew mostly as slaves.*... What the comparison does is to humiliate Israel completely" (*Amos*, Old Testament Library [Philadelphia: Westminster, 1976], 157; italics mine).

40. Gene Rice, "Was Amos a Racist?" *The Journal of Religious Thought* 35 (1978): 35–44.

41. Regina Smith, "An Afro-centric Perspective on Amos 9:7a" (Paper delivered at the annual meeting of the Society of Biblical Literature, Anaheim, Calif., November 1989). The article is to appear under the same title in the fall 1991 issue of the *Journal of the Interdenominational Theological Center*.

42. It should be noted that the Hebrew uses a *hē*-interrogative with the imperfect, *hyhpk*, as the verb in this first clause, which is also understood for the second clause. There is no use of *ykl*, can, in this part of the verse. Thus, the clause should be translated as either "The Cushite change his skin...?" or, as I have proposed, "Would the Cushite change his skin...?" As I argue below, this is more in line with the argument the prophet is making.

43. This sense of being contrary to fact is noted with the *gam-correlativum* in the first part of the clause (see IDB, 169c).

44. Carroll calls this an argument "charged with ideological matters" (*Jeremiah*, 305), but he never makes clear what they are. Likewise, Thompson states, "A negative answer must be given" (*Jeremiah*, 374). Neither of them, however, speaks to the unthinkable nature of the claim; nor do they discuss why the example is chosen by Jeremiah.

accusation. This is seen in the fact that they usually add the word *can* to the beginning of the rhetorical question (i.e., "Can the Cushite . . . ?") although it is lacking in the Hebrew. Because the implied answer to the rhetorical questions of changing is no, they conclude, therefore, that the passage bespeaks negative or unfortunate situations of inability to change.

In so doing these exegetes ignore the basis of Jeremiah's charge, namely that the people of Judah, the addressees in this diatribe, are *lmdy hr*, "learners of evil." Thus, what is being charged is that the Cushite and the leopard have learned the advantages of being who they are, rulers of territories who are respected by and awesome to their neighbors. In a similar manner, those who have lived the life of sinning have learned the advantages of being sinners. In other words, Jeremiah's argument—namely, that there is no incentive for change on the part of the people—can be recognized only if we understand that this is the case for the Cushite. To Jeremiah and to his listeners, it is unthinkable that the Cushites would want to change the way they look. Thus, the use of the Cushite in this passage suggests that Israel should use the Cushites as "yardsticks" for assessing themselves.[45]

Another such passage that cites Africans as the basis for valuation of Israel is Isaiah 43:3. Within the oracle of salvation, Deutero-Isaiah is trying to convince the people of Israel how much Yahweh loves them. One of his proofs is the actions of Yahweh in ransoming Israel with the three African nations, Egypt, Cush, and Sheba.[46] In this instance, not only does the motive clause in verse 3b ("Because you are precious in my sight") make this clear, but the dynamics of the situation also bespeak it. In other words, the mention of these three nations being used as "ransom for Israel" could only be of comfort to Israel if these nations were highly valued.

Similarly, the Psalms contain the notion that when Cush accepts Yahwism, a high point will be reached. This notion is seen in Psalm 68:31 where Egypt and Cush are specifically listed as bringing gifts to and worshiping Yahweh. In other words, true universalism will have

---

45. Bishop Dunston's treatment of this unit is classic. He claims that it proves beyond a doubt that the desire for blacks to be white is unnatural (see *The Black Man*, 47).

46. While McKenzie notes that this passage is intended to show that Israel is "highly valued to Yahweh," he finds it strange that Egypt should be used here and in Ezek. 29:17-20 as the medium for exchange (*Second Isaiah*, 50–51). What becomes apparent from the current study is that it is the value that Israel places upon these African nations that is at the basis of the argument of Deutero-Isaiah.

Another clue to the correctness of this reading is seen in the use of prophetic reversal by the writer in the treatment of these African nations. Isaiah of Jerusalem, in chaps. 19–20, used the prediction of the downfall of these nations as a sign to Judah that its basis of hope in their military might was hopeless. In this passage, Deutero-Isaiah uses the same motif; the fall of these African nations is the symbol of Israel's salvation. In this prophetic book, prophetic reversal is also used in the treatment of "wilderness" and the like.

been achieved when these two nations come to accept Yahweh as their deity.

Thus, one sees that throughout the poetic sections of the prophetic, psalmic, and wisdom literatures there are numerous references to Egypt and Cush that seem to cite these nations as standards against which to evaluate Israel. Whether it is to give the example of the vastness of territory to be considered, military might and power, wealth, wisdom, or as a point of comparison for Israel in which its esteem is boosted, these nations are cited as paradigmatic. In this one sees that not only is there African presence within the Hebrew Canon, but the significance of this presence appears to be that Israel utilizes these nations as the "yardstick" for comparison.

African Individuals in the Narratives of the Hebrew Canon

It is now time to turn our attention to the appearance of African individuals and nations within Hebrew Canon narratives to see whether the paradigms uncovered in the poetic passages are operative there also. Since there is neither time nor space in this study to examine all such narratives, I will simply review a few examples in this context. I will not explore examples that have received special treatment elsewhere in this volume, unless my treatment offers something new to the discussion.

There are several narratives in which an African functions to raise the esteem of an Israelite. One such instance is the stories in Genesis 16 and 21 that feature Abraham (or Abram), Sarah (or Sarai), and Hagar. In these stories Abraham's wife, Sarah, has an Egyptian servant, Hagar, working for her. In the first narrative, since Sarah is barren, she offers Hagar to Abraham as a way to fulfill Yahweh's promise that Abraham will have many descendants (Gen. 15:5b). On the one hand, the reader must assume that Hagar is the very best person Sarah can find to help fulfill the promise. To assume otherwise misses the significance of the union between Abraham and Hagar.

On the other hand, this story must be understood within the context of the writer speaking about the prehistory of the nation Israel. Given the political and economic realities of ancient Egypt and ancient Israel, both in the time the story was written (tenth century B.C.E.) and in the time it is describing (nineteenth to seventeenth centuries B.C.E.), the Israelites' having an Egyptian as a servant was most uncommon. In addition, since Abraham and Sarah are depicted as nomads, having a servant at all is most unusual. The premise of the story, then, is that the forebears of the nation Israel were rich enough to afford an Egyptian servant. Thus, the mention of Hagar functions as a mechanism to raise the esteem of the forebears.[47]

Another Pentateuchal narrative that makes mention of an African is Numbers 12:1-10, the passage in which Moses' Cushite wife is mentioned. This passage is controversial and frequently misinterpreted. This is because most exegetes hold 12:1 to be a totally separate argument unrelated to verses 2ff. Most of the expositions of this passage revolve around either of two themes. The first is the attempt to de-Africanize this woman, to argue that she must come from some Cush other than the Cush in Africa.[48] The other type of argument, which affirms this woman's African heritage, concentrates on the conflict between Miriam and Moses in regard to this marriage and views it as a racially motivated conflict.[49]

Verse 2 of this passage concerns the different status of Moses over against his siblings. Miriam asks, "Hasn't Yahweh spoken not only through Moses but also through us?" The implication is that Moses views himself as having a higher status than his siblings. The response of the deity to this complaint, found in verses 6-8, confirms that Moses is indeed of a higher status than Miriam and Aaron.

Placed in this light, it would appear that the reference to the Cushite wife in verse 1 is the first piece of evidence offered by Miriam in her charge that Moses has an inflated position. In other words, she claims that Moses' marriage to the Cushite woman may increase his social status, but it should not increase his status before Yahweh. After all, Yahweh also speaks to Miriam and Aaron. Read in this light, Miriam's reference to the Cushite wife is not a racist claim against this woman; rather it is a disclaimer that association with the Cushites is not the prime way to gain status. The prime way is to be addressed by Yahweh.

---

47. This argument takes issue with the traditional classist interpretations of Hagar, the Egyptian servant/maid of Sarah. Most of these interpretations, including feminist and womanist readings, concentrate on the socio-economic designation, maid, and ignore the ethnological designation, Egyptian, and, thus, miss the nuancing suggested here. For examples of the former, see Phyllis Trible, "Hagar: The Desolation of Rejection," in her *Texts of Terror: Literary Feminist Readings of Biblical Narratives*, Overtures to Biblical Theology (Philadelphia: Fortress Press, 1984), 9–37, and J. Cheryl Exum, " 'Mother in Israel': A Familiar Story Reconsidered," in Letty M. Russell, ed., *Feminist Interpretation of the Bible* (Philadelphia: Westminster Press, 1985), 76–77. For examples of the latter, see Renita J. Weems, "A Mistress, a Maid, and No Mercy (Hagar and Sarah)," in her *Just a Sister Away: A Womanist Vision of Women's Relationships in the Bible* (San Diego: LuraMedia, 1988), 1–22, and Katie G. Cannon, "On Remembering Who We Are," in Ella P. Mitchell, ed., *Those Preachin' Women* (Valley Forge, Pa.: Judson, 1984), 43–50. For a treatment of the historical-critical dimensions of this complex see the article by John W Waters in this volume.

48. See Martin Noth, *Numbers*, Old Testament Library (Philadelphia: Westminster Press, 1968).

49. For example, see Cain Hope Felder, *Troubling Biblical Waters: Race, Class, and Family* (Maryknoll, N.Y.: Orbis Books, 1989), 42, and Phyllis Trible, "Bringing Miriam out of the Shadows," *Bible Review* 1 (1989): 21–22.

This interpretation appears to be sound on two grounds. First is the fact that the punishment meted out to Miriam as a result of this challenge to the status of Moses is that she is turned "leprous, white as snow" (v. 10). Thus, the punishment for complaining about Cushites as a means of status makes her the exact opposite of the Cushite, white as snow.[50] This ironic twist could not be accomplished unless verse 1 were part of the unit. Second, the interpretation rests upon the understanding that in the Hebrew Canon to be white as snow is a curse.[51]

Another set of passages that rely on the association with Africans as a way to establish the positive status of a biblical character is the fourfold reference to Solomon marrying the "daughter of Pharaoh." In the first instance (1 Kings 3:1), the mention of the marriage comes on the heels of the notice that the kingdom was established in the hands of Solomon (2:46b). The impression is that the marriage is one of the first major official acts of the king. The second notice (1 Kings 9:16) is a parenthetical interpolation into the details of the forced levy of Solomon and is used to explain how Gezer became part of his territory. Interestingly, the notice is in conjunction with a mention of Egyptian military might and of the fact that Pharaoh gives conquered territory to Solomon as part of his daughter's dowry. The third notice of the marriage (1 Kings 9:24) is used to illustrate Solomon's wealth and building activities, while in the fourth instance (1 Kings 11:1) the marriage begins the list of foreign wives in the Deuteronomic negative evaluation of Solomon.

Most researchers have concentrated on the identification of the Pharaoh who made such an alliance with Solomon.[52] They also note that while the practice of the Egyptian Pharaohs was to consolidate their power through political marriages, this always occurred through their sons and not through their daughters. In fact the Amarna letters[53] attest to the fact that such marriages as the one credited to Solomon were forbidden.[54] Surely such was known to the readers of the day. Thus, one must ask, what function is served by having such notices of Solomon marrying an Egyptian princess?

---

50. So Felder, *Troubling Biblical Water*, 42.

51. Such is seen in the oft-mistranslated Isaiah 1:18. In this verse, part of a judgment speech, the charge begins with the word ʿm, "if." Thus, the prophet proclaims, "Come to judgment, if your sins are as scarlet [= negative], then they will be made white as snow [= the punishment]." Since all other instances of ʿm found in this unit are read as "if," there appears to be no reason, other than the desire to keep the phrase "white as snow" as a blessing, to translate it here as "contrary to fact/though," as do most exegetes.

52. For example, see Bright, *History*, 212; A. Malamat, "Aspects of the Foreign Policies of David and Solomon," *Journal of Near Eastern Studies* 22 (1963): 10–11.

53. These letters, found at Tell el-Amarna in Egypt, contain diplomatic correspondence between the kings of the city-states in Syria-Palestine and the Pharaohs of Egypt during the eleventh century B.C.E., when Egypt controlled that territory.

54. See the discussion in John Gray, *I & II Kings*, Old Testament Library (Philadelphia: Westminster, 1970), 118.

It would appear that in stressing this marriage these writers are making a twofold claim. On the one hand, the writers are making the claim not only that Solomon adopted the governing practices of the Egyptians, political alliance through intermarriage, but also that he was able to achieve what other nations could not, in this instance the marriage to an Egyptian princess. Therefore, Solomon's esteem is raised through this association. He can achieve the impossible. On the other hand, he is portrayed as one who can take the Egyptian governing model and perfect it; in other words, he can play their game better than they. Thus, this four-fold notice of Solomon's marrying an Egyptian princess functions as the prime example of Solomon's diplomatic genius. This is especially seen in that while all of his other wives are listed in terms of their nationality (11:1b), this woman is listed in terms of her gentilic relationship.[55]

Another narrative in which Solomon's esteem is established in terms of his relationship with an African woman is found in 1 Kings 10 in the visit of the Queen of Sheba. Again, while most research has focused on the historical questions of the visit and the visitor,[56] the question of esteem and valuation appears to be foremost in the minds of the writer and final editor of these materials.

As one looks at the narrative it appears that there are several keys to the question of valuation. First is the fact that the writer is trying to establish, or further ground, Solomon as one who is wise. The vehicle used is that of having him pass the test of African riddles and wisdom. The assumption, therefore, of the narrator is that this is the most difficult test to be posed. The African queen states: "The report was true which I heard in my own land of your affairs and of your wisdom, but I did not believe the reports until I came and my own eyes had seen it; and behold, the half was not told me; your wisdom and prosperity surpass the report which I heard" (vv. 6-7). To the ancient reader that speech was seen as true validation of Solomon as the wise and prosperous king. Thus, this narrative uses as its basis for argument the high value ancient Israel placed upon African wisdom. Similarly, its function is to firmly establish in the mind of the reader the importance or value of Solomon.[57] In this

---

55. When women are so identified, the intention of the writer is to stress the political aspect of her identity. See in this regard my argument on the genealogy of Bathsheba in 2 Sam. 11:3 (*David in Love and War: The Pursuit of Power in 2 Samuel 10–12*, Journal for the Study of Old Testament Supplement Series, no. 75 [Sheffield, Eng.: Sheffield Academic Press, 1990], 87).

56. See for example Simon J. de Vries, *1 Kings*, Word Biblical Commentary, no. 12 (Waco, Tex.: Word, 1985), 139; G. H. Jones, *1 and 2 Kings*, New Century Bible Commentary (Grand Rapids, Mich.: Eerdmans, 1984), 1:221; James A. Montgomery, *Kings*, International Critical Commentary (Edinburgh: T and T Clark, 1976), 215–16.

57. It is most interesting that while there are three narratives in 1 Kings that serve the purpose of validating Solomon as a master of wisdom (3:3-15, 16-28; 10:1-10, 13), two of them rely upon women as the key characters posing the most difficult problems or tests to be passed. Similarly, in the arrangement of the Solomonic traditions, both of these sets

regard the location of Sheba in Africa has more grounding, since there was no ancient Israelite veneration of Arabian wisdom. In other words, the narrative makes sense only if one sees this woman as an African.

By the same token this narrative utilizes the motif of the wealthy African. The queen comes laden with "a very great retinue, with camels bearing spices, and very much gold, and precious stones" (v. 2a). When Solomon shows her his royal palace, possessions, and the Temple, she is described as being in such a state that "there was no more spirit in her" (v. 5b). As with the instance of wisdom, his wealth is placed in comparison to hers. Thus, her reaction is another case of the utilization of comparison between an African and an Israelite for the purpose of certifying that the latter is "able."

As with the prophetic materials, most notably the treatment of Eze-kiel, the Chronicler negatively utilizes the motif of the military might of the African nations to show the power of Yahweh. In redacting the Deuteronomic materials in Kings, especially regarding battles where an African nation appears, the Chronicler makes Africans the foil of Yah-weh's power. In the instance of Shishak's attack upon Judah during the time of Rehoboam (2 Chron. 12:2-3; par. 1 Kings 14:25), the Chronicler adds key words, which are italicized in the following:

> In the fifth year of King Rehoboam, *because they had been unfaithful to Yahweh*, Shishak king of Egypt came up against Jerusalem *with twelve hundred chariots and sixty thousand horsemen. And the people were without number who came with him from Egypt—Libyans, Sukkim, and Cushites.*

In this way the Chronicler makes the theological claim that apostasy is the explanation for the attack, not the prowess of the Africans, and by implication that Yahweh is in control of the African military force and can use it to punish Israel.

The converse of this situation is accomplished in the Chronicler's redaction of the Asa materials. In this regard we read in 2 Chronicles 14:9-15 that "Zerah the Ethiopian came out against them with an army of a million men. . . . And Asa cried to Yahweh his God . . . so Yahweh defeated the Ethiopians before Asa and before Judah, and the Ethiopians fled."

This battle is not mentioned in the 1 Kings account of Asa. In this instance of 2 Chronicles, loyalty to Yahweh can lead to the defeat of a mighty army like that of the Cushites, even during the lifetime of a king like Asa, who had to pay Benhadad for assistance because he was threatened by Baasha (1 Kings 15:16-24; par. 2 Chron. 16:1-6). In other words, given the latter details regarding the reign of Asa and the motif of the military might of the Ethiopians, it becomes clear that belief in

---

of narratives serve as brackets, separating the negative reports (chaps. 1–2 and 11) from the positive (the Temple building and governance reports).

and reliance upon Yahweh are all that is needed, or so the Chronicler would like the reader to see.

Similar to the prophetic tendency to react against the influence of Egyptian wisdom on Israel, the P writer redacts the plague narratives in Exodus 7–10 in a most interesting manner. A characteristic of this redaction is that after Moses or Aaron performs a "sign" to convince Pharaoh to let the people go, the Egyptian magicians can at first replicate it.[58] Eventually this is not the case, demonstrating that Yahweh is even more powerful than they. Thus, the Exodus motif not only gives Yahweh the opportunity to establish an identity as God (Exod. 6:7), but one of the main ways of doing this is the debunking of Egyptian wisdom. It thus appears that one of the redactional aims of the P writer is to demonstrate this point graphically.[59] By the same token, the greatness of the feat of the Exodus is better grasped when one views ancient Israel's awe of the Egyptian military prowess.

Conclusion

Africans not only have a presence in the Israelite poetic and narrative materials—indeed, those materials show that Israel held African nations and individuals in very high regard. On the one hand, these nations represented the southernmost part of the world, as Israel knew it. They symbolized military might, political stability, and wealth. Their wisdom was highly regarded. These nations were utilized as a standard of measurement for Israel, which reveals that the authors and redactors of the texts viewed these nations and their leaders as having great value. If an Israelite wished to show approval of something or someone, favorable comparison to Africans was one way of doing that. Further, these African nations and leaders were used as foils to reveal how great Yahweh was.

On the other hand, not all writers of the Hebrew Canon were favorably disposed to this tendency to utilize African nations as the measurement of valuation and validation. Within the preexilic and some of the exilic prophetic traditions we see a constant attempt to fight against it. It appears that while the Deuteronomist readily utilizes the standard, the Chronicler and P attempt to minimize it or to use it negatively. Fi-

---

58. See Exod. 7:8-13, 20-24; 8:5-7, 16-19. Interestingly, while Z. Zevit does an excellent job in comparing the P redaction of the plague with the creation motif and its implications for P's portrayal of Egypt, he misses the structural implications noted here. The arguments in both pieces are complementary in their regard of P's anti-Egyptianizing (see Z. Zevit, "The Priestly Redaction and Interpretation of the Plague Narrative in Exodus," *Jewish Quarterly Review* 66 [1976]: 193–211).

59. See my treatment of this motif in more detail in *In the Beginning: The Pentateuch's Last Historian* (Louisville: Westminster/John Knox, forthcoming).

nally, we see that in both the attempts to utilize and those to minimize the influence of Africans and African nations, the motif is readily apparent.

The task that now lies ahead is to take these understandings of the use of Africans and African nations and apply them more systematically to other passages. In this way, new and possibly richer interpretations will be realized.

PART IV

Reinterpreting Biblical Texts

— 9 —

Who Was Hagar?

John W Waters

Introduction

Biblical stories have long provided a basis for research into the world of the ancient Near East. Often biblical research reflects contemporary interests and technology. There are many biblical stories that could serve to demonstrate this principle. One such story that has become rather popular in recent times is to be examined in this analysis. It is the story of Hagar, one of several wives of Abraham (Abram). Several feminist theologians have examined the Hagar cycle of stories: Some present Hagar as a very strong woman; others treat her as a weak, submissive slave. This wide divergence of opinion makes Hagar a prime subject of study. Rosemary Ruether, a feminist theologian, provides some insight for an investigation of the patriarchal period in which the Hagar cycle of stories is set. She writes:

> Feminist theology is engaged in a critique of the androcentrism and misogyny of patriarchal theology. What does this mean? First of all it means that, in patriarchal theology, the male is taken to be the normative and dominant representative of the human species. The male is the norm for imaging God, for defining anthropology, sin, redemption, and ministry. The female is seen as subordinate and auxiliary to the male. Therefore women never appear in patriarchal theology as representatives of humanity as such. Their normative position is that of absence and silence. When patriarchal theology mentions women, it does so to reinforce its definition of their "place" in its system.[1]

---

1. Rosemary R. Ruether, "The Future of Feminist Theology in the Academy," *Journal of the American Academy of Religion* 53, no. 4 (1985): 704. Elisabeth Schüssler Fiorenza

The story of Hagar, who bears a son for Abraham, is well-known. Most scholars seem to agree that she is a slave in the household of Abraham and Sarah (Sarai). A careful reading of the two biblical versions of this story (Gen. 16:1-6 and 21:8-21) suggests the need to reexamine some of the basic assumptions found in most of the studies of these stories, to posit some unique features in these stories, and to raise some historical questions that could clarify the role of Hagar. This threefold task constitutes the aim of the present analysis. One issue that is of paramount concern is the socio-economic status of Hagar, an Egyptian by birth, and it is proper to examine the long-held assumption that Hagar was a slave in the household of Abraham.

Much of the activity in the earlier sections of the Old Testament is set in North Africa. This fact is scarcely mentioned in the majority of commentaries written by European and American biblical scholars. The fact becomes clear if one studies the physical geography of the Bible or if one reads it with the African perspective in mind. That kind of study will reveal that the writers of the Old Testament underscore the importance of Africa in many places. For instance, the so-called Table of Nations (Gen. 10) provides the universe of the early Hebrew/Israelite traditions, and in that universe "the sons of Ham" (i.e., Egyptians) are major actors. Egypt, then, plays a special role in the life and development of the Israelites. These preliminary remarks on the role of Africa and Egypt in the Old Testament set the stage for the story of Abraham, Hagar, and Sarah.

Very early biblical traditions report that Abraham sojourned in Egypt. In Genesis 12 Abraham and Sarah journey to Egypt, and there Sarah is taken into Pharaoh's household. It is Yahweh, the God of Abraham, who brings the unnamed Egyptian Pharaoh to his senses, and he gives Sarah back to Abraham. The same story is presented several times (see Gen. 20:1-7; 26:6-11).

Tradition has it that Abraham is the "father" of the Hebrew nation. The story of the rise of the Hebrews, later to become known as the Israelites, is thought to begin with the "call experience" of Abraham in Genesis 12. Abraham is made heir to a promise made by Yahweh that out of him will come a great nation: "And I will make of you a great nation, and I will bless you, and make your name great, so that you will be a blessing" (Gen. 12:2). In Genesis 13 a further promise is made:

The Lord said to Abraham, after Lot had separated from him, "Lift up your eyes, and look from the place where you are, northward and southward and eastward and westward; for all the land which you see I will give to you and to your descendants forever. I will make your descendants as

provides a survey of the feminists' use of the Scriptures in her "The Ethics of Biblical Interpretation: Decentering Biblical Scholarship," *Journal of Biblical Literature* 107, no. 1 (1988): 3–17.

the dust of the earth; so that if one can count the dust of the earth, your descendants can be counted" [Gen. 13:14-16].

The barrenness of Abraham's first wife, Sarah, is attested in several traditions. The promise made to Abraham and Sarah's barrenness provide a context from which to examine several biblical concepts. Abraham is to become a blessed man, the founder of a great nation. He must be prosperous, live a long, productive life, and have sons. Yet his wife is barren. The Genesis storytellers are skillful in unfolding the resolution to this divine-human dilemma. It is clear that Abraham, at some point, must produce a male heir. When Hagar is introduced into the story, she is destined to become a surrogate mother. The Hagar cycle of stories appears in both the J (Yahwist [16:1-16]) and the E (Elohist [21:8-21]) strands. Hagar is presented as both an Egyptian maid of Sarah and as a slave within the household of Abraham. Sarah gives Hagar to Abraham in order that he may have an heir. Subsequently, Sarah, who is already in advanced years, has a son.

The stories are fascinating in themselves. Translators and commentators have made assumptions that heighten the fascination. European and American biblical scholars are in an apparent universal agreement that Hagar is an Egyptian slave under the control of Sarah. Nevertheless, these commentators have failed to deal with the chronology of events as these relate to the general history of the ancient Near East, and Egypt in particular. In addition, the socio-economic conditions of Egypt at this time should be examined prior to consigning Hagar to a condition of slavery.

The Abrahamic period in Israel is usually designated as lasting from 2000 to 1720 B.C.E. This is the time of Egypt's Middle Kingdom, during which period the areas of Damascus (Syria) and Canaan remained under the domination of Egypt. This is also the time of the twelfth dynasty in Egypt. Since Egypt was in a strong military position at that time, it certainly would not have allowed its citizens to be held as slaves by those who were under its domination. As a matter of fact, most of the slaves in Egypt during the Middle Kingdom were Asiatic.[2]

Very little is known about Hagar. It is appropriate to raise a series of questions whose answers could provide insight for a more balanced understanding of the cycle of stories bearing her name. Among questions of interest are: Who is Hagar? Why must she be a slave to Abraham's Sarah? What are the real reasons that Sarah drives Hagar and her son from Abraham's household? Why is Abraham so willing to allow his

---

2. I. E. J. Edwards, et al., *The Cambridge Ancient History*, vol. 1, pt. 1, 3d ed. (London: Cambridge University Press, 1970), 49; John Bright, *A History of Israel*, 2d ed. (Philadelphia: Westminster Press, 1972), 67–112; Martin Noth, *The History of Israel*, rev. ed. (New York: Harper and Row, 1960), 110–27; John. A Wilson, "Egypt," in H. Frankfort, et al., *The Intellectual Adventure of Ancient Man* (Chicago: University of Chicago Press, 1946), 31–92.

first-born son to be driven out into the desert? Is there a basis here for reexamining the ethical character of both Abraham and God? Do we have here an example of ethnic bias or is it simply a matter of Sarah protecting her own socio-economic welfare?

The Texts

The two biblical texts of primary importance are Genesis 16:1-16 (J) and Genesis 21:8-21 (E). In the Genesis 16 text, Hagar's son's name is given, Ishmael. There are additional biblical references to Ishmael both within and outside of Genesis 16. The New Testament makes it clear that the Hagar tradition remains significant within a Jewish understanding of history (Gal. 4:22f.). There, the apostle Paul presupposes that Hagar is to be regarded as a slave.

The Hagar story in Genesis 16, for the most part, is from the J source. There are some inserts from P (the Priestly source), especially verses 3 and 15-16.[3] Yahweh is the prominent name for God in this version of the story (see vv. 5, 7, 9, 10, 11, 13). It is the prominence of the name Yahweh that is the basis for referring to this as a J source story (the J derives from the German spelling for Yahweh). The second version of the Hagar story is primarily from the E source, Genesis 21:8-21. Here, the primary name for God is Elohim. The connecting link between the two texts is found in the J version, 16:9. There are some major differences in the texts, and there are textual and other problems associated with them. Many of these problems are addressed in the standard commentaries.

The present discussion will be restricted to select verses and terms. In 16:3, the text reads, "Sarai, Abram's wife, took Hagar the Egyptian, her maid, and gave her to Abram her husband as a wife." The term used here for wife ('*ishshah*) has a broad meaning. Elsewhere, it is used as "concubine" (Judg. 19:1, 27) and "harlot" (e.g., Josh. 2:1; 6:22; Judg. 11:11). It is clear in both versions of the story that the "angel of the Lord" is God. Both versions affirm a theophany for Hagar. This in itself is most unusual, since in the Old Testament, theophanies are given almost exclusively to men. The two texts contain several place names. The opening of chapter 16 sets the events in the land of Canaan (v. 3). Other designated locations are "the spring on the way to Shur" (v. 7) and Beer La-hai Roi, a well between Kadesh and Be'red. It is at the latter place that Isaac will live (25:11).

---

3. Gerhard von Rad, *Genesis: A Commentary* (Philadelphia: Westminster Press, 1972), 191; Cuthbert A. Simpson, "Introduction and Exegesis to Genesis," in George A. Buttrick, ed., *The Interpreter's Bible* (Nashville: Abingdon Press, 1952), 1:117; and David A. Leach, *Genesis: The Book of Beginnings* (Valley Forge, Pa.: Judson Press, 1984).

Chapter 21 states that Hagar "wandered in the wilderness of Beer-sheba" (v. 14). The text ends with Hagar's son living "in the wilderness of Paran" (v. 21). Thus, the two versions of the Abraham-Hagar-Sarah encounter are set within the context of the countries around the Mediterranean Sea. This "world" is rather limited. Many of the place names given can no longer be identified. Often, the origin of the names has significance. The explanation given within the texts does not conform, in all too many instances, with current knowledge of the history and geography of this part of the world.

The opening verses of chapter 16 seem to be set at Mamre. According to Genesis 13:18, it is here where Abraham settles. Presumably, Hagar flees from Mamre in the direction of Shur (v. 7). Shur is far south of Mamre; this oasis is located near the northeastern boundary of Egypt (see Gen. 20:1; 25:18). Kadesh (v. 1), another well-known oasis, is located approximately sixty miles south of Beer-sheba. The other place names in chapter 16 are obscure. By contrast, the setting of the story in E (chap. 21) is in the vicinity of Beer-sheba. This is implied by verse 14. The location would be ideal for grazing the flocks of Abraham. In this account, Hagar is sent away by Abraham and wanders in the wilderness of Beer-sheba.

The Traditional Interpretation

In the first two verses of chapter 16, the J writer establishes the context of the story and the major characters, Sarah, Abraham, and Hagar. From Genesis 12 forward it is clear that Abraham is a very wealthy, prominent person. His "household" is extensive. Although, subsequently, he will have more than one wife, it is clear that Sarah is first and most preferred. Although married for years, Sarah has yet to bear children. This in itself would have adversely affected the esteem of her husband; for Abraham to die without a direct male heir would, according to the custom of the time, have been a tragedy. Thus, the J writer sets out to examine a real socio-economic and theological problem. What would have happened to all of Abraham's possessions had he died without an heir and how would the "promise" made to Abraham by Yahweh be realized?

In J's account, Sarah, apparently recognizing the serious dilemma, provides a surrogate, Hagar, so that Abraham might have a male heir. Sarah is presented initially as the caring, concerned wife who wants only what is best for her husband (vv. 1-3).[4] However, the relationship between Sarah and her maid, the surrogate, changes once the pregnancy

---

4. Margaret Wold argues that Sarah yielded to society's pressure and that what she did went beyond the normal desire for motherhood. See this discussion in her *Women of*

is apparent. Hagar treats Sarah with contempt, and Sarah confronts Abraham about Hagar's attitude. The following text, verses 4-6, shows Sarah treating Hagar so "harshly" that she flees for her life. The E source presents Sarah as a jealous, conniving wife who does not wish to have her son play with an "inferior." She has her husband "put out" the surrogate mother and child (21:9-10).

In both J and E, Abraham is presented as a man who consents readily to his wife. It is the wife who takes the initiative. The husband is a willing pawn in her hands. J presents an Abraham who exhibits little interest in the realization of the "promise." He shows no remorse about the fate of the woman who is to present him with an heir apparent.

E appears to be bothered by Abraham's lack of compassion for the woman who has given birth to his son. Indeed, Abraham is displeased by Sarah's demand that he cast Hagar and her son out of the household (v. 11), but Abraham does not protest the demand either to Sarah or God. Eventually, with little sign of compassion or concern, Abraham "cast out" his Egyptian wife and son before daybreak and with little provision to survive (v. 14).

There are profound dissimilarities and a few similarities between the portraits of Hagar in the E and J traditions. In J, she is a bold, proud, resolute Egyptian woman who will not allow herself to be treated "harshly" by her mistress. Here, upon becoming pregnant, Hagar assumes an air of equality with her mistress (v. 4). It is she who will provide Abraham with the necessary heir of the promise. Hagar leaves Abraham's household of her own accord. In contrast, in E Hagar is a "slave woman." She is ejected from the household, and she and her son wander about in the wilderness of Beer-sheba. There she gives up all hope for herself and her child (vv. 15-16). In both versions, Hagar experiences a theophany and becomes a recipient of a "promise." E ends on the note that Hagar is able to obtain an Egyptian wife for her son. This note implies a resourceful Hagar who is in keeping with the portrait in the J tradition.

Ishmael, Hagar's son, is also portrayed differently in J and E. For instance, if one reads the J and E accounts and Genesis 17, it becomes clear that there is a wide discrepancy regarding Ishmael's age.

The issue of an heir for Abraham is the historical context of both the J and E versions of the story. Central here is the promise God has made to Abraham that he will have numerous descendants. Most Old Testament scholars agree that the real issue is that of a successor and

---

Faith and Spirit: Profile of Fifteen Biblical Witnesses (Minneapolis: Augsburg, 1987). See also Katherine C. Bushnell, *God's Word to Women: One Hundred Bible Studies on Woman's Place in the Divine Economy* (North Collins, N.Y.: Ray B. Munson, 1976). Although of less value, some interesting observations are made by Kevin Harris in his *Sex, Ideology and Religion: The Representation of Women in the Bible* (New York: Barnes and Noble, 1984).

heir to Abraham. The stories, in addition, provide some insights into the relationship of the Ishmaelites and the Israelites.

Cuthbert Simpson disagrees with the general assessment of the value of the Hagar cycle of stories. He asserts that the story has no original connection with Abraham. For him, the story originated among the Ishmaelites, who used it to tell of their anonymous ancestor.[5] Nevertheless, both the J and E accounts focus on who is to be Abraham's heir. The texts acknowledge a direct relationship between the Israelites and the Ishmaelites. This relationship begins rather early and is continuous (see Gen. 17:20; 25:12-16; 1 Chron. 1:29-31). The Ishmaelites are presented also as being related to the Midianites (Gen. 37:28-36; Judg. 8:24-28). The Midianites are important to Moses and his becoming acquainted with the god Yahweh (Exod. 3:1ff.).

Sarah's barrenness provides a context from which to begin a description of the formation and development of the Ishmaelites. This is a Bedouin group whose existence is attested as late as the time of Gideon (Judg. 8:24-28). Among the civilizations of the ancient Near East, barrenness of a wife was seen as a disgrace. A wife could be reduced to the status of a slave if she did not produce a son for her husband. Several Old Testament passages present the image of a barren wife: Genesis 11:30; 15:1-3; 16:17-18; 18:1-15; 21:1-6 (all of which relate to Sarah); Genesis 25:21 (Rebecca); Genesis 29:31—30:24 (Leah and Rachel); Judges 13 (the wife of Manoah); 1 Samuel 1-2 (Hannah); and 2 Kings 4:8-17 (the Shunammite woman). In most of these stories, it is God who intercedes so that the woman may have a child. In each instance, the first child is a son.

Rachel (Gen. 30), like Sarah, provides her maid to her husband. Rachel gives Bilhah to Jacob so that, through Bilhah, she would become a mother. There are significant differences between the Rachel cycle and that of Sarah, but both stories provide an environment in which a barren wife has some options. Sarah and Rachel choose to exercise the same option—provide a "substitute" wife for the husband. This practice appears to have had widespread acceptance. According to the Code of Hammurabi (par. 146), a slave girl could become a concubine. This new status, however, did not provide her equality with her mistress. Many of the ancient social customs as related to wives and female servants/slaves are clouded and confused. In particular, the Old Testament, in its early

---

5. Simpson, "Introduction and Exegesis to Genesis," 606. In *Texts of Terror* (Philadelphia: Fortress Press, 1984), Phyllis Trible, who writes from the context of feminist experience, assigns Hagar a "slave" role. Trible treats the two versions of the story as though one is a continuation of the other. Most Old Testament scholars would question this approach. Of course, Trible's purpose is to see the story as one of "terror." In doing this, she dismisses many of the contributions made by modern biblical scholarship for an understanding of the variants. See also Trible's "Depatriarchalizing in Bible Interpretation," *Journal of the American Academy of Religion* 41 (1973): 30–48.

period, is not clear on the status of the servant who bears a child by her master upon the request of her mistress.[6]

In both versions of the text, Hagar is the mother of a son of Abraham. In J, where Hagar is described as a maid, she is given by Sarah to Abraham. Tradition describes this arrangement as one in which Hagar becomes a concubine. Genesis 16:3 states: "Sarai, Abram's wife, took Hagar the Egyptian, her maid, and gave her to Abram her husband as a wife." Therefore, Hagar becomes Abraham's "wife," but clearly not in the same sense that Sarah is his wife also. Hagar is Abraham's wife, but she remains also a "maid" (servant) under the control of her mistress, Sarah. This "new" status of Hagar gets her into trouble with Sarah (v. 4).[7]

The Bible reminds us that a female servant in the capacity of Hagar has few rights. As the possession of the wife (matron) of the household, she is to carry out every reasonable demand made of her. J shows Hagar overstepping the customary bounds. E presents Hagar in a less abrasive fashion. However, even here, Hagar has no permanent status. It is Sarah who controls her destiny. Thus, when Sarah decides Hagar must go, she goes. The E source is careful not to describe Hagar as a wife to Abraham (v. 9). Here, she is referred to as a "slave" woman. In the thinking of E, a slave woman has no rights.

Ishmael plays an important role in the two texts, but very little is said of him in either. The name is given him by a divine being who confronts Hagar (16:7-11). The name is to be descriptive of the character and life style of its recipient. Ishmael is to be the progenitor of the Bedouins, "a wild ass of a man" who will spend his life in warfare (v. 12). J records the birth rather succinctly in verse 15.

E presents a portrait of Ishmael (21:8-21) that defies reason. It is clear that Ishmael is several years older than Isaac (21:8). By the given chronology of the material as it relates to Abraham, Hagar's son would be much older than the text implies (v. 9). Several commentators suggest that in verse 9 Ishmael is abusing Isaac. The text does not indicate this.[8] J. H. Hertz suggests that in verse 9 the phrase "was playing" should be translated "making sport." He claims the Hebrew most often refers to

---

6. In a discussion of the barren wife motif, Mary Callaway examines it rather carefully as it appeared in the ancient Near East. The examination includes both legal and epic literature. The common factor is the desire for offspring. Examples are cited from Ugaritic and Akkadian texts. See Mary Callaway, *Sing, O Barren One: A Study in Comparative Midrash* (Atlanta: Scholars Press, 1986). Callaway cites the *Krt* and *Aqht* texts.

7. Much can be examined that relates to the "arrangement" made between Sarah and Hagar. Both women have received a good deal of scholarly attention in recent years. Among some of the more interesting studies are: Mary Callaway, *Sing, O Barren One*; Conrad Hyers, *And God Created Laughter: The Bible as Divine Comedy* (Atlanta: John Knox Press, 1987); and Margaret Wold, *Women of Faith and Spirit*.

8. See E. A. Speiser, *Genesis: Introduction, Translation, and Notes*, The Anchor Bible, vol. 1 (Garden City, N.Y.: Doubleday, 1964), 155.

an act of impurity or idolatry. He suggests understanding the passage in this way: "Ishmael laughed derisively at the feasting and rejoicing."[9]

Ishmael loses his position as heir apparent to Abraham. He does this when Abraham's wife, Sarah, has a son. For Ishmael to cease to be a threat to both Isaac and Sarah, he has to be separated from the household. Both versions of the story allow this to happen by making him a Bedouin who will do quite well on his own (see 16:12; 21:20). For Sarah, it is an economic issue. Her welfare is tied to that of Isaac.

Some Critical Observations

Both texts present two women of different temperaments. Sarah is presented initially as a concerned, caring wife. In the J account, her attitude changes once Hagar becomes pregnant. Then, Sarah becomes the calculating, noncompassionate wife who seeks only for her best interest. Why this change in attitude and character? Let us now compare the portraits of Hagar. In the J document she is a very strong, "arrogant" woman. It is her pride and willpower that allow her to flee from the household of Abraham. In E, Hagar is a whimpering slave woman who happens to have mothered the son of Abraham. How does she come to be chosen to bear the son?

The two versions of the legend permit some insight into the role of women during the early patriarchal period. The childless state of Sarah can be compensated by her husband having a child by her personal maid. The practice appears to have been somewhat common (see Gen. 30). Children born through such an arrangement would become children of the wife. Thus, Sarah's initial arrangement would be acceptable. It is clear, however, that Sarah cannot go through with the arrangement. The blame is put on Hagar. "She looked with contempt on her mistress" (16:4). It is this look of contempt that prompts Sarah's appeal to Abraham. Thus, once Sarah has given Hagar to Abraham to bear a child, Sarah appears to lose control over her. Abraham, however, insists that the "power" to deal with Hagar still rests with Sarah (v. 6).

In E, Sarah demands that Hagar and her son be put out of the household. Without mentioning Hagar by name, Sarah tells Abraham, "Cast out this slave woman and her son" (v. 10). It is clear that both Hagar and her son are thought of as inferior to Sarah and her son. Thus Sarah says nothing of a Hagar who has shown "contempt." It is clear that Sarah seeks only for her best interest and that of her son. There is no compassion, no remorse, no concern. No one is to be permitted in the household

---

9. J. H. Hertz, ed., *Genesis: Pentateuch and Haftorahs with Commentary* (London: Oxford University Press, 1929), 176.

who could be considered a rival heir. Sarah's request to Abraham is in violation of both custom and law.[10]

By examining the reaction of Sarah in the two versions we can gain some insights into various issues of the times—social customs, the status and standing of subjugated people, and the matter of inheritance. In the versions there is ambiguity as to who has what authority over Hagar. Hagar has become a wife to Abraham, but she remains a servant to Sarah (16:3). What is the status of Hagar? The J text suggests that Hagar assumes a status equal to that of Sarah. In reality, she assumes a superior status, one she acquires as the potential mother of Abraham's heir. Verse 5 suggests that Sarah is extremely uncomfortable with the results of her plan for Abraham and Hagar. Western Old Testament scholars tend to cite the legal customs of Babylonia to justify the action of Sarah. The Code of Hammurabi becomes the point of reference. The justification is based on the Babylonian birth of Abraham.[11]

In J, Hagar is an Egyptian maid; in E, she is a slave woman. The character of Hagar shown in the two versions is at opposite extremes. Each portrait of Hagar is incomplete. Which story best describes the relationship of Hagar to the household of Abraham?

The fact is that Hagar bears Abraham a son, an heir. Whatever her previous status, she now has a permanent place in the household of Abraham. It is this new status that disturbs Sarah. In J, Sarah abuses Hagar to the degree that Hagar leaves on her own accord. In E, Hagar is driven out of the house by Abraham in clear violation of the Law.

Is Hagar simply a servant or is she a slave? Little is known of the origin of slavery, but we certainly know that a slave is a person owned by another person. A slave is the personal property of a specific person. The slave's function is dependent upon the owner's will.[12] Yet neither text provides any description of the function of Hagar, other than that of childbearer, within the household of Abraham and Sarah. The texts insist that Hagar is Egyptian. In Egypt at this time there was no rigid caste system,[13] though Egyptians could hire themselves out. There is no evidence as to how Hagar becomes a part of Abraham's household. Speculation abounds that this occurred during Abraham's Egyptian sojourn (Gen. 12:10ff.). Such claims have not been proved as objective historical fact. The question thus arises: How would Abraham, as a traveler/sojourner in Egypt, acquire an Egyptian as a slave? As stated earlier, most of the slaves during this period in Egypt were Asiatic. Sarah, as the

---

10. Bruce Vawter, *A Path through Genesis* (New York: Sheed and Ward, 1956), 165.

11. Von Rad, *Genesis*, 192; Hertz, ed., *Genesis*, 140; and W. Gunther Plant, *The Torah: A Modern Commentary* (New York: Union of American Hebrew Congregations, 1974), 148.

12. Edwards, et al., *The Cambridge Ancient History*, vol. 1, pt. 1, p. 853; Roland de Vaux, *Ancient Israel: Social Institutions* (New York: McGraw Hill, 1965), 80–90.

13. Wilson, "Egypt," 75.

wife of a wealthy caravaneer, would be afforded a maid. Could this maid be an Egyptian who was a slave during the time of the Middle Kingdom? It is in the later retelling of the story that Hagar evidently becomes a slave.

The Hagar of J retains character and dignity. She displays an independence, some would argue arrogance, that would be more typical of a hired Egyptian servant. The Hagar of E reflects an attitude and character of someone whose status is that of a slave. Here, there is no independence, no determination, no resourcefulness. The dichotomy of the two Hagars is most apparent.

In reading the Old Testament, it is possible to see an increasing tendency to portray the Hebrews/Israelites as superior to all their neighbors. This "air" is incorporated in the concept of "the chosen people." Examples abound. One example is 1 Kings 4:30f.: "Solomon's wisdom surpassed the wisdom of all the people of the east and all the wisdom of Egypt. For he was wiser than all other men."

The sense of superiority finds its way in to the cycle of tales dealing with Hagar. Hagar's status as carrier of Abraham's son threatens Sarah's position in the household (J). Sarah remains the favorite wife, although she is barren (see 1 Sam. 1:1-8). Sarah resolves to put Hagar in her place. Obviously, given Hagar's new status, Sarah needs permission from Abraham to do so. Having obtained this, Sarah treats Hagar harshly. The term *'innah* suggests excessive severity.[14] In reality, Sarah humiliates Hagar. This action reestablishes Sarah's superior status in the household. The humiliation causes Hagar to flee from the household. She refuses to be reduced to the level of a house slave.

In E (21:9f.), the sight of Isaac playing with Hagar's son provides the impetus for Sarah's action against Hagar. Seeing the two sons together, Sarah realizes the legal ramifications of the son of Abraham born to Hagar. Hagar's son is a legitimate first heir to Abraham. The children of Abraham are playing together, innocent of any social or economic distinction. Sarah displays a fit of jealousy that results in Hagar and her son being ejected from the household. Sarah implies that her son is too good to play with the child of a slave. Of course, the real reason is Sarah's economic self-interest.

Both versions of the story connect the Egyptians with the Ishmaelites. This connection is made through Hagar. In the tradition of the Old Testament, a great deal is made of blood lines. J does not describe the son and his descendants in positive tones (16:12). The text implies that a nomadic, Bedouin existence is inferior to that of a settled one. According to the two texts, the Israelite life style is superior to any other in the region. In both J and E, it is a Hebrew/Israelite who emerges as the

---

14. John Skinner, *A Critical and Exegetical Commentary on Genesis*, The International Critical Commentary, vol. 1, 2d ed. (Edinburgh: T and T Clark, 1930), 285; and Vawter, *Path*, 139.

superior, more cultured being. This is true even when the texts attempt to examine the legal and moral ramification of actions taken. The biased view is most evident.

The Theophany

In both J and E, the fate of Hagar and her son is announced by God. There is an appearance of God. Hagar says in 16:13b, "Have I really seen God and remained alive after seeing him?" In 21:17, the narrative states, "And God heard the voice of the lad; and the angel of God called to Hagar from heaven." The earlier tradition has no problem allowing God to be seen by specific human beings. Hagar has a theophany. In each case, she becomes the recipient of a promise made by God. The promise is identical to the promise given to the patriarchs by God.

Martin Noth has devoted extensive study to the theme "promise of the patriarchs." He points out the uniqueness of this Pentateuchal tradition. The tradition was associated with clan cults in and around Palestine. These cults centered around great "fathers." Within each cycle of stories dealing with the promise made to the patriarchs are several recurring concepts: (1) promise of the inheritance of land; (2) promise of abundant posterity who would enjoy this inheritance; and (3) fulfillment of the promise.[15] The promise to the patriarchs is set within the context of an appearance of the divine to a specific patriarch at a specific location. This appearance, this theophany, demonstrates a personal relationship of the patriarch with God. This "tradition" can be observed in other ancient New Eastern religious traditions as well.

In both J and E, Hagar encounters and confronts the divine. The theophany in J begins at verse 7. The text begins with the words: "The angel of the Lord." This translation is more than misleading. It provides a theological judgment that was foreign to the thought of early Israel. The tradition saw no distinction between "the angel of the Lord" and Yahweh. For the Israelites, there were no intermediary beings who would intrude in the affairs and activities of humans. As pointed out earlier, in J this angel of Yahweh ("the angel of the Lord") is identified with Yahweh in verse 13.[16] In contrast, in the retelling of the legend in E, God hears the child of Hagar weeping. "The angel of God" speaks to Hagar from heaven (vv. 17f.). Verse 18b makes it clear that in the mind of the narrator, it is God who speaks to Hagar.

In both accounts, there is a promise of many descendants and of land (16:10f.; 21:18). Hagar, as a woman, is heir to a promise identical to that

---

15. Martin Noth, *A History of Pentateuchal Traditions* (Englewood Cliffs, N.J.: Prentice-Hall, 1972), 54–58.

16. Von Rad, *Genesis*, 193; and Speiser, *Genesis*, 117.

of the patriarchs. It is significant that Hagar is the only Old Testament woman who has a recorded theophany and is a recipient of the promise of possession of land and a large number of descendants.[17] Thus, Hagar is portrayed as the first genuine matriarch of the Old Testament. This North African woman, an Egyptian by birth, demonstrates that the divine promise could be given to a non-Israelite or a woman. However, Hagar is only one of many very strong women whose personalities color the stories of early Israel. It has to be assumed that these women also shared in the tradition of the divine promise.

Concluding Observations

In both the J and E versions, Abraham is presented as a wealthy man who submits to the will of his first wife, Sarah. In J, Abraham shows no compassion for Hagar and their son, though he does provide the child a name. E presents Abraham in a somewhat more favorable light. The demand made by Sarah for him to "cast out this slave woman and her son" (v. 10) is very displeasing to him (v. 11). However displeasing, Abraham does what he is told to do by Sarah. The narrator inserts that Abraham concedes to Sarah's demand based on the intervention of God (v. 12). The implication is that Abraham would have rejected Sarah's demand, understanding it to be unreasonable and unjustifiable. In both cycles, Sarah is to be seen as one who doubts God (see Gen. 18). It is clear in E that there is doubt in the mind of Sarah as to who will be the son of the promise. Were there no doubt, Hagar and her son would not be seen as a threat. Abraham, according to tradition, had at least one other wife, Keturah (Gen. 25:1). There were six sons born to him by Keturah. The tradition is clear, however, that it was Isaac who inherited the wealth, thus confirming the economic basis for Sarah's concern (25:5). The text implies that there were many other concubines and sons. All were sent away from Isaac. A rather interesting note occurs in 25:9. There it is Isaac and Ishmael who bury Abraham. The implication is that Ishmael showed no bitterness at having been dispossessed by Isaac's mother.

There is need for additional study on the role of Abraham. He violates Near Eastern law as it relates to first-born sons. An additional study should examine Abraham the father of the house and his relationship to his sons and wives. Is he a strong businessman who ill manages his own

---

17. There are two Old Testament women who experience a theophany: Hagar, whose experience is recounted in two traditions, and the wife of Manoah, the Danite (Judg. 13:12-25). Unlike Hagar, the wife of Manoah does not become a recipient of the promise of land and descendants. The son born is Samson. A rather interesting discussion of the role of women in the Old Testament can be found in John H. Otwell, *And Sarah Laughed: The Status of Women in the Old Testament* (Philadelphia: Westminster Press, 1977).

home? (This is the case with King David centuries later.) What is it that makes him submit, almost unquestionably, to the whims of his erratic wife Sarah? In Egypt he encouraged lying (12:10-19). Should he now be shown to be an inept father? A man who lacks sensitivity, one who would put a woman and her child out into the world with virtually no means of survival, prior to daybreak, should not be thought of as "the father of the faithful." There are many reasons to study and evaluate Abraham further.[18]

The portrayal of God in both versions of the Hagar material is of interest. It is Yahweh who compels Hagar to return to a household from which she has fled (16:9). The God of the Israelites "stops" her and directs her to return to a subservient life within the household of Sarah. It is clear that Hagar has been abused by Sarah (v. 6). Yet now God tells her to "submit" to Sarah (v. 9). Nothing is said of any protection for Hagar within this hostile environment. Why does Yahweh not offer her some kind of protection?

God tells Hagar she will have a child. Clearly, this is no revelation to her (see v. 4). Verse 11 ("the Lord has given heed to your affliction") implies divine disapproval of what has happened; yet there is no reference to future treatment. E presents God as supportive of the action of Sarah. God tells Abraham, "whatever Sarah says to you, do as she tells you" (v. 12). E is interested in justifying Isaac's claim to Abraham's fortune. The E source does not realize or chooses to ignore the negative connotation of the position assigned to God.

Is Yahweh immune from moral judgment? Should not Yahweh be judged by the ethical standards of the period? Abraham, in E, appears to have more immediate concern for Hagar and his son than God does. Sarah's request that Hagar and Ishmael be "cast out" is in opposition to Near Eastern law, yet it is God who provides permission for Abraham to execute the plan. Would it not be in the best interest of God to have Abraham demonstrate some humane treatment to Hagar and his son? It is inexcusable to put this mother and her son out with so little (21:14). As a wealthy man, Abraham could at least have provided some means of transportation and some financial assistance to them.

There are many reasons to examine the role assigned to God in both the J and E accounts. Such an examination needs to be set within the context of the "fairness" and "justness" of the God of Israel, Yahweh, when dealing with non-Israelites.

One of the central issues in the story of Hagar is the rights of the first-born son. A great deal is taken for granted in relating the story. Usually,

---

18. In many ways, Abraham demonstrates a remarkable "lack of faith" in God. See Charles T. Fritsch, *The Book of Genesis*, The Layman's Bible Commentary, vol. 2 (Richmond, Va.: John Knox Press, 1959), 62f.

references are made to the Code of Hammurabi and the Nuzi texts.[19] Genesis 21:10 implies an equal right to inheritance between Isaac and Ishmael. Sarah is presented as opposing such a right for Ishmael.

Given what is said in Genesis 21:10, there is a need for further examination of the view of the role of the first-born son in the ancient Near East and in the Old Testament. The examination as it relates to Ishmael should be done on at least two levels: Ishmael as the son of a free Egyptian woman; and Ishmael as the son of a slave woman. There are other examples in the Old Testament in which it is clear that the first-born son does not become heir to the father's estate.

The right to inheritance in the ancient Near East is not a clear matter, though some would lead us to believe otherwise. There are numerous examples in the annals where the sons of a wealthy man wage battle to determine who will gain control of their father's wealth. Other examples describe sons jockeying for power and control prior to the death of the father.[20]

The status of Hagar in the household of Abraham and Sarah needs clarification. J describes her as an Egyptian maid (vv. 1, 3, 6, 8). E describes Hagar as a slave woman (*'amah*) (vv. 10, 12, 13). Israel knew slavery as an institution from early in its history. The most common term used to refer to slaves was *'ebed*. The term is translated most often as "slave," "servant." It occurs some 799 times in the Old Testament. In Genesis 9:25, the meaning is clear: "Cursed be Canaan; a slave [*'ebed*] of slaves [*'abarim*] shall he be to his brothers" (see also Gen. 40:10; etc.).

---

19. Mary Callaway has examined the Nuzi tablets along with an Egyptian text that relates to a female slave bearing children for the husband of her mistress. See Callaway, *Sing, O Barren One*, 14. Callaway cites John Van Seters, "The Problem of Childlessness in Ancient Near Eastern Law and the Patriarchs of Israel," *Journal of Biblical Literature* 87 (1968): 401–8. At Nuzi, a contract dealing with Kelimninu and Shemnema describes an arrangement quite like the Sarah-Hagar arrangement. Of course, the Nuzi texts are post-Abrahamic. See James B. Pritchard, ed., *Ancient Near Eastern Texts Relating to the Old Testament*, 3d. ed. (Princeton, N.J.: Princeton University Press, 1969), 220; and Bright, *A History of Israel*.

20. Within the biblical tradition, it is clear that the "right of the first-born son" is often violated. This is clear in the Esau-Jacob cycle (Gen. 27–28) and regarding the sons of Jacob, where favoritism is shown Joseph (Gen. 37f.). Solomon is not among the older sons of David. He, like so many other sons, plotted to become heir apparent. The conflict is very real between Adonijah and Solomon for control of the crown (see 1 Kings 1:5-23). After the death of David, Solomon has Adonijah put to death (see 1 Kings 2:13-25). Sennacherib was murdered by certain of his sons (2 Kings 19:37) and was succeeded by Esarhaddon (680–69 B.C.E.), a young son who proved to be an exceedingly vigorous ruler (see Pritchard, ed., *Ancient Near Eastern Texts*, 289). The matter of the sons battling after the death of the father-king is familiar in ancient Near Eastern history. An examination of the annals of Assyria demonstrates this (see John Bright, *A History of Israel*, 314f.). The annals discuss the claims of several sons upon the death of Asshurbanapal. Martin Noth (*The History of Israel*, 310f.) examines this phenomenon during the Persian period. Other examples abound. See also Norman K. Gottwald, *All the Kingdoms of the Earth* (New York: Harper and Row, 1959), 186f. Especially interesting are the footnotes.

In numerous texts, it is clear that '*ebed* means a servant, a "worker" who is in the employ of someone else. However, this is the term used to describe the experience of Israel in Egypt (see Exod. 13:3, 14; 20:2; etc.). These and similar passages are translated with reference to the "house of bondage." Clearly, slavery or servitude is being described. Deuteronomy uses '*ebed* to describe the experience in Egypt (see Deut. 5:15; 15:15; etc.).

There is a feminine form of '*ebed* that is found in the Old Testament (e.g., Gen. 26:14; Job 1:3; Ezek. 9:8, 9; Neh. 9:17). '*Abduth* translates as "servitude" and "bondage." In neither J nor E is this term applied to Hagar.

Translators suggest that the Hebraic *shiphahah* and '*amah* are synonymous. The root word *sph* appears to have original meanings of "pour" and "effusion." In its Arabic cognate, the term implies "to commit fornication."[21] One lexicon raises the question of whether the original meaning of the root of the term used in J is "concubine." That lexicon translates '*amah* as "maid," "handmaid." This is equated with *shiphahah*. E chooses to use '*amah*. According to the aforementioned lexicon, '*amah* at times suggests greater servility than the term used by J. It is noted also that J does not make use of the term '*amah*.[22]

The etymology of both terms needs to be examined. Hebrew is a "concrete" language. It is concise and clear. Some rational explanation is needed for the use of the two descriptive terms applied to Hagar. Why is it that neither text makes use of the more common term for slave? Is it that within both traditions there remains the belief that Hagar was an Egyptian citizen?

Regardless, in J, Hagar is no ordinary household slave.[23] In both traditions, she is Egyptian. In E, Hagar obtains an Egyptian wife for her son. Customarily this was the function of the father. Her acquiring a wife for her son (21:21) implies she has financial resources, for there was a cost involved in such an arrangement.[24] Here is another indication that in the original story Hagar is more than a "slave woman."

Is Hagar an Egyptian slave in the household of Abraham? The Old Testament evidence suggests that in the sense of being in bondage, she is not. In J, Hagar displays an attitude of a "free" person. She does not submit to the whims of Sarah. In E, she has the resources to acquire a wife for her son. Could a slave display either characteristic?

In the ancient Near East, enslavement was largely the result of warfare, and most slaves belonged to the king.[25] There are, how-

21. Frances Brown, et al., *Hebrew and English Lexicon of the Old Testament* (Oxford: Clarendon Press, 1962), 1046.
22. Brown, *Hebrew and English Lexicon*, 51. For an extensive treatment of the subject see Roland de Vaux, *Ancient Israel*, 80–90.
23. Skinner, *Genesis*, 285.
24. Speiser, *Genesis*, 155; and von Rad, *Genesis*, 234.
25. *Encyclopaedia Britannica*, 15th ed., s.v. "Slavery, Serfdom, and Hired Labour."

ever, examples of people selling themselves and/or their children into servitude.

How is it that Hagar comes to be in the service of Abraham and Sarah? The Old Testament does not provide sufficient data to ascertain an appropriate answer. Is Hagar a North African by birth? Both traditions maintain that she is. E relates the relationship between the Egyptians and the Ishmaelites through Hagar. Was Hagar a slave in the sense that Israel was a slave in Egypt? Probably not. The language and "feeling" of the story suggest that she was a free person.

Then why is it that—regardless of the language and feeling of the story—traditional Old Testament scholarship describes her as an Egyptian slave? Is it the racial bias of the translators and commentators? In Western biblical scholarship, the real culprit is the King James Version of the Bible. Given the negative view of Africa at the time this translation came into existence, a person in the Bible who had an African heritage was described usually as a slave. This is not to say that there are not exclusivist currents within the Bible itself. It is, for instance, inherent within the biblical tradition that non-Israelites are inferior to God's "chosen people," the Israelites. That notion, however, does not go unchallenged in the Bible. The prophet Amos strongly challenges this notion within the biblical tradition (see Amos 3:2; 9:7; 14; etc.). In short, the long tradition of designating Hagar as a slave would seem largely to come from sources outside the Bible itself.

Additional study would reveal more about the nature of Egyptian slavery during the time of Abraham. Such a study would provide a context from which to examine effectively the various possibilities for Hagar within the household of the Chaldean, Abraham, and his wife.

Excursus

In recent times, many attempts have been made to demonstrate the existence of racism within the biblical traditions. Charles Copher, Cain Hope Felder, and others have provided various analyses and studies to demonstrate the presence of blacks in the biblical world. What has been ascertained is the increasing tendency within the development of the Old Testament to look with disdain upon the peoples of Africa. From the modern perspective, this is described as a "racist tendency." Racism, as it is known in our time, is a phenomenon of the modern period. The various theories of racism are discussed in numerous places. It may be more practical, in terms of the Old Testament world, to examine the issue of ethnicity. There are very real ethnic positions taken within the Old Testament. An ethnic group is a group in which there is a common and distinctive culture. Ethnic concerns, such as cultural and speech differences, are identifiable. Religious distinctions also constitute an ethnic issue.

The Hebrews/Israelites are told to shun many groups. Various reasons are given within the texts. The Midianites are presented as a people to be destroyed by Israel (Num. 25:6, 16f.; 31:1-2). The Edomites are thought to be descendants of Esau. They are of a mixed ancestry (see Gen. 14:6; 32:3; 36:21f.; Judg. 5:4; Deut. 2:12). The justification for Israel's negative attitude toward the Edomites, their relatives, is that prior to the conquest of Canaan by Israel, the Edomites refused to allow the Israelites to pass through their territory while en route to Canaan (Num. 20:18-21). This justifies the harsh treatment of the Edomites during the time of the United Kingdom.

Specific texts regarding other ethnic groups would indicate a similar pattern. One could argue that a "theology of war" or a "theology of economic survival" justifies the pronouncements and attitude of Israel toward non-Israelites. A passage in Numbers indicates a growing dislike for Africans. Numbers 12:1 reads: "Miriam and Aaron spoke against Moses because of the Cushite woman whom he had married, for he had married a Cushite woman." The text is emphatic that Moses is now married to a Cushite. In the Table of Nations in Genesis, Cush is a son of Ham (Gen. 10:6). The sons of Cush, listed in Genesis 10:7-12, are seen as the peoples of central and southern Arabia. It is clear that in the Old Testament, Cush is Ethiopia. The Cushites became a powerful force and during the twenty-second Egyptian dynasty began to encroach on the territory of Egypt. The twenty-fifth Egyptian dynasty, ca. 715–656 B.C.E., was an Ethiopian dynasty.[26] In the earlier Old Testament traditions, there is a tendency to use the term *Cush* to refer to Egypt as well as Ethiopia. Cush, Nubia, Put (Phut), and Egypt were not always distinct geographical entities. It was during the twelfth dynasty that Cush was conquered and annexed by Egypt (ca. 1991–1786 B.C.E.). Thus, during the early patriarchal period in the life of Israel, Cush was a geographical part of Egypt.

Between the Hebrews/Israelites and the Egyptians there were periods of conflict and periods of peace until Egypt became too weak to interfere in the affairs of its northern neighbors. The ethnic identity of ancient Egyptians is hard to specify because Egypt had an open-door policy and its population was thus quite diverse and mixed. Egypt, from its earliest existence, served as a magnet attracting countless peoples. Its culture was the most advanced in all the ancient Near East. Western Old Testament scholars consistently have displayed the tendency to see Egypt in European dress. Few have discussed Egypt as a north African

26. John A. Wilson, *The Culture of Ancient Egypt* (Chicago: University of Chicago Press, 1951), 292f.

country or culture. It is through these types of attitudes that racism has entered Western biblical scholarship.

In both the J and E versions of the texts, it is apparent that Hagar is Egyptian. Simpson, however, argues that the term *Egyptian* is an insertion into the text made by the P redactor. He states categorically that Hagar is a woman of the desert, not an Egyptian.[27] In both the J and E versions it is apparent that Hagar's precise status is not clear. Yet Hertz argues that Sarah and Abraham acquired Hagar as a slave during their stay in Egypt. His reference is Genesis 12.[28]

Sarah's command in Genesis 21:10 provides a basis for an examination of the issue of ethnic "purity," as well as an examination of Sarah's vested economic interest. Sarah expresses opposition to equality for the two sons of Abraham. (Compare the story of Jephthah in Judges 11:1ff.) Sarah's economic survival rests with her own son.

Ishmael, as the first son, would have had certain property rights based on ancient Near Eastern law.[29] Given that, it would seem that some justification would be expected when Abraham drives him off the land. Both versions of the story make it clear that the Ishmaelites will fair well. Simpson, who is bothered by this, argues that Ishmael was not originally associated with Abraham, but with Isaac. He states that the E account has scarcely anything to do with Ishmael.[30] The Ishmaelites were identified with the people of Egypt. They were a nation of mixed ancestry. It seems to be the hallmark of Western (Eurocentric) biblical scholars to seize upon every opportunity to read their racial biases into the interpretation and translations of the ancient biblical text. This is especially true in terms of the early stages of the development of Israel. Thus, through the translations of the texts and interpretive commentaries on the texts, the Western (Eurocentric) concern with race is expressed through the biblical texts.

27. Simpson, "Introduction and Exegesis to Genesis," 604.
28. Hertz, ed., *Genesis*, 140.
29. Speiser, *Genesis*, 165.
30. Simpson, "Introduction and Exegesis to Genesis," 606, 607.

— 10 —

The *Haustafeln* (Household Codes) in African American Biblical Interpretation: "Free Slaves" and "Subordinate Women"

Clarice J. Martin

Few New Testament narratives have exerted as profoundly a malefic and far-reaching impact on the lives of African Americans as have the *Haustafeln*—the table of household codes or domestic duties found in Colossians 3:18—4:1; Ephesians 5:21—6:9; and 1 Peter 2:18—3:7. This essay assesses the varying hermeneutical approaches of African Americans toward the slave regulation enjoining "submission," on the one hand, and toward the regulation enjoining submission of "wives" (and, by extension, women), on the other hand.

I begin with a brief assessment of the interpretation of the *Haustafeln* in recent decades. Second, I review interpretations of the slave regulation in the *Haustafeln* by proslavery apologists and those abolitionists who opposed them. African American hermeneutical approaches to the slave regulation are assessed within this context. Third, interpretations of the regulation regarding wives (and women) are examined. Fourth, the hermeneutical issues engendered by divergent approaches to the slave regulation and the regulation about women are explored.

Finally, implications of my analysis for theological reflection and praxis are examined.

Two methodological assumptions should be noted regarding the *Haustafeln* as a paranetic unit. First, by *Haustafeln* I mean the more complete domestic codes in Colossians 3:18—4:1; Ephesians 5:21—6:9; and 1 Peter 2:18—3:7, where the *Haustafeln* genre is most explicit. I exclude 1 Timothy 2:8-15; 5:1-2; 6:1-2; Titus 2:1-10; 3:1.[1] Second, it is my position that the *Haustafeln* and the letters in which they are found are not Pauline, but deutero-Pauline. The question of whether the *Haustafeln* are Pauline is, of course, linked to the question of the authenticity of Colossians, Ephesians, and 1 Peter. I would argue that Colossians and Ephesians are deutero-Pauline, that is, written by circles of Paul's students on the model of the Pauline letter,[2] and that 1 Peter is pseudonymous.[3]

The Interpretation of Haustafeln *in Recent Decades*

The topic of "household management" in the *Haustafeln* has come under renewed scrutiny in recent decades. Particular attention has been given to the social world (*kosmos*) in which the codes originated.[4] The concern that these codes have been used to reinforce a thoroughgoing chauvinism in church and society has become more urgent.[5] Frank Stagg's observation that the *Haustafeln* and similar texts have been used to turn the "good news" into the "bad news" for women is perhaps more than a rhetorical repartee.[6]

1. There is some dissension in the literature regarding which New Testament narratives should be included in the *Haustafeln*. David L. Balch concludes that Col. 3:18—4:1; Eph. 5:21—6:9; and 1 Peter 2:18—3:7 represent the more "complete codes." The material in 1 Tim. 2:8-15; 5:1-2; 6:1-2; Titus 2:1-10; 3:1 is not organized as precisely, even if it does contain Hellenistic moral instructions and principles for family living. See Balch, *Let Wives Be Submissive: The Domestic Code in 1 Peter*, Society of Biblical Literature Monograph Series, vol. 26 (Chico, Calif.: Scholars Press, 1981).

2. Helmut Koester, *Introduction to the New Testament*, vol. 2, *History and Literature of Early Christianity* (Philadelphia: Fortress Press, 1982), 3. The subject of the authorship of these letters has been regularly discussed in standard works such as Werner George Kümmel, *Introduction to the New Testament*, rev. ed. (Nashville: Abingdon, 1973).

3. Koester, *Introduction to the New Testament*, 292–95.

4. See William R. Herzog, III, "The 'Household Duties Passages': Apostolic Traditions and Contemporary Concerns," *Foundations* 24 (1981): 204–15; Norman R. Peterson, *Rediscovering Paul: Philemon and the Sociology of Paul's Narrative World* (Philadelphia: Fortress Press, 1985), 89–199. Peterson's analysis of social structures and social relations in Philemon is instructive for our understanding of the slave (*doulos*) in the Greco-Roman world of the first century and, thus, in the *Haustafeln*.

5. See Robin Scroggs, "Paul, Chauvinist or Liberationist?" *The Christian Century* 89, no. 1 (1972): 307–9; Elisabeth Schüssler Fiorenza, *In Memory of Her: A Feminist Theological Reconstruction of Early Christian Origins* (New York: Crossroad, 1985), 251–84.

6. Frank Stagg, "The Gospel, *Haustafel*, and Women: Mark 1:1; Colossians 3:18—4:1," *Faith and Mission* 2, no. 2 (1985): 60.

In Ephesians and Colossians the exhortations in the *Haustafeln* are set forth in three pairs and outline reciprocal relationships between husbands and wives, fathers and children, and masters and slaves. The Petrine code has only one of the three pairs (husbands and wives), and slaves are exhorted but not masters (see 3:1-7; 2:18-25). In the *Haustafeln* the literary structure of the statement of domestic duties underscores the nature of the "power dynamic" in the social relationships set forth. The essential concern of the passages is the relationship of the "weaker" or "inferior" groups to the dominant male-master figure. The male, who was head of the Greco-Roman household, exercised full authority over the wife, child, and slave. In effect, as William Herzog has so aptly observed of the text from Colossians (3:18—4:1), the "concern of the text is the relationship of three subordinate groups to the one dominant figure of the household. . . . The rhetoric of the passage is 'male-master rhetoric,' and the structure of the passage reflects this orientation."[7] E. A. Judge summarizes the matter succinctly: What we hear in the *Haustafeln* is "the voice of the propertied class."[8] The data can be diagrammed as follows to illustrate the hierarchical dynamic:

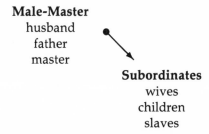

Male-Master
husband
father
master

Subordinates
wives
children
slaves

It is very pertinent at this point to recall the characteristic perceptions of the three subordinate members of the household code in the Greco-Roman world of the first century. In the social world of the first century, certain assumptions existed about the established order of social relationships. As Wayne Meeks notes, the Greco-Roman household (*oikos*) was hierarchical, and, according to the political and moral thought of the period, the structure of superior and inferior roles was believed to be basic to the well-being of the whole society.[9] As a patriarchal society the Greco-Roman world was one in which a few men exercised power over other men, women, children, slaves, and colonized people.[10]

---

7. Herzog, "Household Duties," 209.
8. E. A. Judge, *The Social Pattern of Christian Groups* (London: Tyndale, 1960), 60, 71.
9. Wayne A. Meeks, *The First Urban Christians: The Social World of the Apostle Paul* (New Haven: Yale University Press, 1983), 76.
10. Schüssler Fiorenza, *In Memory of Her*, 29.

The paterfamilias, or male-ruled family unit,[11] was believed to represent the appropriate ordering of the household. It was generally accepted that wives, children, and slaves should submit fully to the rule of the husband-father-master and practice his religion.[12] The household was believed to be an economically independent, self-sufficient unit that was the basis of the state. Several households constituted a village, and several villages a city-state or *politeia*.[13]

Aristotle, whose philosophical discussion of "proper household science" has influenced Western political philosophy and American legal concepts decisively, argued that the primary parts of the household are: master and slave, husband and wife, father and children.[14] Aristotle argued that patriarchal domination of the male over the female (wife), child, and slave was natural and enhanced the proper functioning of the household and, ultimately, the functioning of the state.[15]

Aristotle's viewpoint is echoed elsewhere in ancient literature, including that of Hellenistic Judaism. Philo, for example, identifies a direct correlation between household and state management:

> For the future statesman needed first to be trained and practiced in house management, for a house is a city compressed into small dimensions, and a household management may be called a kind of state management [*politeia*]. . . . This shows clearly that the household manager is identical with the statesman.[16]

Hellenistic Jews, including Philo and Josephus, also sought to articulate ethical imperatives in the pattern of household codes. The view that Hellenistic Judaism borrowed its scheme of ethical instruction is well attested.[17] The Hellenistic Jewish scheme emphasized worship and obedience to the one God (not the "gods") and duties relating to husbands and wives in marriage, children, masters and slaves, and the young and old.[18]

The question of how the codes *functioned* in the earliest Christian community has yielded a number of suggestions. Clearly, the New Testament writers borrowed the *Haustafeln* genre, but to what end? At least three proposals have received significant support.

---

11. Paterfamilias refers to the male-headed ("pater" = father) family household. For a more detailed discussion of the character and function of the paterfamilias, see G. E. M. de Ste. Croix, *The Class Struggle in the Ancient Greek World* (Ithaca, N.Y.: Cornell University Press, 1981), 69–111.

12. Schüssler Fiorenza, *In Memory of Her*, 263.

13. Ibid., 255.

14. Aristotle *Politics* 1.1253b. For a fuller discussion of Aristotelian philosophical thought and the New Testament codes see Balch, *Let Wives Be Submissive*, 33–49.

15. See *Politics* 1.1254b.

16. Philo *On Joseph* 38–39 (cited in Schüssler Fiorenza, *In Memory of Her*, 257).

17. Eduard Lohse, *Colossians and Philemon*, Hermeneia (Philadelphia: Fortress Press, 1971), 155.

18. Ibid.

First, William A. Herzog argues that the early Christian community, as a "minority community" in a "majority culture," drew upon the resources, precedents, models, and paradigms of the society of which it was a part as it reassessed the meaning of life in the *ekklēsia* of God.[19] The household codes were utilized and thus Christianized as the church underwent a process of resocialization in light of its new vision of community and world.[20]

An important feature of this resocialization and the Christianization of the social relationships between the patriarchal head and his subordinates is "agapeic love." Gerd Theissen has argued that the "agape [*agapē*] love" of Christianity reduced the "frictions" in status inequality[21] and structural hierarchies as they existed in the patriarchal society. For him, this "love patriarchalism"[22] meant, in effect, that hierarchical relationships of male dominance and female, child, and slave subordination were accepted and maintained as normative, but with the understanding that there was now an "inner equality" in Christ.

The ethical teachings of the Christianized household codes thereby conveyed *a new motive for action* in accord with the prescribed behavior. One was to act "as is fitting in the Lord" (Col. 3:18; Eph. 6:1), "fearing the Lord" (Col. 3:22), "as to the Lord" (Eph. 5:22). In sum, the hierarchical structural pattern of a male superior and wife-child-slave inferiors remained intact. The patriarchal structure was now, however, Christianized through the integrative power of *agapē* love. Thus, the New Testament writers who utilized the household codes were neither interested in reforming the social order nor interested in social revolution. They sought to transform hierarchical relationships *within the context* of the prevailing social differences and hierarchies.[23]

Second, some scholars have argued that the New Testament writers used the *Haustafeln* as a form of apologia for the Christian faith. This is

19. Herzog, "Household Duties," 156.

20. Herzog is here integrating and expanding the insights of Peter Berger and Thomas Luckmann in *The Social Construction of Reality: A Treatise in the Sociology of Knowledge* (Garden City, N.Y.: Doubleday, 1966). Berger and Luckmann contend that human beings pass through three stages of socialization: primary socialization, secondary socialization, and resocialization. When new revelations lead persons to question basic and traditional structural patterns and assumptions, "resocialization" occurs and the processes of primary and secondary socialization undergo change. Where resocialization occurs, the community will still draw upon models of the world of which it is a part.

21. According to Meeks, "status" is the most useful category for assessing social stratification in the Greco-Roman world. Status variables include power (the capacity to achieve goals in social systems), occupational prestige, income or wealth, education, family and ethnic group position, etc. See Meeks, *First Urban Christians*, 54.

22. Gerd Theissen borrows this analytic concept from Troeltsch. See Theissen, "Soziale Schichtung in der korinthischen Gemeinde: Ein Beitrag zur Soziologie des hellenistischen Urchristentums," *Zeitschrift für die Neutestamentliche Wissenschaft* 65 (1974): 270; Ernst Troeltsch, *The Social Teaching of the Christian Churches*, trans. Olive Wyon (Chicago: University of Chicago Press, 1960), 1:75, 78.

23. Schüssler Fiorenza, *In Memory of Her*, 78–79.

particularly true of 1 Peter 2:11—3:12, where the *Sitz im Leben* is one of high socio-political tension between the Christians and the surrounding pagan world.[24] The prominent motif of suffering in 1 Peter suggests that the recipients of the letter were undergoing some form of religious persecution, scorn, or abuse—possibly by government officials and/or non-Christian neighbors. In 1 Peter 3:15 Christians are explicitly encouraged to be prepared to make a defense (or apology) of their faith by both their word and their conduct so that their pagan detractors cannot revile them.[25] The household codes function in this context to reinforce and secure "proper household management," and thus conformity to generally accepted societal norms. Such conformity would minimize the perception that the Christians were a threat to the Greco-Roman social order.

Elisabeth Schüssler Fiorenza offers a third proposal for the function of the *Haustafeln*. In her view, the Jesus movement (originally a renewal movement within Judaism) was dominated by an ethos of what she calls "the discipleship of equals."[26] In this view, the disciples of Jesus did not respect patriarchal family bonds. Faithful discipleship was an eschatological calling for both women and men. Jesus' true family is defined in Mark 3:31-35 as those who do the will of God: "Whoever does the will of God is my brother and sister and mother." The discipleship of women is again affirmed in Luke 11:27-28. Here a woman in the crowd calls out to Jesus: "Blessed is the womb that bore you, and the breasts that you sucked!" Jesus' response ("Blessed rather are those who hear the word of God and keep it") suggests that "biological motherhood" is not enjoined of women; rather, women, like men, are called to faithful discipleship.[27]

The liberation of women as well as men from disease reinforced the idea that the *basileia* (kingdom) vision of Jesus was a vision of a community marked by a "praxis of inclusive wholeness."[28] The child and slave who are typically relegated to the lowest rung on the patriarchal household ladder become, in the ministry of Jesus, a primary paradigm for authentic discipleship. Jesus' paradoxical saying in Mark 10:15 conveys this sentiment well: "Whoever does not receive the kingdom of God like a child shall not enter it." The point of the saying is not that the believer should become naive and childlike; rather, the saying is a challenge to relinquish claims of power and domination over others.[29] Similarly, that structures of domination should not be normative is seen in the sayings

24. Balch, *Let Wives Be Submissive*, 81.
25. Ibid.
26. Schüssler Fiorenza, *In Memory of Her*, 140–54.
27. Ibid., 146.
28. Ibid., 118, 121.
29. Ibid., 148.

about those who would be "great" or "first" among the disciples (Mark 10:42-45; 9:33-37; par. Matt. 20:26-27; Luke 22:24-27). The truly "great" are those who become servants or slaves (*douloi*). "True leadership in the community must be rooted in solidarity with and work for those who are 'servants and slaves' in the community."[30]

The argument that the earliest gospel stratum pronounces blessing and inclusive wholeness for those on the margins of society is compelling. The promise of life in a *basileia* community is its promotion of a nonpatriarchal structuring of social relationships that calls *all* to empowerment under God.[31] In my view, this inclusive community places priority on allegiance to the Christian *communitas* and not to original ties to one's family. Women are thus defined by their new allegiance to the *basileia* community and not by traditional familial roles (Gal. 3:28-29).

What happened, then, to facilitate the possible transition from an earlier and perhaps more liberatory vision of inclusive wholeness in the ministry of Jesus to the adoption of the Greco-Roman patriarchal household order in the *Haustafeln* (with their reinforcement of patriarchal domination) in the latter decades of the first century? Elisabeth Schüssler Fiorenza argues that while the early Christian vision of a "discipleship of equals" attracted numbers of women and slaves to Christianity, it also created new tensions and conflicts within the patriarchal household.[32] The Christian movement did create "an alternative vision and praxis" to that of prevailing society and religion, but it also threatened the solidity of the established structures of hierarchy within Greco-Roman households. In short, Christians and Christian missionaries—female and male—were threatening the social order of the patriarchal household.[33]

By the latter decades of the first century, then, the "disruption" of the patriarchal household—which was occasioned, in part, by an in-

---

30. Ibid.

31. Questions about Schüssler Fiorenza's "discipleship of equals" thesis have been raised by Cain H. Felder and John Koenig. For example, within the context of a "discipleship of equals," why did Jesus select twelve *men* as disciples? Or in what sense are we to understand and interpret the terms *equals* and *egalitarian*? For review of the issues see Cain H. Felder, "Toward a New Testament Hermeneutic for Justice," *Journal of Religious Thought* 45 (1988): 26–27; John Koenig, in "Review Symposium. Elisabeth Schüssler Fiorenza's *In Memory of Her.* Four Perspectives," *Horizons* 11 (1984): 144–46. For a response by Schüssler Fiorenza and further discussion of the issues see *Horizons* 11 (1984): 154–57, and Schüssler Fiorenza, "The Biblical Roots for a Discipleship of Equals," *Duke Divinity School Review* 45, no. 2 (1980): 87–97.

32. Schüssler Fiorenza, *In Memory of Her*, 251.

33. Ibid., 265. A useful example of the potentially "subversive" impact of the Christian movement on the Greco-Roman socio-religious patriarchal ethos is found in Acts 16:16-24. Paul and Silas are brought before magistrates by the owners of a slave girl in Philippi. Accused of creating a disturbance in the city and advocating customs that were illegal for Romans to adopt and follow (16:20-21), Paul and Silas are censured by the owners for healing the slave girl, making her economically useless to her owners. Further, by freeing her from her spiritual bondage as well as her owners, "Paul interfered with the property rights and ancestral laws of the household" (Schüssler Fiorenza, *In Memory of Her*, 265).

creased participation of women and slaves in the Christian missionary movement—prompted a clamping down on women and slaves to restore "peace" in the community. The *Haustafeln* in Colossians, Ephesians, and 1 Peter—all written after C.E. 70—reflect an attempt to restrict the enthusiasm of women and slaves and thus restore order to the patriarchal household. Patriarchally appropriate behavior was enjoined to persuade imperial authorities that Christian communities were not a threat to the state (1 Peter 2:11—3:12). The *Haustafeln* were also used to reinforce the hierarchical, patriarchal ordering of the husband-wife, father-child, and master-slave relationships and to justify them christologically.

"Free Slaves"

If African Americans have persistently interpreted and reinterpreted any regulation in the New Testament in light of American social and religious history, it has been the slave regulation in the *Haustafeln*: "Slaves be submissive to your masters" (Col. 3:22-25; Eph. 6:5-8; 1 Peter 2:18-25). The eighteenth and nineteenth centuries in particular witnessed antithetical hermeneutical approaches to this regulation by black slaves, on the one hand, and by white proslavery apologists and their sympathizers, on the other hand. While the slavemasters pleaded that black slaves "be submissive" to their masters in conjunction with the "biblical mandate" in the *Haustafeln*, many slaves insisted that the true message of the Christian gospel that they embraced was a message of inspiriting and empowering freedom under God. Above all, "free slaves" and not "submissive slaves" was the ringing cry of African Americans in these centuries. Charles Hodge, in his essay "The Fugitive Slave Law,"[34] published in 1860, appealed indirectly to the *Haustafeln* to argue that the slaves' obedience to their masters is requisite:

> The obedience which slaves owe their masters, children their parents, wives their husbands, people their rulers, is always made to rest on the divine will as its ultimate foundation. It is part of the service which we owe to God. . . . In appealing therefore to the Bible in support of the doctrine here advanced, we are not, on the one hand, appealing to an arbitrary standard, a mere statute book . . . but we are appealing to the infinite intelligence of a personal God, whose will, because of his infinite excellence, is necessarily the ultimate ground and rule of all moral obligation.[35]

---

34. Charles Hodge, "The Fugitive Slave Law," in *Cotton Is King and Pro-slavery Arguments Comprising the Writings of Hammond, Harper, Christy, Stringfellow, Hodge, Bledsoe, and Cartwright on This Important Subject* (Augusta, Ga.: Pritchard, Abbott and Loomis, 1860), 809–40.

35. Ibid., 819–20.

Also utilizing the *Haustafeln* to buttress his proslavery apologetic, George D. Armstrong declared in his letter of rebuttal to abolitionist C. Van Rensselaer that slaveholding is not *malum in se* (a thing evil in itself). Appealing to Paul's Letter to Philemon as well as to the slave regulation in the *Haustafeln*, he sought to provide divine sanction for slavery:

> In our examination of what the New Testament teaches on the subject of slavery, we have found (1) That slaveholding does not appear in any catalogue of sins or "offences" given us by inspired man; (2) That the Apostles received slaveholders into the Christian church, and continued them therein, without giving any intimation, either at the time of their reception or afterwards, that slaveholding was a sin or offence; (3) That Paul sent back a fugitive slave to his own master again, and assigned as his reason for so doing, the master's right to the services of his slaves;[36] (4) That the Apostles frequently enjoin the relative duties of master and slave, and enforce their injunctions upon both alike, as Christian men, by Christian motives.[37]

Further, the use of the *Haustafeln* to justify slaveholding was not confined to the religious spheres of American social discourse. Legal magistrates sometimes wove Scripture into the fabric of their legal statutes to reinforce the master-slave system in general, and to legitimate the dehumanization of blacks as "property" without civil and legal rights in particular. Judge A. Leon Higginbotham, Jr., author of *In the Matter of Color: Race and the American Legal Process, the Colonial Period*,[38] describes a case that illustrates this practice in judicial settings.

The famous North Carolina court case State v. Mann[39] was concerned with the issue of whether it was a criminal offense to subject a slave woman to "cruel and unreasonable battery." The court argued that a slave was to labor "upon a principle of natural duty" without regard to his or her own personal happiness. This sentiment is not surprising in a period when one of the chief functions of judicial proceedings involving slaves was convincing each slave that he or she "had no will of his [or her] own.... The power of the master must be absolute to render the submission perfect."[40]

---

36. Paul's Letter to Philemon is used to justify points two and three.

37. The allusion to the *Haustafeln* and similar narratives enjoining the submission of slaves is clear in the fourth point. See George D. Armstrong, "On the Proper Statement of the Scriptural Doctrine of Slavery," in George D. Armstrong, ed., *A Discussion on Slaveholding: Three Letters to a Conservative and Three Conservative Replies Together with Two Rejoinders, on Slaveholding, Schemes of Emancipation, Colonization, Etc.* (Philadelphia: Joseph M. Wilson, 1858), 4–5.

38. A. Leon Higginbotham, Jr., *In the Matter of Color: Race and the American Legal Process, the Colonial Period* (New York: Oxford University Press, 1978).

39. State v. Mann, North Carolina, 13 N.C. 263 (1829) 8.

40. State v. Mann, North Carolina, 13 N.C. at 255.

Proslavery jurists argued that in order for the slave to remain a slave, he or she must be convinced that the master's power is in no way usurped: "[Slavery] is conferred by the laws of man at least, if not by *the law of God*."[41] Obedience and submission to the master—self-designated as "God's overseer"[42]—were synonymous with "exhibiting good Christian character." In short, blacks could be "saved by Christ," but never "free from their masters."[43]

As H. Shelton Smith has noted in his critical survey of the impact of white racism upon human relations in the South,[44] the Bible was the southern churchperson's major argument in defense of human bondage.[45] Old Testament narratives such as the oft-misquoted and misinterpreted curse of Ham (Gen. 9:18-29)[46] became the *argumentum ad invidiam par excellence* (a definitive appeal to prejudices) for proslavery moralists to prove that subordination of blacks was preordained by God centuries earlier. Leviticus 25:44-46 also provided such grist for the proof-texting mill. The supposition of the proslavery argument based on Leviticus 25 could be aptly summarized: "If God gave the Hebrews 'written permission' to buy, hold, and sell men and women in perpetual servitude, why should we not do so as well?" Again, the *literal* reading of biblical narrative in support of slavery was thus designed to provide moral and legal sanction for the South's defense of slaveholding.

African Americans and their white abolitionist sympathizers also appealed to Scripture in their abolitionist apologia. Based on ardent appeals to such narratives as the *Haustafeln*, their hermeneutic promulgated a rejection of the literalist rendering of the slave regulation and a reinterpretation of such narratives. H. D. Ganse argued, for example, that the instructions to slavemasters in the *Haustafeln*

41. Ibid. at 266–67; italics mine.
42. Higginbotham, *Matter of Color*, 128. Higginbotham observes that the Reverend Thomas Bacon of Virginia shared this sentiment with his slaves, telling them, "And pray, do not think that I want to deceive you, when I tell you, that your *masters* and *mistresses* are God's *overseers*—and that if you are faulty toward them, God himself will punish you severely for it in the next world, unless you repent it and strive to make amends, by your *faithfulness* and *Diligence*" (p. 37).
43. See Higginbotham, *Matter of Color*, 37, and William W. Hening, *Statutes at Large of Virginia* (Richmond: Franklin, 1819–20), 2:26. It should be recalled that in Virginia baptism did not affect the bondage of blacks and Indians (see Higginbotham, *Matter of Color*, 36).
44. H. Shelton Smith, *In His Image but...Racism in Southern Religion, 1780–1910* (Durham, N.C.: Duke University, 1972).
45. Ibid., 129. This fact has been well-documented in the literature. Larry Morrison has noted: "Nearly every pro-slavery pamphlet, or article, or speaker made at least some reference to a biblical sanction of slavery." See Morrison, "The Religious Defense of American Slavery before 1830," *Journal of Religious Thought* 37 (1981): 16–29.
46. For a discussion of the many problems with the so-called Hamitic hypothesis, see Winthrop Jordan, *White over Black: American Attitudes toward the Negro, 1550–1812* (New York: W.W. Norton, 1968), 17–20, 35–37, 41–43.

and similar narratives were used to "limit" power and not to "confer it."[47]

A favorite New Testament narrative used in the argument against slavery was Acts 17:26: God "made from one every nation of men to live on all the face of the earth, having determined allotted periods and the boundaries of their habitation." First Corinthians 12:13 was also a favorite text: "For by one Spirit we were all baptized into one body—Jews or Greeks, slaves or free—and all were made to drink of one Spirit." The unmistakable emphasis on the "universal parenthood of God" and the "kinship of humankind" was a persistent theme in abolitionist rhetoric.[48]

Throughout the pre– and post–Civil War eras, and in the midst of passionate and often riotous debates about the "biblical warrant" for slavery, African Americans rejected the proslavery, literalist hermeneutic used to sanction involuntary servitude, proclaiming, to the contrary, that the Bible witnessed to an all-powerful, liberating God who in Jesus Christ was concerned for the ultimate and holistic liberation of all of humanity. That the slaves sought to distinguish their own experiential Christianity from the "biblical" Christianity of their slavemasters is neither surprising nor enigmatic. Albert J. Raboteau states the matter succinctly: "Slaves were distrustful of the white folks' interpretation of the Scriptures and wanted to be able to search the Scriptures for themselves."[49]

In the mid–nineteenth century a young, white, Presbyterian clergyman named Charles Colcock Jones preached the New Testament narratives enjoining "submission of slaves to their masters." He preached these sermons on his father's Georgia plantation. His narration of the response of the slaves to his efforts is recorded in his *Tenth Annual Report*, written in 1845, and corroborates Raboteau's thesis:

> Allow me to relate a fact which occurred in the Spring of this year, illustrative of the character and knowledge of the Negroes at this time. I was preaching to a large congregation on the Epistle to Philemon; and when I insisted upon fidelity and obedience as Christian virtues in servants, and upon the authority of Paul, condemned the practice of running away, one-half of my audience deliberately walked off with themselves, and those that remained looked anything but satisfied, either with the preacher or his doctrine. After dismission, there was no small stir among them: some solemnly declared "that there was no such epistle in the Bible," others,

---

47. H. D. Ganse, *Bible Slaveholding Not Sinful: A Reply to "Slaveholding Not Sinful" by Samuel B. Howe* (New York: R and R Brinkerhoff, 1856), 36–37.

48. Peter J. Paris, *The Social Teaching of the Black Churches* (Philadelphia: Fortress Press, 1985), 10–11. Paris makes the point that the emphasis on the "kinship of humankind" has always been a characteristically ubiquitous theme in African American biblical interpretation.

49. Albert J. Raboteau, *Slave Religion: The Invisible Institution in the Antebellum South* (New York: Oxford University Press, 1978), 239–42.

"that it was not the gospel," others, "that I preached to please masters," others, "that they did not care if they ever heard me preach again."[50]

James Evans also argues that African Americans rejected a literalist interpretation of the slave regulations in New Testament narrative. Blacks, he argues, neither "gave up the Bible" nor gave up "the quest for freedom,"[51] but they accepted Paul's statement within *its own sociohistorical context*.[52] African Americans saw and heard in the biblical witness a mandate for human freedom and justice that only enkindled their efforts to secure their own liberation.

Evans's analysis of three suppositions that guided African Americans' approaches to the dictum "Slaves obey your masters" clarifies the hermeneutic operative in their interpretation of this regulation. First, it was believed that the slave regulation neither exemplified the whole gospel nor manifested its central thrust. Second, the relation of human bondage and the gospel was not considered to be the primary focus of the epistles in which the slave regulations are found. Third, Paul himself was not Christ, but a "dedicated, fully human servant of the Lord." Therefore, the apostle cannot be presumed to have possessed the "fullness" of the gospel, though he "strove to attain it."[53]

The white, Western, Christian proslavery hermeneutic stood in diametrical opposition to the more liberatory hermeneutic of African Americans regarding the nature of humanity and the integrity of human personhood. Peter Paris succinctly describes an unmistakable affirmation of the fundamental integrity of humanity in African American biblical interpretation:

> The universal parenthood of God implied a universal kinship of humankind. *This is the basic proposition of the hermeneutic designated as the black Christian tradition.* The black churches have always discerned this doctrine to be the bedrock of the biblical perspective on humanity, and they have given prominence to biblical passages that make it unequivocally clear. Accordingly, the black church has never hesitated to disavow any interpretation of Scripture that would attempt to legitimate racism, slavery, or any other form of human bondage. . . . Racism has never found asylum in the black churches.[54]

---

50. I am indebted to Milton C. Sernett for this quotation. See Sernett, *Black Religion and American Evangelism: White Protestants, Plantation Missions, and the Flowering of Negro Christianity, 1787–1865*, ATLA Monograph Series, no. 7 (Metuchen, N.J.: Scarecrow and The American Theological Library Association, 1975), 201. The quotation is taken from Charles Colcock Jones, *Tenth Annual Report* (1845), 24–25.

51. James Evans, "Black Theology and Black Feminism," *Journal of Religious Thought* 38 (1981): 46–47.

52. Ibid.

53. Ibid., 47.

54. Peter J. Paris, "The Bible and the Black Churches," in Ernest R. Sandeen, ed., *The Bible and Social Reform* (Philadelphia: Fortress Press, 1982), 134–35.

African American insistence on freedom from the hierarchical subordination implicit in the *Haustafeln* master-slave regulation, and from all
forms of tyranny and oppression, was unequivocal. The utilization of a
hermeneutic that nurtured this liberatory vision has remained a central
tenet of African American biblical hermeneutical theory and praxis.

"Submissive Wives" and "Submissive Women"

Traditionalist, literalist interpretations of the slave regulations in the
Haustafeln by proslavery moralists, as I have shown, contributed to
an oppressive and marginal existence for African American men and
women in the eighteenth and nineteenth centuries. Similarly, the legacy
of traditionalist, literalist interpretations of the regulations concerning
the "submission of wives" in the *Haustafeln* has been marked by the
marginality and domination of women.[55] In both instances, the codes
have been interpreted as affirming ontological equality (in the one case
between the master and slave and in the other case between the husband and wife), but a functionalist distinction between the roles of the
master-husband and the slave-wife is still retained as universally binding
forever. That is, the notion of female's "inner equality" with males was—
and is—viewed as compatible with women's hierarchical subordination,
marginality, and inequitable treatment in the domestic, ecclesiastical,
and socio-political spheres.

Christianity has profoundly encouraged the marginalization, subjugation, and exploitation of wives in Western culture. Stressing that the
"rulership" of wives by husbands has divine sanction based on the Genesis account of creation (Adam had chronological precedence over the
woman, named the woman, and she was designated his "helper," so the
arguments state),[56] and that several New Testament narratives reinforce
the patriarchal and hierarchical model for contemporary husband-wife
relationships (1 Tim. 2:11-15; 1 Cor. 14:34-35), Christian ethics has pro-

---

55. Elizabeth Carroll's definition of domination is pertinent to my discussion of male
dominance. Describing domination as a situation wherein persons assume the right to
control individuals or groups that may differ from the dominant group in race, national
origin, class, religion, or sex, Carroll observes: "All domination results from the human
inability to deal with differences in any way except through the imposition of power.
The 'different' is categorized as the inferior, and some form of dependency relationship
is imposed. Structures of dominance are ordinarily hierarchical." See Carroll, "Can Male
Dominance Be Overcome?" in Virgil Elizondo and Norbert Freinacher, eds., *Women in a
Men's Church* (*Concilium* 134 [New York: Seabury, 1980], 43).

56. For a helpful rebuttal to these still widespread positions see Gilbert Bilezikian,
"Hierarchalist and Egalitarian Inculturations," *Journal of Evangelical Theological Studies*
30, no. 4 (1987): 421–22. Bilezikian notes, for example, rulership has been conferred by
God over both female and male.

mulgated those characteristics in women that often render them passive, acquiescent, dependent, and infantile as both wives and women.

The Bible has been used to curb women's movement toward full partnership in home, church, and society; to inhibit efforts to insure the more equitable distribution of power in societal institutions; and to discourage efforts to redefine and nurture more balanced and positive cultural images and roles of women. These facts are evident in the domestic, ecclesiastical, and socio-political spheres of American culture. As Elizabeth Carroll has noted, women are subordinated in the "domestic regimes" as well as in public and sacred space. Ideologies of male supremacy promote males as those who are powerful, active, self-sufficient, fully human; women are supportive players in the "essentially male drama," with female nature defined as relative to the "normative" male nature, and secondary to that of the male.[57]

A survey of contemporary biblical interpretation on the *Haustafeln* regulation enjoining wives' submission to husbands confirms that the code continues to be utilized to legitimate a hierarchical, subordinationist ethos in the domestic sphere. Charles C. Ryrie, for example, argues that the wife's subordination to her husband is not an interim ethic, but constitutes an interminable norm, meant for all times:

> In domestic relationships, then, God has appointed an order which includes the husband as the head and the wife in a place of honor through a place of subordination.... The early church clearly considered the subordination of the wife in domestic relations the normal and fixed status.[58]

Ryrie quickly accedes that this observation should in no way lead one to conclude that Paul views women as inferior, but rather, the headship of the husband is to be exercised through the "filter of Christian love." He observes: "Peter illustrates it by commending the example of Sarah who obeyed Abraham and called him Lord."[59]

Fritz Zerbst argues that the *Haustafeln* prescribe the "divine arrangement" for husband-wife relations. While men are not told to "subject" wives to themselves or that they should exercise "power" over women,

---

57. Carroll, "Can Male Dominance Be Overcome?" 46. The point here is that women's "full integration" into church and society is no more sufficient than the "full integration" of blacks into society unless there is a more just and equitable distribution of power and responsibility for the good of the whole society. Full integration into a hierarchical, oppressive society only means that a hierarchical, oppressive society is now more fully integrated by blacks or women. To achieve a fuller partnership of women in church and society we must restructure institutions and structures within both church and society, so that power, leadership, and opportunity are shared in mutuality by women and men.

58. Charles C. Ryrie, *The Place of Women in the Church* (New York: Macmillan, 1958), 65–66.

59. Ibid., 66–67.

it is clear that subjection on the part of the wife remains.[60] Zerbst argues that since teaching and proclaiming the Word involve, in some sense, "rule-over" others, women's ordination especially is prohibited as a violation of women's subjection.[61]

In traditional interpretations of the regulation regarding women in Ephesians 5:21-33, the head-body relationship between Christ and the church is the paradigm for understanding the husband-wife relationship in marriage. And yet, verse 23 ("For the husband is the head of the wife as Christ is the head of the church, his body, and is himself its Savior") has remained a thorny problem in the history of the interpretation of the pericope. What does "headship" (*kephalē*) mean here? Some traditionalist interpreters argue that the term is synonymous with "authority" (*exousia*), while others reject this interpretation in favor of "source." Egalitarian interpreters argue that any imposition of an "authority structure" on what is meant to be a relationship marked by reciprocity would be a distortion of the christological paradigms adduced in the passage.[62]

Equally problematic in the interpretation of the regulation regarding wives is the meaning of "to be subject" (*hupotassō*) (see Col. 3:18; 1 Peter 3:1). Is "submission" synonymous with obedience? Is it voluntary? Reciprocal?[63]

Instead of rehearsing the literature on the linguistic peculiarities and significance of *kephalē* and *hupotassō*, I wish to move the discussion to another level, and ask a more fundamental and a priori question. Should we continue to accept as binding a Christianized pattern of hierarchical domination in the marriage relationship? Or is this a case—as with the slave regulation in the *Haustafeln* genre—where a literalist interpretation of the "letter" imposes an outmoded social ethos of another period onto the contemporary church? Before I turn to a discussion of the hermeneutical tensions engendered by these questions, I must briefly consider

60. Fritz Zerbst, *The Office of Women in the Church: A Study in Practical Theology* (St. Louis: Concordia, 1955), 77–78. I am indebted to Willard M. Swartley for the observations of Ryrie and Zerbst. See Swartley, *Slavery, Sabbath, War and Women: Case Issues in Biblical Interpretation* (Scottsdale, Pa.: Herald Press, 1983).

61. Zerbst, *The Office of Women*, 80–81.

62. In addition to commentaries on Ephesians, the reader may consult the following: Catherine Clark Kroeger, "The Classical Concept of *Head* as Source, Appendix III," in Gretchen Gaebelein Hull, *Equal to Serve: Women in the Church and Home* (Old Tappan, N.J.: Fleming Revell, 1985); J. Massyngbaerde Ford, "Biblical Material Relevant to the Ordination of Women," *Journal of Ecumenical Studies* 10, no. 4 (1973); Stephen Bedale, "The Meaning of *Kephalē* in the Pauline Epistles," *Journal of Theological Studies* 5, no. 2 (1954); Gilbert Bilezikian, "Hierarchalist and Egalitarian Inculturations."

63. See Ruth A. Tucker and Walter Liefield, *Daughters of the Church: Women and Ministry from New Testament Times to the Present* (Grand Rapids, Mich.: Academie, 1987), 454–55; Randy L. Maddox, "The Word of God and Patriarchalism: A Typology of the Current Christian Debate, " *Perspectives in Religious Studies* 14 (1987): 197–216; Carl B. Hoch, Jr., "The Role of Women in the Church: A Survey of Current Approaches," *Grace Theological Journal* 8, no. 2 (1987): 241–51; David L. Balch, "Early Christian Criticism of Patriarchal Authority: 1 Peter 2:11—3:12," *Union Seminary Quarterly Review* 39 (1984): 161–73.

the ways in which the *Haustafeln* regulation about wives has, by extension, reinforced notions of the propriety of women's submission and subordination to men in Western culture in general.

The dictum regarding women's subordination in the *Haustafeln* is directed to wives; however, it should never be assumed that the regulation has been used to legitimate the subordination of wives only. In fact, this injunction has been used more broadly, in conjunction with similar dictums in New Testament narratives, to reinforce patterns of male domination of women in church and society.

Again, both in the last century and in contemporary society, the Bible has been used against women's movement toward equality within church and society. As women have protested against socio-political discrimination, civil degradation, and inequality within the church, the Bible has been offered as the raison d'être for the perpetuation of women's subordination and marginality.[64] Indeed, several texts from the New Testament continue to be used in conjunction with the *Haustafeln* to restrict the leadership and authority of women in all dimensions of the church's life. The Pauline injunction in 1 Corinthians 14:33b-35 is cited most frequently:

> As in all the churches of the saints, the women should keep silence in the churches. For they are not permitted to speak, but should be subordinate, as even the law says. If there is anything they desire to know, let them ask their husbands at home. For it is shameful for a woman to speak in church.

Similar New Testament admonitions continue to be promulgated in homiletical and exegetical reflections about women in numerous denominations in the United States. Thus, 1 Corinthians 11:3 ("But I want you to understand that the head of every man is Christ, and the head of a woman is her husband, and the head of Christ is God") is cited along with 1 Timothy 2:11-15 ("Let a woman learn in silence with all submissiveness. I permit no woman to teach or to have authority over man; she is to keep silent . . . ") as mandating a fully masculine model of ecclesiastical leadership.

Assumptions that women's skills, rights, and gifts are not to be valued to such a degree as to warrant re-creating the social and ecclesial order to incorporate them more fully and justly into the fabric of our society are not relics of the past, but are still widespread. Traditionally, women have played a supportive role to men, and are generally prevented from creating and shaping ecclesiastical policy. This "trivialization of women"[65]—in part an outgrowth of a biblical literalism—has

---

64. Schüssler Fiorenza, "The Biblical Roots for a Discipleship of Equals," 88.

65. Carter Heyward and Suzanne R. Hiatt, "The Church Ponders Evermore the Trivialization of Women," *Christianity and Crisis*, June 26, 1978, 160.

thus perpetuated a very real and dangerous ethos in ecclesial communities. This ethos argues that not only should women's supportive roles in theological and ecclesiastical institutions and structures be nurtured as normative, but women have no natural right to shape and influence policy and lives in church and society. "The masculine model is the rational, orderly head and leader; the feminine model the emotional, chaotic, submissive heart, which follows and supports."[66] Feminist critiques of patriarchy and androcentrism constitute a radical call for the church to take seriously its agency as a vehicle through which God can achieve the full humanity of all persons.

Since the chief concern of my study is a review of divergent African American hermeneutical approaches to the slave regulation and to the regulation concerning wives (and women) in the *Haustafeln*, it is appropriate to note that African American women, with women in Western culture in general, have often tasted the pungent fruit of androcentric, hierarchical domination.

Black women are no strangers to arguments that the Bible sanctions their submission as wives and women in the domestic and socio-political spheres. They, too, have challenged literalist interpretations of women's subordination in the *Haustafeln* and similar narratives. Julia Foote, the well-known A.M.E. writer and preacher (born in 1823 in Schenectady, New York), allowed no one to dissuade her from accepting the challenge of public ministry. In an essay entitled "A Word to My Christian Sisters," she encouraged black women to be faithful to their ministry:

> Sisters, shall not you and I unite with the heavenly host in the grand chorus? If so, you will not let what man may say or do, keep you from doing the will of the Lord or using the gifts you have for the good of others. How much easier to bear the reproachment of men than to live at a distance from God. Be not kept in bondage by those who say, "We suffer not a woman to teach," thus quoting Paul's words [1 Cor. 14:34], but not rightly applying them.[67]

Jarena Lee, another illustrious writer and A.M.E. preacher in the nineteenth century, also repudiated literalist interpretations of the regulations regarding women's subordination, and stated her case for traversing the bounds of the traditional female role of "homemaker":

> Oh how careful ought we to be, lest through our by-laws of church government and discipline, we bring into disrepute even the word of life. For as unseemly as it may appear now-a-days for a woman to preach, it should be remembered that nothing is impossible with God. And why should it

---

66. Ibid.
67. Julia Foote, "A Word to My Christian Sisters," in William L. Andrews, ed., *Sisters of the Spirit: Three Black Women's Autobiographies of the Nineteenth Century* (Bloomington: Indiana University Press, 1986), 227.

be thought impossible, heterodox, or improper for a woman to preach? seeing the Saviour died for the woman as well as the man. If a man may preach, because the Saviour died for him, why not the woman? seeing he died for her also. Is he not a whole Saviour, instead of a half one? as those who hold it wrong for a woman to preach, would seem to make it appear.[68]

Jarena Lee, Julia Foote, and their sisters in the ministry had to reconcile their own inner conviction of a "call" to preach the gospel with traditional societal expectations that "feminine decorum" required them to either remain at home or exercise leadership primarily in the religious societies and women's organizations in the church. Like their white female counterparts in mainline Protestant denominations in the nineteenth century, African American women participated in churches and ecclesiastical structures marked by a male-dominated clergy and authority.[69]

We should note that in spite of dictums prescribing a limited role for African American women in churches and ecclesiastical structures, black women have always exercised power and influence in African American religious communities.

This exercise of power and influence has been documented by sociologist Cheryl Townsend Gilkes in her essay "The Role of Church and Community Mothers: Ambivalent American Sexism or Fragmented African Familyhood."[70] Gilkes defines the "church" or "community" mothers who function in sacred and secular community settings as powerful, older, respected black women. In the secular sphere, these mothers are usually heads of black women's organizations, and they may also hold positions of power and authority in more broadly based community and civil rights organizations. In sacred arenas, particularly the church, the women may be pastors, evangelists, pastors' wives and widows—but they are most often leaders of organized church women (they are missionaries, deaconesses, on mother's boards, etc.).[71]

---

68. Jarena Lee, "The Life and Religious Experience of Jarena Lee," in Andrews, ed., *Sisters of the Spirit*, 36.

69. The problem of black women's fulfillment of their spiritual quests in the nineteenth century has been described cogently by William L. Andrews: "Christian tradition granted women spiritual gifts such as the power of prophecy and charismatic preaching. The problem for women in nineteenth-century America was, in what sphere would they have the freedom to exercise their gifts? . . . Organizations run by and for women, such as women's auxiliaries in Protestant churches, missionary societies, and various agencies for moral reform, [were] greeted with enthusiasm in most quarters of antebellum America. In these kinds of organizations women could put their faith into practice without overstepping the bounds of proper feminine decorum or overreaching the traditional limits that mainstream Protestantism had placed around female leadership in the church" (p. 13).

70. Cheryl Townsend Gilkes, "The Role of Church and Community Mothers: Ambivalent American Sexism or Fragmented African Familyhood," *Journal of Feminist Studies* 2, no. 1 (1986): 41–59.

71. Ibid., 41–42.

Of particular relevance to our study is Gilkes's analysis of the diverse patterns of power shared by African American women across a broad spectrum of denominations. Women community workers are also usually churchwomen, and yet wide cleavage exists between the sphere of authority exercised by women community workers and by churchwomen.

Churchwomen often do not have the same access to authority within the church and ecclesiastical structures as they do in the socio-political sphere. Gilkes's comments are insightful:

> The paradoxes and ambivalence surrounding the appropriate roles of women in public life are more obvious within the churches. Within larger Baptist and Methodist denominations, women are organized under a system of relatively unyielding male authority. . . . Within the Sanctified Churches . . . there is a broader range of attitudes and practices concerning the position of women. Church mothers are not only role models and venerable elders—but also older venerated Spirit-filled women who hold considerable power within nearly autonomous and well-organized parallel women's worlds. . . . Some church mothers are church founders, preachers, and congregational leaders with full authority within congregational and denominational structures.[72]

In spite of the recognition of black women's labor in these ecclesial arenas, however, theological ambivalence remains regarding women's participation in the most authoritative arenas of the ecclesiastical community. Gilkes's allusion to the Church of God in Christ is illustrative of this ambivalence toward power-sharing in many African American religious communities. In the Church of God in Christ, with its powerful network of active women as "church mothers," women are still expected to accommodate themselves to male power and authority. Thus the official church manual states: "Women may teach the gospel to others [and] . . . have charge of a church in the absence of its pastor . . . without adopting the title of Elder, Reverend, Bishop, or Pastor."[73]

As Gilkes so eloquently states: "The entire tone of the official church manual's section, 'Women in Ministry,' reflected the ambivalence of men who were aware that 'the "proper" place of women in the church is an age-old debate.' "[74] Again, I would hasten to add that such ambivalence regarding African American women's fuller participation in the policy-making and ordained ranks of denominational hierarchies is not

72. Ibid., 50–51.
73. Church of God in Christ, "Women in Ministry," in *Official Manual with the Doctrines and Discipline of the Church of God in Christ* (Memphis: Church of God in Christ Publishing House, 1973), 159, 160 (cited in Gilkes, "The Role of Church and Community Mothers," 52).
74. Gilkes, "The Role of Church and Community Mothers," 52. The observation is by Bishop O. T. Jones, in Charles H. Pleas, *Fifty Years Achievement (History): Church of God in Christ* (Memphis: Church of God in Christ Publishing House, ca. 1957), 35.

peculiar to the Church of God in Christ, but transcends denominational boundaries in African American faith communities.

Hermeneutical Paradoxes, Issues, Tensions

One vexing question remains before us. Why is the African American interpretive tradition marked by a forceful critique and rejection of a literalist interpretation of the slave regulations in the *Haustafeln*, but not marked by an equally passionate critique and rejection of a literalist interpretation regarding the subordination of women to men in the *Haustafeln*? New Testament narratives that prescribe hierarchical patterns of dominance-subordination between men and women have *not* been perceived to be as troublesome and offensive as those that prescribe hierarchical patterns of dominance-subordination between slavemasters and slaves. If liberating biblical traditions regarding the kinship of humankind under God have comprised a treasury of antislavery apologia in the struggle for African American emancipation in the eighteenth and nineteenth centuries, why have we not witnessed the creation of a treasury of pro-women apologia to insure the full empowerment of African American women in the religious and socio-political spheres of African American culture and American national history? The question has remained a troubling and perplexing one for many.

James Evans's aforementioned insights that outlined African American hermeneutical strategies for reinterpreting the slave regulations are pertinent here. First, if African Americans believed that the slave regulations did not exemplify the whole gospel with regard to slavery, that it was not an institution that should exist *in perpetuum*, why continue to believe that the regulations regarding women's subordination exemplify the gospel *in perpetuum*? Second, if the relation of human bondage and the gospel was not the primary focus of the *Haustafeln* in which the slave regulations were found, why should we continue to believe that the regulations regarding women's subordination comprise a primary focus of the gospel in the *Haustafeln*? Finally, if writers of the *Haustafeln*—fully dedicated servants though they were—"did not possess the fullness of the Gospel," but "strove to attain it," and so were limited by their own socio-historical context with regard to the master-slave relationship, why not conclude that the writers of the *Haustafeln* were limited by their own socio-historical context with regard to the place of women in husband-wife relationships and female-male relationships? Why do androcentric interpretations and versions of Christian religious traditions in African American religious history continue to render African American women invisible (or marginal) partners in ecclesiastical structures and theological institutions of higher learning? What factors have contributed to the African American communities' paradoxical interpretation of the slave regulation and the regulation regarding women in the *Haustafeln*? Theologian Jacquelyn Grant articulates the question succinctly: "How can a Black preacher preach in a way which *advocates* St. Paul's dictum concerning women while *ignoring or repudiating* his dictum concerning slaves?"[75] The question can be stated more broadly: How can black male preachers and theologians use a liberated hermeneutic while preaching and theologizing about slavery, but a literalist hermeneutic with reference to women?[76]

I suggest that at least two factors have contributed to and undergird the paradoxical hermeneutical tensions in traditional African American approaches to the slave regulation and the regulation regarding women in the *Haustafeln*.

First, African Americans have exhibited a dominant orientation toward paradigms in biblical narratives that affirm *explicitly* the liberatory and just acts of God as a locus of hermeneutical authority. Thus, the Exodus paradigm (Exod. 14 in particular) has functioned as a vivid and explicit symbol that confirms that God is a God who liberates, who secures justice for the people of God, and who demands a radical obedience that upholds justice for everyone within the community of the people of God. In light of the socially restricting and often brutalizing forces to which African Americans have been subjected psychologically, socially, economically, and politically,[77] it is not at all surprising that they could identify with the struggles and the victory of the Israelites. That the Exodus paradigm has functioned as a source of encouragement and empowerment for black people is well known. James Cone identifies "liberation" (and the liberation motif in the Exodus event) as the central pillar of Christian theology itself.[78]

That the explicit paradigm of God's liberating activity has constituted a paradigmatic "canon" for African Americans is attested by Warren H. Stewart in his book *Interpreting God's Word in Black Preaching*. According to Stewart, "God as liberator" is an "ancient yet contemporary pivotal point around which Black theology revolves."[79]

---

75. Jacquelyn Grant, "Black Theology and the Black Woman," in Gayraud S. Wilmore and James H. Cone, eds., *Black Theology: A Documentary History, 1966–1979* (Maryknoll, N.Y.: Orbis, 1979), 421.

76. Evans, "Black Theology and Black Feminism," 47.

77. Peter Paris, "The Bible and the Black Churches," 133.

78. James Cone, *A Black Theology of Liberation* (Philadelphia: Lippincott, 1970), 17–22. For a discussion of the ways in which the Exodus paradigm addresses the fundamental and lasting human need of freedom and independence, see B. van Iersel and Anton Weiler, eds., *Exodus: A Lasting Paradigm* (entire issue of *Concilium* 189 [Edinburgh: T and T Clark, 1987]).

79. Warren H. Stewart, *Interpreting God's Word in Black Preaching* (Valley Forge, Pa.: Judson, 1984).

The point that I make here is that whereas the legitimacy of the slave regulation in the *Haustafeln* could be challenged rather handily based on *explicit* paradigms about liberation from slavery in such narratives as Exodus 14, biblical narrative does not contain an equally explicit and *consistent* paradigm about the liberation of women from patriarchy, androcentrism, and misogyny.[80]

A second factor that has contributed to African American ambivalence toward the authority of the regulation regarding women in the *Haustafeln* is that many African Americans have accepted uncritically a socialization that tolerates and accepts the patriarchal model of male control and supremacy that typifies the Eurocentric, Western, Protestant tradition in general.[81] A patriarchal ethos that inhibits the advancement of women in the socio-political and ecclesiastical spheres has often been mirrored by African American male culture as more normative than exceptional. Assumptions that men have the right and duty to dominate and to shape all dimensions of discourse in social and especially religious institutions and structures are easily documented in African American social and cultural history.[82]

How, Then, Will We Live? A Womanist Perspective

Increasingly, womanist theologians are redefining and expanding their understanding of religious history, ethics, theology, and biblical interpretation. A womanist is a black feminist (or feminist of color) who claims her roots in black history, religion, and culture.[83] Informed by biblical, theological, ecclesiastical, anthropological, and economic sources (among others), womanist theology searches in particular for the voices, actions, opinions, experiences, and faith of black women.[84] Womanist theologians take seriously the socio-historical context in which black women have found themselves as moral agents,[85] using this context as

80. See Phyllis Trible's analysis of biblical narratives that have as their focus tales of terror and suffering with women as victims, in *Texts of Terror: Literary Feminist Readings of Biblical Narratives* (Philadelphia: Fortress Press, 1984); Carolyn De Swarte Gifford, "American Women and the Bible: The Nature of Woman as a Hermeneutical Issue," in Adela Yarbro Collins, ed., *Feminist Perspectives on Biblical Scholarship* (Chico, Calif.: Scholars Press, 1985), 11–33.

81. Grant discusses this point at length in "Black Theology and the Black Woman," 420–23.

82. The literature on this subject is massive, and the reader is invited to consult sources in African American history, religion, and literature.

83. For an excellent analysis of the origin and development of the term *womanist* in Alice Walker's writings, see Delores S. Williams, "Womanist Theology: Black Women's Voices," *Christianity and Crisis*, March 2, 1987, 66–76.

84. Ibid., 67.

85. Toinette M. Eugene, "Moral Values and Black Womanists," *Journal of Religious Thought* 44, no. 2 (1988): 23–34.

an operative norm for feminist reflection. Further, they identify ways in which the plurality of experiences of African American women is both consistent with and in contradistinction to mainstream American socio-political and theological culture.[86] A womanist reflection on the hermeneutical paradoxes, issues, and tensions in the slave-woman regulation in the *Haustafeln*, then, takes seriously the need to create and implement responsible ethical guidelines for the dismantling of the gender hierarchy of African American men and women.

If it is true that the regulations in the *Haustafeln* are provisional; if it is true that they are "wineskins" and not "wine";[87] if it is true that the codes should not be "absolutized, universalized, or eternalized,"[88] either with regard to slaves or women—then *African American believing communities need to assume a new and more profoundly integrative praxis that moves women "from the margins" of the church and ecclesial structures "to the center."*[89] I propose at least three strategies for promoting more equitable, just, and liberative faith communities.

First, in recognition of the origin of the New Testament household codes and of the paradoxical and competing hermeneutic employed in the slave-woman regulation in the *Haustafeln* in Western culture, African American biblical interpreters must develop and adopt a liberationist biblical hermeneutic instead of a hierarchalist hermeneutic with regard to the interpretation of biblical narratives about women and women's "place" in ecclesiastical arenas and hierarchies. New Testament theologian Willard M. Swartley identifies two traditional hermeneutical approaches to the *Haustafeln*.[90] The first is that of the "hierarchic interpreters," who argue that subordination of wives and women to men is a biblical teaching that mandates long-term ethical guidelines for cultural obligation. I have presented arguments representing this viewpoint above under the heading " 'Submissive Wives' and 'Submissive Women.' "

---

86. For additional resources on womanist theological reflection see Katie Cannon, *Black Womanist Ethics* (Atlanta: Scholars Press, 1988); Delores S. Williams, "Women's Oppression and Lifeline Politics in Black Women's Religious Narratives," *Journal of Feminist Studies in Religion* (1985): 59–71; Kelly D. Brown, "God Is as Christ Does: Toward a Womanist Theology," *Journal of Religious Thought* 46, no. 1 (Summer–Fall 1989): 7–16; Jacquelyn Grant, *White Women's Christ, Black Women's Jesus: Feminist Christology and Womanist Response* (Atlanta: Scholars Press, 1989); Renita J. Weems, *Just a Sister Away: A Womanist Vision of Women's Relationships in the Bible* (San Diego: LuraMedia, 1988); Clarice J. Martin, "Womanist Interpretations of the New Testament: The Quest for Holistic and Inclusive Translation and Interpretation," *Journal of Feminist Studies in Religion* 6, no. 2 (1990): 41–61.

87. Stagg, "The Gospel, *Haustafel*, and Women," 60.

88. Ibid.

89. Bell Hooks, *Feminist Theology: From the Margin to the Center* (Boston: South End Press, 1984).

90. Swartley, *Slavery, Sabbath, War, and Women*, 258–69.

The second hermeneutical approach to the *Haustafeln* is that of the "liberationist interpreters." According to this view, espoused by Paul Jewett and others,[91] New Testament teaching on the subordination of women is a part of the various writers' historical limitations. It does not express the ideal found in Galatians 3:28-29. These teachings should not be taken as prescriptions for our social order today. According to Jewett:

> Paul "went all the way in living out the truth that in Christ there is neither Jew nor Greek," but Paul only began to work this out for slave and free, male and female. His limitations here should not restrict us: it is high time that the church press on to the full implementation of the apostle's vision concerning the equality of the sexes in Christ.[92]

David and Elouise Fraser, in their essay "A Biblical View of Woman: Demythologizing Sexegesis," argue that the functional subordination of women to men is the result of the fall and does not grow out of God's intention in creation. Never meant to be a permanent ethic for male-female social relations, but a part of sin's curse, it is ultimately abolished in the work of Christ. "The church should never be content until the full personal and social implications of the eschatological reality of Galatians 3:28-29 are established and practiced in this age."[93]

In contradistinction to the Greco-Roman, hierarchalist paradigm, a nonhierarchalist paradigm should be achieved. In this paradigm partnership and a supportive male mutuality in all of life under God empower the whole people of God.[94]

$$\text{female} \xrightarrow{\quad\quad\; God \;\quad\quad} \text{male}$$

If it is true that the earliest Christian communities nurtured a vision of a redeemed community of inclusive wholeness for women and men alike, then perhaps Frank Stagg is correct: "The preoccupation for male authority over women is pagan, anti-Gospel. It cannot be redeemed; it can only be aborted. It is a negation of the 'Gospel of Jesus Christ.' "[95] We need to look forward and seek to implement the best and most noble ideals of the gospel, extending the range of egalitarian, nonhierarchical social relationing to reciprocal relationships that are mutually empowering and liberating.

---

91. Paul K. Jewett, *Man as Male and Female: A Study in Sexual Relationships from a Theological Point of View* (Grand Rapids, Mich.: Eerdmans, 1974); this view is also shared by Virginia R. Mollenkott, *Women, Men, and the Bible* (Nashville: Abingdon, 1977).

92. Jewett, *Man as Male and Female*, 139.

93. David and Elouise Fraser, "A Biblical View of Women: Demythologizing Sexegesis," *Theology, News, Notes* (Fuller Theological Seminary), June 1975, 14–18.

94. For concrete suggestions on how partnership with God, humanity, and creation can be achieved, see Letty M. Russell, *Growth in Partnership* (Philadelphia: Westminster Press, 1981).

95. Stagg, "The Gospel, *Haustafel*, Women," 63.

A second and related strategy for promoting more just, equitable, and liberative faith communities is to encourage black males and black females to assume an advocacy stance in identifying liberatory biblical traditions that promote ideological and existential empowerment for black women at every level of ecclesiastical governance.[96]

The identification and emulation of more liberatory biblical traditions have been practiced by black women for centuries. The nineteenth-century A.M.E. preacher Jarena Lee cited Joel 2:28-29 as legitimating her call for the ordained ministry:

> I could not believe that it was a short-lived impulse or spasmodic influence that impelled me to preach. I read that on the day of Pentecost was the Scripture fulfilled as found in Joel 2:28-29, and it certainly will not be denied that women as well as men were at that time filled with the Holy Ghost. . . . Women and men are classed together, and if the power to preach the Gospel is short-lived and spasmodic in the case of women, it must be so equally in the case of men. . . . But the Bible puts an end to this strife when it says: "There is neither male nor female in Christ Jesus" [Gal. 3:28].[97]

It is true that the biblical narratives are androcentric and that the early Christian movement is presented through a patriarchally tinged filter. The absences and silences about women's historical and theological experience and contribution in the early Christian movement must never be overlooked;[98] rather, we must create and nurture strategies and paradigms that can provide clues to the more empowering and inclusive traditions in the early Christian movement.

Finally, we must encourage black women to prepare for graduate theological education in preparation both for the ordained ministry and for careers as theologian-scholars.[99] Nurturing a vision for such vocational alternatives should be accompanied by concretized strategies for providing financial and moral support for the task, as well as a commit-

---

96. New Testament scholar Cain H. Felder makes some concrete suggestions in this area. See his essay "The Bible, Black Women, Ministry," *Journal of Religious Thought* 12 (1985): 9–21. In *Just a Sister Away*, Renita J. Weems provides helpful exegetical and hermeneutical insights for analyzing biblical texts with her exploration of the complexities of human social relationships. African American biblical interpreters must continue to wrestle with the fact that the historical particularity and patriarchal/androcentric conditioning of biblical texts should raise methodological and practical questions about the task of biblical interpretation. Which texts can or should have theological significance and authority for African American faith communities? For a useful discussion of some of the methodological issues, see Letty M. Russell, ed., *Feminist Interpretation of the Bible* (Philadelphia: Westminster Press, 1985); and Elisabeth Schüssler Fiorenza, *Bread Not Stone: The Challenge of Feminist Biblical Interpretation* (Boston: Beacon Press, 1984).

97. Jarena Lee, "Women in the Gospel," in Andrews, ed., *Sisters of the Spirit*, 208.

98. Elizabeth Fox-Genovese, "For Feminist Interpretation," *Union Seminary Quarterly Review* 35 (1979–80): 10.

99. I use this term in the broadest sense to refer to academic careers as biblical scholars, theologians, ethicists, philosophical theologians, church historians, etc.

ment to create leadership positions for women in our churches, ecclesial structures, and theological institutions.

According to sociologist Delores Carpenter, personal qualities, education, and support of family and friends comprise important motivating factors toward the ordination of women. A major negative influence is sexism, including the lack of support of other clergy and especially male clergy. Strategies that address structural barriers, sexism, and resistance by male clergy are requisite.[100]

> If black people are going to create new roles in the ministry, black men will have to recognize that the present status of black women in the ministry is not acceptable. Since the gospel is about liberation, it demands that we create structures of human relations that enhance freedom and not oppression.... Liberation is not an individual's agenda but, rather, the commitment of the black community.[101]

A true understanding of the mission of the church requires that African Americans embrace a resocialized vision of the liberating character of the new creation of God for humanity in the most comprehensive and inclusive sense. A foremost and urgent need in African American faith communities is the need to alleviate the oppression and marginalization of women.[102]

The black church need not be captive to elements in Western, post-Enlightenment culture that eliminate women as creators and shapers of theological discourse or of ecclesiastical policy and agendas. A serious hermeneutical reassessment of our paradoxical approach to the slave-woman regulation in the *Haustafeln* challenges us to reexamine our very understanding of the Christian gospel itself. The task is urgent. How, then, will we live?

---

100. Delores S. Carpenter, "The Professionalization of the Ministry of Women," *Journal of Religious Thought* 43, no. 1 (1986): 72–73.

101. James H. Cone, "New Roles in the Ministry: A Theological Appraisal," in Wilmore and Cone, eds., *Black Theology*, 387–97.

102. Delores S. Williams, "The Color of Feminism: Or Speaking the Black Woman's Tongue," *Journal of Religious Thought* 43, no. 1 (1986): 57.

— *11* —

An African American Appraisal of the Philemon–Paul–Onesimus Triangle

Lloyd A. Lewis

In a sermon entitled "Finding Our Margin of Freedom," Samuel D. Proctor, distinguished pastor of Abyssinian Baptist Church in New York City, spoke of a central hope of black people:

> It does not matter where we were born, what kind of rearing we had, who our friends were, what kind of trouble we once got into, how low we sank, or how far behind we fell. When we add it all up, we still have some options left, we still have some choices we can make.[1]

Proctor is raising a pertinent issue here since he speaks of those things that in most cases determine an individual's position in society. Galatians 3:1-29, his text for the sermon, has the function of challenging that which is static and those things that are often appealed to as social determinants, as justifiers of the status quo.

Nonetheless Paul has been a particularly difficult character for those African Americans who would venture into the skies of biblical interpretation. For many of us he offers more bane than blessing. By this I mean

---

1. Samuel D. Proctor and William Watley, *Sermons from the Black Pulpit* (Valley Forge, Pa.: Judson Press, 1984), 38.

that the positive nature of his gospel of freedom in Christ is clouded by what appear to be insuperable thunderheads. Not all of this tempest, however, is due to what Paul himself has written. One needs only to consider the fact that a second generation of "Paulinists" took up Paul's mantle to address their problems and that successive generations interpreted Paul according to their contexts and problems. Because of this, biblical scholars, and African American biblical scholars in particular, have often had to strip away layers of interpretation of Paul by church fathers, preachers, and politicians in order to let Paul himself speak.

The Letter to Philemon is a particularly good example of the issue of the conflict between a text and the methodology of its interpretation. The connection between the names of several characters in Philemon and those mentioned in Colossians 4:7-18 has often reduced the significance of Philemon to one of providing links to justify the inclusion of Colossians within the Pauline homologoumena—those letters whose Pauline authorship is not contested. Thus Philemon becomes an exegetical stepchild, made all the more odious to many black exegetes by its ambiguous position on slavery. But what if we were to delve into Paul's language in Philemon and link what he says in the letter with what he says in Galatians? What if, instead of Colossians, Galatians becomes the interpretative key to Philemon?

It is the thesis of this short study that the relationship between Paul, Philemon, and Onesimus—a relationship that is fraught with the social barriers that stand between a master and his slave—is mitigated by Paul's careful use of language that reinforces the image of the church as a particular type of family.[2] His purposeful use of this language, drawn from Galatians, becomes instrumental in his dealings with both Philemon and Onesimus.

Paul's Predicament and Use of Familial Language

How can we characterize the problem that Paul faced? According to the Letter to Philemon, Onesimus, a slave, had run away from his master, Philemon (v. 15). While in Ephesus, Onesimus met Paul in his imprisonment and was subsequently converted to Christianity (v. 10). Paul then returned Onesimus to Philemon as the herald of the apostle's own impending visit (v. 22).

The letter itself is clearly meant to curry the favor of an offended Philemon. Paul bases his appeal on the closeness that he had enjoyed

---

2. The extent of Paul's use of metaphorical language to describe the church is illustrated by Paul Minear, *Images of the Church in the New Testament* (Philadelphia: Westminster Press, 1960).

with Philemon in the past. Love, the chief virtue of the Christian community, figures prominently in Paul's discussion with Philemon (vv. 1, 5, 7, 9, 16). The past relationship between the two men had resulted in a type of closeness and mutual dependence between them so that Paul could speak confidently of his knowledge of the kind of response that he would receive from his friend (v. 21).

Paul, however, is quite specific in the way he makes his appeal to Philemon on behalf of Onesimus. In Philemon 15f. Paul discusses returning the runaway Onesimus to his master with the instructions that the master should receive his servant "as a beloved brother." We know that Onesimus's status has changed, for since his conversion he now shares membership in the church with both Philemon and Paul. Again, Paul speaks of this change metaphorically. Onesimus is his "child" whom he has "begotten." His new status is contrasted with his former social status as a slave; by virtue of his relationship in the church, Onesimus is now more than a slave (*hyper doulon*). Yet there is no overt statement by Paul that he anticipates the immediate emancipation of Onesimus. The far more pleasing juxtaposition of "once a slave . . . now free" is lacking in this letter. Thus both exegetes and ethicists alike have the problem of determining Paul's attitude to slavery as an institution, especially as practiced among Christians.

Paul sees no need to comment any further to Philemon on the status of Onesimus. His statement would effect what Paul wanted done, and his words would indicate most clearly what the desired relationship should be. By a metaphorical use of language Paul could communicate his wishes to his friend and modify his friend's behavior. Thus it seems for Paul to call Onesimus his brother was a highly calculated move.

Language is a powerful tool in social relations in part because it can provoke emotions that are purely subjective.[3] When one talks about the connotative function of words one is talking about this very factor. Because of varying personal experiences, for example, the word *brother* may evoke radically different responses from different individuals. But when a group makes a denotative definition of a word, it is attempting to standardize the individual perceptions that one may have from hearing a word. The repetition of words by a group, especially words that have become a type of code or argot[4] for use within the group, has important instrumental effects.

If language is instrumental, that is, if it helps to create or sustain social realities, then what type of social reality was Paul creating for the church by calling it in many cases a family? Paul used a social symbol,

---

3. William P. Alston, *Philosophy of Language* (Englewood Cliffs, N.J.: Prentice Hall, Inc., 1964), 47.

4. On the instrumental nature of language, see especially Oscar Uribe-Villegas, *Issues in Sociolinguistics* (The Hague: Mouton Publishers, 1977), 64.

the household, and used it as part of an elaborate metaphor both to describe the comprehensive nature of the Christian community and to mark its borders. In doing so Paul was following a pattern established in the Old Testament and later Jewish literature in which the story of the delivery of Israel at the Red Sea was combined with the language of family to describe the nation of Israel under the parenting of God.[5] God is Father; the members of Israel are his children and therefore siblings of one another. Paul also followed a pattern used by several different groups within Israel who sought to maintain continuity with the promises made to Abraham while addressing their group's particular situation.

Those at Qumran, for example, sought to isolate themselves from the wider nation of Israel while remaining in contact with the promises made to Israel. By identifying themselves as the children of God over against Israel they were able to create a social structure that was able to sustain this identity.[6] In a less isolationist way Philo and Josephus, though interested in protecting the cultic uniqueness of Israel, used the same language to allow wider contact with the non-Jewish world.[7] Paul, like the community at Qumran, wished to emphasize the continuity of the church with the promises made to Abraham while making possible an attitude toward the non-Jewish world that could justify a Gentile mission. The naming of the church as a family was one important means of accomplishing this.

Blood kinship, the claiming of common ancestry, is one means of creating order in a social group. On other occasions in which social order is needed and where no blood relationship exists, patterns of organization must be synthesized. Sometimes an individual uses family language in addressing another simply as a means of indicating sentiment without any overt attempt on the part of the user to create any lasting relationship between the speaker and the one who is addressed. The older woman who casually calls a young woman "my child" has no intention of creating any artificial family and uses the term in a social setting solely to express endearment or to recognize the fact that she is the elder in a situation. Legal adoption presents another case in which kinship language is used although blood relationship does not exist. Here a person becomes by law a member of a family, severing by doing this all ties with a former

---

5. There are numerous Old Testament texts that can be cited here, for example, Exod. 4:22-23; Hos. 11:1-3; Lev. 25:35-38, where the Exodus event is a sufficient warrant to require care for a fellow Israelite.

6. See in the Qumran literature, for example IQH IX, 29–33; IQH IX, 35f. Note the restrictive way that the Qumran community uses the word *brother* in IQS I, 24f. The members of the Dead Sea Scroll group had radically particularized the Jewish metaphor to speak only of themselves.

7. In order to accommodate his concerns Philo essentially maintains two sets of borders. He speaks of a universal fatherhood of God accomplished through creation (*Migr. Abr.* 28; *Det. Pot.* 54). At the same time he can point to the fact that this kinship with God precludes engaging in idolatrous religious practices (*Spec. Leg.* 1, 322).

family, and assuming the rights and duties of a child, often for a childless couple. Yet a third instance in which family language may be used occurs in a wide variety of situations in which, without legal action or family ties, people organize themselves into groups that use family language in referring to one another and adopt attitudes that reflect family feeling and family expectations.[8] Unlike those who use the language of family as a simple form of social convention, there is a clear understanding that there are definite rights and duties that those who belong to the group have and definite expectations that they can have of one another. At the same time those who belong to these groups regularly do not cease to belong to their blood families. Anthropologists use the technical name *pseudo-families* to refer to such groups. These groups' use of family language becomes a way of conveying the hopes and limits of those who are within the group.

If we briefly survey the images that Paul uses in speaking about the church as a family[9] and if we analyze the 112 times that Paul describes members of the church as "brothers" and the fact that he hardly ever uses this language to speak of actual blood kinship, we can come to the conclusion that Paul's intention was that within the church of Jesus Christ the primary relationship would be a pseudo-familial relationship among peers. Paul's Christians call one another "brother" and "sister" precisely because they are children of the same Father.

Galatians on the Family of God

As stated above, it is my concern that Philemon be read in the light of what Paul states in Galatians, particularly Galatians 3:1—4:7, where Paul speaks about the family of God and about the results of inclusion in it. In Galatians, Paul attempts to draw a dichotomy between two communities—those who have received the proclamation of the crucified Christ and those who remain under the Law. As a by-product of this argument, and also as a justification of the full inclusion of the Gentiles, Paul had to prove that adherence to the Law does not make one God's child.

The opening passages of Galatians 3 set three questions before the Galatians (vv. 2, 3, 5). By opposing "hearing with faith" to "works of

---

8. I am very purposefully using "pseudo-kinship" to define the model that the church presents. In this I am drawing on anthropological studies, especially Julian Pitt-Rivers, "The Kith and the Kin," in Jack Goody, ed., *The Character of Kinship* (Cambridge: Cambridge University Press, 1973), 95.

9. I mean here such words as *child, brother, sister, father,* and *mother*—terms Paul uses to speak of members within the church; and *sons of God, daughters of God,* and *children of God*—terms he uses to speak of the relationship that members of the church have with God.

Law" in verses 2 and 5, Paul is certainly opposing the two terms *faith* and *works*, which are prominent in his arguments both in Galatians and in Romans. In essence, however, Paul is opposing circumcision and the ritual acts associated with membership in Israel according to the Law of Moses to "hearing with faith," the reception of Paul's preaching to the Galatians, the occasion when they received the first installment of the Spirit. This message was received through faith, and it was on the basis of faith that the Spirit was received by the Galatians. Paul establishes elsewhere that there is a connection between the works of the Law and the flesh. Here he introduces the notion that faith is connected to the reception of the Spirit. Paul indicates this in Galatians 3:6-29, where he uses the very example of Abraham to prove that the true children of Abraham, that is those who belong to the family of Abraham, are not those who are Abraham's physical descendants, but rather are those who, like Abraham, respond to God in faith (Gal. 3:7).

The negative argument, which parallels that of verses 6–9, begins in verse 10. Here Paul uses the Old Testament again to show that a curse rests upon those who keep the Law. The function of the crucifixion of Jesus was not simply to break the Law but to redeem those who were under the Law (Gal. 3:13). Paul, thus, has introduced a second rearrangement within the household of faith, that of freedom from the Law, a matter that he will develop more fully in Galatians 4:8—5:11.

The opposition of Christ to the Law (v. 13) served a dual purpose (the two *hina* clauses that follow). First, it assured that the blessing of Abraham would come upon the Gentiles. Second, it guaranteed that the promise of the Spirit might rest upon the believing community through faith. But by doing this Paul has purposefully connected the promise made to Abraham with the Spirit and has asserted that this is accomplished in Christ.

Paul illustrates this in verse 15 by using the analogy of a will; by this example he shows the reliability of the guarantee made to Abraham by God. On a purely jural level, a will is a trusted document. But in this case the guarantor of the will is God. Thus, as in 3:16, Paul can assume the reliability of the promise made to Abraham that in him all the nations would be blessed. Yet Paul could also argue that the promise had been particularized in Christ. In 3:16 he makes this claim in a midrash on Genesis 12:7. He bases his argument on the Septuagint's version of 12:7, where the word *seed* is in the singular, rather than in the plural. This language is crucial in determining the true boundaries of the family of Abraham, and thus of his heirs, the true Israel. The promise that is connected with Abraham is now focused on one person, Jesus the Christ. This move by Paul defines the meaning of the word *promise* as he uses it, for Paul seems to assert that the proclamation of the risen Christ is an occasion for the presence of the Spirit,[10] the means by which all the nations are blessed in the faithfulness of Abraham's descendant Jesus Christ.

At this point we can see how family language has functioned thus far in Paul's argument and how he has reformed it. Paul has rearranged the borders of the family of Abraham. Since Christ was the unique "heir" to Abraham, those who are in him receive the promise made to Abraham— the Spirit. They are a second generation of heirs and are Abraham's legitimate heirs. Paul identifies the promised inheritance as the Spirit, which is now available to those outside the natural family of Abraham, since the true family of Abraham is determined by faith, like that of Abraham, and not by blood. Paul has defined the content of the promise made to Abraham. He has also particularized the meaning of *heir* and *child of Abraham* so that these terms enhance the position of the Gentiles who, like Abraham, were justified apart from the Law through faith.

To sharpen his point even further, in verses 23ff. Paul uses the picture of a household to contrast the Law with the life of the Christian under Christ. Here the Law is seen as a servant within a household, thus showing the relationship between believer and Law. The figure is that of a minor child who is compared to the child who had reached maturity. The Law has the function within a household of a "custodian," a domestic servant, who protected the child and kept it from trouble. The authority of the servant ended when the child reached maturity, and Paul means for us to understand the same thing about the Law. The Law remained in force until faith took over. But faith, as we have seen, was found in the coming of Jesus Christ. Therefore the Law no longer holds any sway over those who are in Paul's church. The Law no longer determines membership in God's family.

This is confirmed by the section that begins at 3:26. Paul asserts as a parallel to his statement in 3:7 that all who are in Christ Jesus are the sons of God through faith. Thus Paul has linked through faith both membership in the family of Abraham and membership in the family of God. Paul here is using material that is traditional and linked to the act of baptism. As we have seen, this statement is based on Paul's assumption that Christ is uniquely the heir to the promises made to Abraham, and that those who are baptized into Christ have put him on. The series of distinctive statements found in 3:28 looks back to the argument in the first contrast found in 3:1-25 while at the same time it anticipates in its contrast between slave and free what he discusses in 4:8—5:1.

The three antitheses of roles within society (Jew-Greek, slave-free, male-female) are mitigated through baptism (3:28). This is important

---

10. See particularly David John Lull, *The Spirit in Galatia* (Chico, Calif.: Scholars Press, 1980), 55. Lull argues the importance of this factor in interpreting what Paul understood about baptism.

to note because the subordinationist roles conveyed in the latter two antitheses reflect the ideal of order in the Greco-Roman world where females were subject to males and slaves were subject to masters.[11] For diasporan Jews contemporary with Paul keeping the Law would define their place in respect to God's promises. Paul has already shown how membership in the family of God is not determined by keeping the Sabbath, circumcision, or other laws. Now Paul suggests that old structures of subordination no longer hold for those who are baptized. The binding nature of the diasporan Jewish household is also superseded by membership in the family of God, where all are considered as one and therefore as peers.

For Paul to speak in Galatians about the adoption of Christians as the children of God means that he advances a type of porous solidarity for members of the church. In accord with one aspect of this language, baptism and the gift of the Spirit set the church apart. Yet at the same time boundaries that apply to the church remain permeable so that others might be included. Status,[12] which undermines the common lot found in being the child of God, is suppressed: It is the common lot that is the focus of Paul's appeal. Paul's use of this language of family, thus, not only defined the community but also indicated the ideal attitudes that members of the church should have toward one another.

The Philemon–Paul–Onesimus Triangle Reconsidered

Now we return to the Letter to Philemon—the starting point of this study. How does the use of family language form attitudes that determine behavior within the Pauline churches? And how, as in the case of Philemon, does this language enter into situations in which the ideals of the church collide with those found in the wider society?

The use of family language in the twenty-five verses of Philemon is extensive. Four times (vv. 1, 7, 16, 20) the word *brother* is used to signify a member of the church. Once (v. 2) a female member of the church is identified as "sister." Paul refers to Onesimus, the runaway slave, as his "child" in verse 10 and claims that he has "fathered" him (*gennao*). The

---

11. Further development of this structure in early Christianity is found in the tables of household duties. See David Balch, " 'Let Wives Be Submissive . . .': The Origin, Form, and Apologetic Function of the Household Duty Code in 1 Peter" (Ph.D. diss., Yale University, 1974).

12. The important role that status played in Hellenistic society cannot be minimized. Wayne Meeks shows that status inconsistency undermined "traditional hierarchy of ranks: language and place of origin, . . . personal liberty or servitude, wealth, occupation, age and sex." One can find in Paul, as Meeks suggests, examples of how early Christianity could enhance social mobility. See Wayne A. Meeks, *The First Urban Christians* (New Haven: Yale University Press, 1983), 22–23.

familiar epistolary greeting speaks of God as Father to Paul, Timothy, and Philemon and his household. In this letter there are no cases in which any family terms are used literally.

In the letter, reciprocal sharing, either of status or goods, is of great importance to Paul. Named individuals are classified as Paul's "fellow prisoners" (v. 23), "fellow soldiers" (v. 2), or "fellow workers" (vv. 1, 24). Paul's appeal to Philemon is made to a "partner" (v. 17). Even Philemon's faith is a commodity that Paul would have him share in partnership with others. There is the potential for the exchange of money between Philemon and Paul (v. 18), and Onesimus travels back and forth between his master and the apostle.

There is also a limited use of language that is concerned with the household of Philemon. When Paul addresses the letter he does so to Philemon and to the church that met at his house (v. 2). Philemon's family seems to be mentioned if we can assume that Apphia is his wife. But the Greco-Roman household contained more than those who might be called "primary kin." Freedmen and slaves were part of the household, too. That Onesimus is Philemon's slave (v. 16) is the central concern for Paul. This is why, when Onesimus crosses into the pseudo-family of the church, the two households, one literal and one figurative, seem to collide.

There is also a fair amount of status-conscious language in the letter. Overt pseudo-family language, as we have seen, makes a distinction between church members and those who are outside the church, as does the use of the word *hagioi* (vv. 5, 7) to indicate that one is a Christian. Paul's position as a prisoner, which he mentions in verses 1, 9, 10, 13, would place him in unfavorable status in the eyes of the world. Elsewhere in his letters Paul may reveal that he is conscious of his apostolic role and his authority as a church leader, but in Philemon he seems to veil these factors purposefully. Though he can command (v. 8) he chooses to appeal (vv. 9, 10) and to avoid compulsion in all that he does.

The convergence of all of these factors highlights the importance of this letter. I believe that John Knox is right when he states that the highly personal nature of the letter often covers the fact that the epistle is official correspondence.[13] We need to begin by looking at the epistolary address and conclusion of the letter and in particular the way in which individuals other than Onesimus are described by Paul. Once that has been done we can consider the body of the letter and the interaction that occurred among Onesimus, Philemon, and Paul.

In the homologoumena other than Philemon, when Paul delivers his credentials he describes himself as "apostle" (Gal. 1:1; 1 Cor. 1:1; 2 Cor.

---

13. John Knox, *Philemon among the Letters of Paul* (New York: Abingdon Press, 1959), 21.

1:1) or as the "slave of Christ" (Phil. 1:1) or in the case of Romans as both "slave" and "apostle" (Rom. 1:1).

In Philemon, however, he uniquely introduces himself as "a prisoner of Christ." Scarcely a metaphor for Christian service,[14] the title refers to the actual fact of Paul's imprisonment. Curiously we know that Paul did not find his imprisonment embarrassing. Indeed, he could see how it aided in the advance of the gospel (Phil. 1:12f.). In Philemon, Paul mentions his imprisonment three times—in the address of the letter and then in verses 10 and 13, where he is concerned with the conversion and mission of Onesimus.

The letter is sent by Timothy, who is simply given the title "brother," the first use of pseudo-family language in the epistle. We have noted above that this word emphasizes the shared status that is found in the church and is synonymous with being one of the baptized. Yet we know that Timothy was notable among members of the church. In 2 Corinthians 1:1, Philippians 1:1, 1 Thessalonians 1:1, and 2 Thessalonians 1:1 he is given as a co-writer of an epistle. We can suppose that this would help to further his influence. Timothy was clearly a man on the move. In 1 Corinthians 4:17 and 16:10 we see that he was an advance man for Paul in his dealings with the Corinthians. Paul also chose him to be an emissary to the Philippians (Phil. 2:20) because of his faithfulness and reliability. In 1 Thessalonians 3:2, 6, he accepts a similar role with the Thessalonians and brings reports and messages to and from Paul. Here, too, he is identified as "brother." His activity as Paul's companion and messenger must have been important to the Roman congregation (see Rom. 16:21).

Clearly not all of those who were members of the church and brothers or sisters in the community had the high visibility of Timothy and were Paul's emissaries. It is, however, inconceivable that anyone would be allowed to send letters or act as an emissary for the church unless he or she were a "brother" or "sister."

Now let us turn to those who received the letter. Philemon is addressed in verse 1 as "our beloved fellow worker." We have noted above how "love" typifies this letter as a whole. Paul praises Philemon for his love (vv. 5, 7) and makes his appeal to him for the sake of love (v. 9). If *beloved* is an attributive adjective, then Paul is expressing his own affectionate regard for Philemon. But opinion varies as to whether the word is an attributive adjective or a substantive, and because of this a strong case might be made that *beloved*, found without a possessive pronoun or noun, is really a separate title that designates those who, like Israel in Romans 11:28, are beloved of God. Romans 16:12, 2 Corinthians 7:1, 12:19, and Philemon 1 are all instances in which these factors occur

---

14. Peter Stühlmacher, *Der Brief an Philemon* (Zurich: Benziger Verlag, 1975), 29.

in the Pauline letters. There individuals are addressed in the vocative case of the term.

Philemon is also Paul and Timothy's *co-worker*, a word that places Philemon and Prisca and Aquila (Rom. 16:3), Urbanus (Rom. 16:9), Epaphroditus (Phil. 2:25), Clement and his companions (Phil. 4:3), and Epaphras, Demas, and Luke (Philemon 24) among the groups of men and women who share with Paul in the work of the gospel. There is no strong reason to suggest that the "co-workers" constituted an office in the Pauline churches. Meeks's suggestion that they constituted a type of staff for the apostles is no doubt as accurate a description as is possible,[15] since there is no record of how they were chosen or of any specific duties that were common to them all. But cooperation among them was essential for their work to be successful, since, as Stühlmacher states, "Paul and Philemon work together for the cause of Christ."[16]

Although Philemon is the principal recipient of the letter, we find that other individuals and, at the end of the introduction, the whole of Philemon's house church are addressed. Apphia, whom we noted before, is named as a recipient of the letter. Though, as stated above, there is a possibility that Apphia may be Philemon's wife, she is addressed in the epistle as "sister," a member of the church. Although as a wife in the household she might have had a special responsibility for governing the servants,[17] Paul lets it be known that he views Onesimus as his peer in the family of God. Archippus is the last of the named individuals who receives the letter. All we know about him we find in Philemon and, as in the case of Apphia, his place within the household of Philemon must remain open to speculation. Nor can we say that his title,"fellow soldier," should be taken literally. Philippians 2:25 speaks of Epaphroditus as "brother," "fellow soldier," and "co-worker." No distinction is made among these titles. Can we not assume that all of these titles emphasize a concept of shared status that was particularly important for Paul to mention?

Paul concludes his address with the familiar doxology found in his letters. Whereas Paul returns momentarily to the singular in verse 2 and indicates that the letter is primarily for Philemon, the greeting as well as the final salutation (v. 25) are fixed bits of liturgical speech. We can therefore see Paul beginning and ending the letter with liturgical formulas that indicate the shared unity of believers.

Now we can look at the end of the letter. Epaphras, who is one of those who greets Philemon, shares with Paul the experience of imprisonment. In the final salutation, Mark, Aristarchus, Demas, and Luke are also

15. Meeks, *First Urban Christians*, 133.
16. Stühlmacher, *Der Brief an Philemon*, 30.
17. Eduard Lohse, *Colossians and Philemon* (Philadelphia: Fortress Press, 1971), 190.

mentioned as Paul's fellow workers; these four, then, share with Paul and Philemon in the work of the gospel and are peers of one another.

This somewhat detailed investigation of the introduction and conclusion of the letter is justified, I believe, for it shows that the density of communal terms is so marked that it can hardly be coincidental. Much has been said about the tactful nature of the Letter to Philemon, but little has been said about why it was so important for Paul to lay aside not only his status but also that of others who were prominent in his retinue in order to settle this master-slave situation. The boundaries of the letter, conventional as they may be, help to drive home how deeply Paul believed that shared status must mark a church. Now let us turn to the body of the letter to see how Paul develops a picture of the relationship between himself and Philemon and Onesimus; that picture will at least ameliorate the situation posed by the defection of Onesimus.

The body of the letter breaks conveniently into two parts. Verses 4-7 are an epistolary thanksgiving. As such they set forth a number of themes that Paul will pick up in the rest of the body of the letter: love (vv. 5, 7, 9, 16); prayer (v. 22); sharing and partnership (v. 17); doing good works (v. 14); deep affection (vv. 12, 20); refreshment (v. 20); and fraternity (v. 20). All of these help to highlight the virtue of Philemon, which Paul is effusive in praising.

In the thanksgiving Paul uses little family language. Philemon is praised because of the love and faith that he exhibits. Whereas in the other letters Paul often cites the triad "faith, hope, love," it is love that is first mentioned in our letter, love that is visible in Philemon's activity on behalf of the saints.

In verse 6 this is made explicit in a phrase that refers to Philemon's fellowship in faith. But is Philemon's fellowship simply his participation in the church, or does Paul mean more? Paul Sampley certainly believes that "partnership" is more than sharing or participation. For Sampley it is a dynamic reciprocal agreement with legal antecedents by which two parties are drawn together for mutual benefit.[18] Paul is aware that among members of the church Philemon has already demonstrated this quality. Should Paul not anticipate the same from him in the issue of the runaway slave?

The concrete example of Philemon's love in verse 5 is recapitulated in verse 7. By Philemon's providing refreshment for the hearts of the saints, Paul has received joy and comfort. The little constellation of words—*heart*, *love*, and *refresh*—will reappear again as Paul identifies Onesimus as his "heart" and prays that Philemon will provide refreshment for him.

---

18. J. Paul Sampley, *Pauline Partnership in Christ* (Philadelphia: Fortress Press, 1980), 81.

Partnership and shared joy are both activities of those who are emotionally bound together. Paul further indicates this when he addresses Philemon as his brother in verse 7, thus showing that in addition to the family and household that Philemon heads, there is another household into which Philemon has been inserted through his conversion—the household of which God is Father.

With the initial "therefore" of verse 8, Paul begins his request of Philemon. In part he builds his request on those qualities found in Philemon that he has effusively praised. Paul's method, however, is to provide an example for Philemon. We know from the introduction of the letter that Paul has voluntarily bracketed his status as an apostle. It is perfectly possible for Paul to "command" a response from Philemon out of boldness. Boldness before others was one of the marks of an apostolic person (2 Cor. 7:4; see also the description of the apostles in Acts 4:13, 29, 31; and 28:31). Issuing commands, however, is not typical of Paul. He refuses to act as a superior to Philemon. Rather, on the basis of love (which we remember he shares with Philemon [vv. 5, 7]) he chooses to "appeal" to Philemon on the issue of the runaway. This is the word that Paul uses most frequently to address fellow baptized persons in the church (Rom. 12:1; 15:30; 16:17), those for whom reciprocal exhortation is an established pattern (1 Thess. 4:18; 5:11). Paul, therefore, voluntarily places himself on the same level as Philemon.

Now in the latter half of verse 9 the de-emphasizing of Paul's credentials is repeated in another way. Paul says he is a *presbutes*. The ambiguity of this word is well known, and strong arguments have been mounted to translate it either as "old man" or "ambassador." Does not the context, however, suggest that "ambassador" would sharpen the continuation of Paul's voluntary self-abasement?

Paul's brotherly exhortation to Philemon has a purpose: the cause of Onesimus. In verse 10 the unique relationship between Paul and Onesimus is described through the use of family language. Paul calls Onesimus his child and reveals to Philemon that he had given life to Onesimus during his imprisonment. We might note that Paul in his own writings rarely refers to himself as a "father" to fellow Christians, and reserves that title for times when he is speaking to those whom he has converted to Christianity (1 Cor. 4:15) or for particularly sharp issues of ecclesial conflict.

Paul's conversion of Onesimus had transferred the runaway into the family of God, but what did this transfer mean to Onesimus? In verse 11 Paul states that Onesimus was "Formerly ... useless to you, but now he is indeed useful to you and to me." Then in verse 12 Paul indicates that he is sending Onesimus to Philemon, Onesimus who is Paul's very heart.

Paul's language in verse 11 includes the well-discussed pun on the runaway's name. Our interest, however, needs to be on why Onesimus was once useless, but now is useful. Surely Paul could not be speaking of the usefulness/uselessness of Onesimus as a slave. Otherwise we would have to read the latter half of verse 11 as a sign that conversion's greatest effect on Onesimus was the power for greater diligence in his chores, and that out of his conversion he had ended up with two slavemasters instead of one. Verse 12 provides stronger clues for solving this riddle. Onesimus was now being sent to Philemon to stand as the representative of Paul. We cannot say categorically whether before his conversion Onesimus was a useless slave in Philemon's household. We can say, however, that the unconverted Onesimus did not possess that status in the family of God that would make him of use to the church and its leaders. But by virtue of his baptism Onesimus now could be of great practical use in the church. Like Timothy he could be sent by Paul to others because he could stand in the place of Paul. And as in the case of Timothy, where Paul's "child" was, one could see Paul's ways.

But what of the relationship between Philemon and Onesimus? Paul hints at this in verse 13 when he states his wish that Onesimus should be returned to serve him in his imprisonment in the place of Philemon. Not only would Onesimus be able to be Paul's envoy to Philemon: The return of Onesimus to Paul would prove that Onesimus could be the envoy of Philemon to Paul.

We have seen above how mutuality has marked this letter, and we have noted Paul's tact in handling a situation that could be both embarrassing for Philemon and socially explosive in his community. Paul continues his appeal in verse 14, now seeking to have Onesimus returned to him as an act of Philemon's own will. What does remain is that final issue of the status of Onesimus, which Paul clarifies in verses 15-16. First, we must understand Paul's perspective in the matter. The flight of Onesimus was a rupture of social codes as they existed within the household of Philemon. Nonetheless Paul could accept that rupture as yielding some fundamental truth about living in the family of God. Now Paul, who in verse 9 had claimed paternity to Onesimus, uses the same term that he applied to Philemon to describe Onesimus. He is no longer a slave; rather he is more than a slave—he is a beloved brother, just as Philemon is Paul's "brother" and is "beloved" by God. Onesimus thus stands on a par with both Paul and his former master.

For Paul, whom Onesimus had not wronged directly, this would be no problem, but for Philemon it could be. Does Paul suggest that conversion is tantamount to emancipation from slavery? Does Paul suggest that the household of Philemon should have a double standard—one set of norms for its life as a household, but another for its life as a house church?

Paul does not answer the question directly, and he does not insist on either of these two options. This, I believe, is very important. What Paul does, rather, is to make himself, in essence, the envoy of Onesimus, identifying himself with the runaway convert so closely that the debts that Onesimus incurred Paul desires to assume (v. 18). Thus Paul has brought to light the implications of being his child and the child of God in a church and community where equal status under the gospel, as shown in Galatians, is a virtue and where an apostle, a runaway slave, and a slaveholder can be interchanged. He now leaves it to Philemon to decide what understanding of Onesimus within his household would best reflect this reality.

Conclusion

I want to return to the power that Dr. Proctor found in the words of Paul. He discovered that Galatians, and the way that Paul wrote the letter, provided a window of hope for the people of his congregation. My purpose in exegeting Philemon was to suggest that the same nonidolatrous language that marked Paul's preaching in Galatians is also evident, though subtly, in a letter that black peoples have heard as a proof-text to justify slavery in the past and to some extent racial bigotry in the present. It is a fact, however, that a different approach to the letter—one that is less interested in inserting Philemon into Pauline chronology and that is more concerned with fitting the letter into Paul's theology and ecclesiology—presents different results. I see in Paul's almost dizzying display of family language even Paul struggling with the fact that a gospel that subverts the fundamental distinction between Jews and Gentiles would not long leave the issue of slavery alone. Here, I think, is a chance for black exegetes to claim Philemon as their own and as an indication of good news and of a new arrangement for blacks. I believe that African American people who study the Bible and who are concerned with issues of human freedom and liberation can take heart from Paul. Careful examination of his language shows that his ambiguity may not be so much a matter of his indecision as his unwillingness to canonize the social roles found in his environment. Rather, he invites the black church into new, nonstatic social configurations. And that, it seems to me, is where the storm clouds begin to part.

Index of Ancient Sources

OLD TESTAMENT —

247

NEW TESTAMENT —

EXTRABIBLICAL LITERATURE —

Index of Topics and Names

Contributors

Randall C. Bailey is Associate Professor of Old Testament and Hebrew at the Interdenominational Theological Center in Atlanta. He is also the author of *David in Love and War: The Pursuit of Power in 2 Samuel 10–12* (Sheffield, 1990). He holds a Ph.D. in Old Testament from Emory University.

Charles B. Copher is Professor Emeritus of Old Testament at the Interdenominational Theological Center, where he currently serves as Adjunct Professor of Old Testament. He also served the ITC as its Vice-president for Academic Affairs and as Dean of the Faculty. He holds a Ph.D. in Old Testament from Boston University.

Cain Hope Felder is Professor of New Testament Language and Literature and Editor of *The Journal of Religious Thought* at the School of Divinity, Howard University, Washington, D.C. He is also the author of *Troubling Biblical Waters: Race, Class, and Family* (Orbis, 1989). He received his Ph.D. in New Testament from Columbia University/Union Theological Seminary, New York.

Thomas Hoyt, Jr., is Professor of New Testament and Director of the Black Ministries Certificate Program at Hartford Seminary in Connecticut. He holds a Ph.D. in New Testament from Duke University. He is a member of the Faith and Order Commission of the World and National Council of Churches, serving as Vice-chair of the latter.

Lloyd A. Lewis is Dean of the George Mercer, Jr. Memorial School of Theology of the Episcopal Church in the Diocese of Long Island. He formerly taught New Testament at Virginia Theological Seminary in Alexandria and holds a Ph.D. in Religious Studies from Yale University.

Clarice J. Martin is Assistant Professor of New Testament at Princeton Theological Seminary and an ordained member of the Presbyterian clergy. She holds a Ph.D. in New Testament from Duke University.

William H. Myers is Professor of New Testament at Ashland Theological Seminary in Ashland, Ohio. He received the Ph.D. in Religious Studies from the University of Pittsburgh.

David T. Shannon is President of Andover-Newton Theological School. He is a former Professor of Old Testament at the Interdenominational Theological Center. He is also the author of *The Old Testament Experience of Faith* (Judson, 1977) and coeditor of *Black Witness to the Apostolic Faith* (Eerdmans, 1985). He holds a Ph.D. in Old Testament from the University of Pittsburgh and a D.D. from the University of Richmond.

John W Waters is a former Associate Professor of Old Testament at the Interdenominational Theological Center. He is currently Minister at the Greater Solid Rock Baptist Church in Riverdale, Georgia. He holds a Ph.D. in Biblical Studies and Old Testament from Boston University.

Renita J. Weems is Assistant Professor of Hebrew Bible at Vanderbilt University. She is also the author of *Just a Sister Away: A Womanist Vision of Women's Relationships in the Bible* (LuraMedia, 1988) and of *Marriage, Sex, and Violence: Hebrew Rhetoric and Audience* (Fortress Press, forthcoming). She holds a Ph.D. in Old Testament from Princeton Theological Seminary.

Vincent L. Wimbush is Professor of New Testament and Christian Origins at Union Theological Seminary, New York. He is also the author of *Paul the Worldly Ascetic: Response to the World and Self-understanding according to 1 Corinthians 7* (Mercer, 1987) and the editor of *Ascetic Behavior in Greco-Roman Antiquity* in the Studies in Antiquity and Christianity series (Fortress Press, 1990). He holds a Ph.D. in New Testament and Christian Origins from Harvard University.